ASPECTS OF DONCASTER 1

ASPECTS *of* DONCASTER

Discovering Local History

Edited by
Brian Elliott

Series Editor
Brian Elliott

Wharncliffe Publishing Limited

First Published in 1997 by
Wharncliffe Publishing Limited
an imprint of
Pen and Sword Books Limited,
47 Church Street, Barnsley,
South Yorkshire. S70 2AS

Copyright © Wharncliffe Publishing Limited 1997

For up-to-date information on other titles produced under the
Wharncliffe imprint, please telephone or write to:

> **Wharncliffe Publishing Limited**
> **FREEPOST**
> **47 Church Street**
> **Barnsley**
> **South Yorkshire S70 2BR**
> **Telephone (24 hours): 01226 - 734555**

ISBN: 1-871647-39-8

Cover photograph: 'Conisbrough Castle', from a late 18th century engraving

Printed in Great Britain by
Redwood Books, Trowbridge, Wiltshire

CONTENTS

INTRODUCTION

by Brian Elliott

From brassbands to buildings on the Brodsworth estate and from medieval lords to mining memories, there is a purposeful variety of subjects in this, the first volume, of *Aspects of Doncaster*. The success of the acclaimed *Aspects* series is based upon a simple but proven premise: local and family history is such a popular interest that a collection of well-researched and well-written articles by both experienced and new writers, relating to a town and the surrounding area, will appeal to a wide readership. In this respect Wharncliffe Publishing have fully supported the project in an attractively presented and well-illustrated format which does not compromise on the quality of production whilst its editors always have an eye on academic standards.

The *Aspects* series was founded in 1993 with the publication of *Aspects of Barnsley* which was so successful that a further three annual volumes were issued. *Aspects of Rotherham*, under Melvyn Jones's editorship, appeared in 1995, exceptional demand meriting a second volume a year later. This year, 1997, the series has been extended to Doncaster, Sheffield and Leeds with further new areas and subsequent volumes being planned.

Doncaster's agrarian history is rightly given some prominence in an area where the influence of farming and of course landownership has been – and continues to be – of crucial importance in the making of the local landscape. Dan Byford's long interest in the drainage of the wetlands to the east of Doncaster has resulted in an authoritive study of open field farming in the Fishlake and Hatfield areas, based on the manor court books. Brian Barber's essay on the landed gentry of our area provides us with a broad and fascinating overview of key families from the seventeenth century to modern times. The comprehensive listing of source material will ensure that his contribution will serve as a most useful guide for future researchers. Likewise John Goodchild's essay on the enclosure of Mexborough will not only be of value to anyone interested in that locality but will also serve as both a subject of comparative reference and an exemplar for further studies of late enclosure.

Buildings of architectural and historic interest, in particular those associated with farms and estates are also given some scope in this opening volume, highlighting the value of fieldwork in historical research. Peter Gordon Smith's study of the Italianate buildings on the Brodsworth estate provides us with further information about the remarkable achievements of Charles Sabine Augustine Thellusson who had established his new mansion of Brodsworth Hall in 1860–61, now of course an award winning property in the care of English Heritage. Alan Whitworth's enthusiasm and extensive knowledge of buildings is reflected in his interesting account of Doncaster area corn windmills. Brian Elliott's survey of surviving local dovecotes will serve as a useful companion to his article in *Aspects of Rotherham 2*, raising awareness of otherwise underrated vernacular buildings and forgotten agricultural practices.

Aspects of medieval/late medieval life are explored in two contributions. Brian Sprakes chronicles the fascinating story of the DeMauley family whilst Tom Beastall provides us with a rare insight in to the enforced retirement, in Tickhill, of Henry Cundall, the last abbot of Roche Abbey. Moving forward in time, David Hey skilfully uses a selection of probate inventories to provide original information about the homes and lives of Doncaster people living in the late seventeenth and early eighteenth centuries. Jenny Moran also makes excellent use of original documents in her pioneering study based on the borough coroner's records.

Transport and communications continue to be important for Doncaster's economic and social development, and Philip Scowcroft provides us with an overview of historic land systems, from the days of packhorse travel to the emergence of the motor lorry.

Doncaster people have been fortunate at having such a variety of entertainment and sporting facilities. In his carefully researched account of local brass bands, Philip Scowcroft takes us to the pioneering days of the movement when Doncaster's contribution is examined in its historical context whilst Kate Taylor's well-researched essay on Doncaster's theatres appears at a time when the future of *The Grand* remains uncertain.

Finally, no *Aspects* volume is complete without some reference to family history or biography. Doris Kitching's childhood memories will no doubt bring back similar recollections to many readers brought up in mining communities but her writings will also serve a useful purpose for future generations.

This volume could not be produced without help from a number of individuals and organisations. Locally, I would like to thank staff at Doncaster Library Local Studies section and Doncaster Archives for such an excellent service and for permission to reproduce certain material. Barbara Bramall, Roni Wilkinson and Paul Wilkinson have made my job a lot easier at the production end and therefore deserve my sincere thanks. I would also like to thank all at Wharncliffe involved in the promotion support services for the book, including Publishing Manager Charles Hewitt and Paula Brennan for sales and promotion. Finally, I would like to express my appreciation to all the contributors who have met deadlines and written excellent articles that will hopefully encourage others to research aspects of Doncaster's history.

Anyone interested in making a contribution to *Aspects of Doncaster 2* should, in the first instance contact **Brian Elliott, c/o Wharncliffe Publishing Ltd, 47 Church Street, Barnsley, S70 2AS**, enclosing a brief summary of the work.

1. FROM PACKHORSE TO MOTOR LORRY: FREIGHT TRANSPORT IN DONCASTER AND DISTRICT

by Philip L Scowcroft

DONCASTER'S POSITION AS A MAJOR road centre, whether for passengers or freight, is owed in the first place to the Romans. The Roman road from Lincoln to York, which linked different Roman military camps at various times, had to cross the River Don somewhere and Doncaster, or *Danum* as the Romans called it, was in the optimum position. It was at the limit of navigation on the Don (and remained so for many centuries) and was a readily bridgeable point between marshlands to the east and high gorges to the west.

A fort, then a civil settlement, was established at or very near the crossing point. A link road, the ancestor of the present A630, ran westwards joining Danum to the smaller Roman fort of Templeborough, between modern Sheffield and Rotherham. During the Middle Ages other main roads focusing on Doncaster were established, from Barnsley, Penistone and Saltersbrook to the west, from Tickhill to the south and from Thorne to the east, along with many branches. By 1500 Doncaster had become an important road centre, however imperfect the condition of the roads themselves (Figure 1).

Figure 1. Doncaster's pre-motorway road network in outline. *Map drawn by Laurie Thorp*

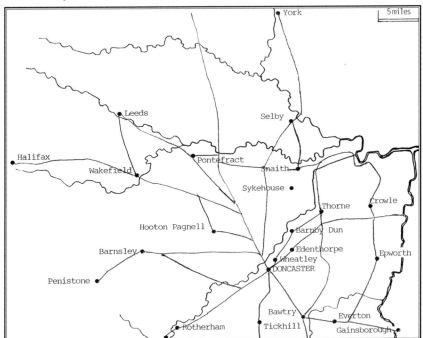

Figure 2. Seventeenth century packhorse train.

It is no accident that to this day the town stands at the crossing of major north/south and east/west routes even though the roads just avoid the town centre.

The primary purpose of Roman roads was military. We know little about the extent to which these and indeed the inland waterways which the Romans developed, again, and at least initially, for military purposes, were used for civilian traffic, whether passenger or freight, during the Roman era and afterwards, but there must have been some of this; and certainly Roman roads formed the basis of England's road network until after the medieval era. By that time the Roman (and other) roads were in a bad state of repair. Until the sixteenth century, when private carriages became reasonably common, this did not matter too much as passenger and freight traffic by land, other than that for the shortest distances, mainly depended on the horse and not on vehicles. For freight transport this meant – unless there was navigable water available – the packhorse (Figure 2). Carts were known as early as 1248 because the tolls of Doncaster's new bridge of that year, the first time the Don had been bridged in stone, mention carts and provided they pay a 'custom' of 1d per cart laden with merchandise for three years – surely a rather short term toll. But as late as 1695 leading carrier Abraham Pilling died, possessed of sixteen packhorses and 'accessories' valued at £104, but no carts (see chapter 8). Carts and waggons existed in some numbers by 1700 but their use, for example for distributing coal, was purely local and because of the often

Figure 3. The ancient 'Saltersbrook' route is acknowledged by a number of place-names, including this example, at Goldthorpe. *Brian Elliott.*

dire road conditions, largely confined to the summer months.

Doncaster was a focus for, and involved with, the packhorse trade in various ways. First, the horses could be bought there at the quarterly horse fairs in what is now Waterdale whilst Thorne, twelve miles away, had two horse fairs annually. Secondly, a variety of produce came through by horse: salt from Cheshire via Saltersbrook (Figure 3) and Barnsley, the most northerly of the trans-Pennine routes from Cheshire, charcoal for the South Yorkshire iron industry, and its finished iron products, Sheffield cutlery, Derbyshire lead, mostly for onward transit down the Don and the Humber (though much of this went to Bawtry before the Don [Dun] Navigation was constructed in the eighteenth century) plus woollen cloth from the West Riding and stockings made in Doncaster itself, cheese from Cheshire and livestock and farm produce for Doncaster's market which was already prosperous and dated back to the eleventh or twelfth centuries. Doncaster bridge tolls set in 1614 indicate the likely scale of the livestock traffic, 2d for every score of beasts and horses, for every score of sheep and for every laden packhorse. Thirdly, Doncaster's status as a market town helped the packhorse trade was it as later to help the stage-coach and stage-waggon trades and the local carters because it had so many inns. One of these inns was in fact called the *Pack Horse* and was situated on the west side of Lower French Gate which was then part of the north–south thoroughfare through the town. This inn dated from the early seventeenth century, if not earlier, and as its name suggested, it was heavily involved in packhorse traffic. At the rear, a gallery extending along the attic storey was used as bedrooms for the packhorsemen and this communicated directly with the courtyard below by external stairs, ensuring that late arrivals and early departures did not disturb too much the rest of the inn's patrons.

Packhorses could go many places a vehicle could not, but the freight each could carry was small compared with a river or canal boat or even a waggon.[1] The Don Navigation and the development of the stage-waggon (Figures 4 & 5), itself encouraged by an improvement in the roads, brought about by turnpike trusts and, from the late eighteenth century, improved roadmaking techniques which between them encouraged wheeled traffic, caused a decline in the packhorse trade after around 1750, certainly for longer distance work – although there is some evidence that horses remained in use for local haulage and smaller loads (like local farmers getting their corn and other produce to markets such as Doncaster's) well after 1800. Doncaster's first long distance stage-waggon was advertised in 1743. This was a London–York service taking five days in summer and six in winter for the full journey and, as was to be usual, also conveying passengers, often poorer folk who could not afford the very expensive travel by stage-coach, as well as goods. Connections to Wakefield were available from Doncaster. Other waggon services gradually appeared, like the London–Doncaster–Pontefract–York one of 1755 which used the rather ironically named *Woolpack Inn* in the Market Place as its staging point. In 1787 Jackson's waggons came to Doncaster from Sheffield and then turned south to London, taking six to eight days for the whole journey. Carts and waggons worked also between Sheffield,

Figure 5. This stage waggon, pulled by eight horses, would be capable of carrying heavy loads.

Figure 4. A typical stage waggon. *Drawn by Laurie Thorp*

Doncaster and York. In July 1791 'flying stage waggons' between Leeds and London provided a faster (and daily) service. By 1815 further services were available from Doncaster to Leeds, Wakefield and Halifax. It seems clear that at least some of the waggons working long distance services through Doncaster were actually based there because in April 1800 all the stage-waggons working from York, Halifax and Wakefield to London with 'the Horses, Geers [sic], Utensils and Implements thereto' were put up for sale by Henry Heaton of Doncaster along with a wharf, warehouse, staith, yard and dwelling house in Fishergate, Doncaster. The waggons, like lorries in our present age, were targets for thieves; a truss of cloth worth £71 15s was stolen when the Leeds stage-waggon stopped overnight in Doncaster on 22 March 1816.

The local stage-coach magnate Richard Wood (Figure 6) was heavily involved in the waggon business too, from 1826 when he purchased a share in Jackson's operation, if not earlier. He was in his prime in the period 1815–35 which was the peak for Doncaster stage-waggon services just as it was for stage-coach services. Wood was a canny man, who could be ruthless when his interests were threatened and he was a survivor.[2] His waggons left the *Reindeer Inn* – on the Great North Road through the town – daily for London and now took only three days. Waggon services from Doncaster now ran also to York, Newcastle, Edinburgh, Carlisle, Leeds and (thrice weekly from the *Wellington Inn* near the Market Place) Manchester. In 1815 seven daily services and eight twice or thrice weekly waggon services left Doncaster for various destinations. This was not a bad network when the received wisdom is that water transport, for which Doncaster's connections were then good as they had been for generations, was always preferred, we are told, to road transport where freight was concerned. But roads were improving and so was waggon tech-

Figure 6. Advertisement in the *Doncaster Gazette* of 15 December 1826, noting the recent expansion of Richard Wood's stage waggon business. Wood's importance as a stage coach operator is also apparent from this. The *Rein Deer Inn* was in Hallgate, the *Black Boy* in French Gate.

nology. In 1821 Anderton's, coachmakers of Frenchgate, Doncaster
were building Johnson's Improved Patent Waggons. Wood was one of
Anderton's customers.[3] The railways put paid to long distance waggon
services; all those involving Doncaster had gone by 1852, a mere four
years after the first railway reached the town.

This did not mean of course that Doncaster and district roads did
not carry freight during the remainder of the nineteenth century and
up to 1914, by which time the motor lorry was beginning to appear.
Indeed they probably carried more than previously with increased
population and increased prosperity, but the traffic was short-haul in
character. Horsedrawn tradesmen's vans and drays were seen
in considerable numbers in town centre streets, though we only hear
about them if they were involved in accidents, usually when the horse
or horses were frightened and bolted. And there were the carrier
services linking surrounding villages with Doncaster, mainly (though
not entirely) on market days. These had already begun by the beginning of the century if not earlier; on 13 January 1813 a waggon bound
from Doncaster market to Barnby Dun was overturned due to the
carelessness of the driver. It was carrying several women, one of whom
was 'hurt severely'.[4]

In 1837, according to *White's Directory*, there were stated to be
twenty-three places connected by carriers to Doncaster. Some of these
would be served by stage-waggons, then still very much in their
heyday, as the twenty-three destinations included places as distant as
London, Leeds, Nottingham and Leicester and others were 'middle
distance' ones like Barnsley, Sheffield, Gainsborough, Selby and York.
Slater's Directory of 1854 by contrast list twenty-six carriers' services,
the most distant being that to Sheffield. A Directory of 1867 sees even
fewer such 'medium hauls', ten to twelve miles now being the usual
maximum operating radius, subject to one or two exceptions (like
Sykehouse) just outside that range. More Doncaster area villages were
now being served, thirty-six altogether, three-quarters of which had
no railway station, by forty-three operators, most of them working just
once a week, on Saturday, market day; Bawtry, whose service ran on
five days per week, Tickhill, which had three operators, and Wroot
were exceptions to that rule. Most of the services (Bawtry was again
an exception) terminated at public houses in the Market Place or
immediately adjacent thereto.

Kelly's Directory of 1877 indicates that thirty-nine places were
served, again within a smaller radius as 1867, by forty-six operators
(Sykehouse, a quite small and remote village west of Thorne, now had
no fewer than five different carriers). In 1893, forty-one places were

served by forty-three operators while in 1908, on the threshold of the motor age, thirty-eight villages were served by thirty-four operators (Tickhill had three operators, Sykehouse, Wroot, Everton, Crowle and Hooton Pagnell two each); twenty-seven of the operations were Saturdays only but Tickhill's three operators each ran thrice weekly and Bawtry's single operator ran four times weekly. Practically all carrier services still ran to inns in or close to the Market Place. Six of the 1908 carriers and eleven others were still in business in 1927 when fifteen villages were served, several of them the more remote ones – Sykehouse had four carriers and Belton three. Thorne's carrier services operated to Doncaster, Snaith and Epworth but most of these had disappeared well before 1900.

The nineteenth century carrier services, admittedly small in scope, have been in general largely ignored by historians, although we read of them in fiction, in Thomas Hardy's *The Woodlanders* and Dickens's *The Cricket on the Heath* for example and in later years even in the detective stories of Dorothy L Sayers; but they played an important part in opening up isolated villages and assisting their economy. Doncaster's carriers doubtless reflect the experience of those of many other places. Where they served villages with a railway station handy (and this did happen) one may expect with their doubtless minimal overheads they were competitive in price with the railways. Most however served villages with no rail access readily available.

By 1927, though, the horsedrawn cart or waggon was being replaced by the motor lorry for the transport of freight, the process being hastened by the many demobilised ex-servicemen with gratuities (and perhaps some mechanical expertise as a result of their service) going into the haulage business after 1918, indeed in some

Figure 7. A Sheard Binnington container van drawn by eight horses at an unidentified location during the first decade of this century. Freight transport then was a labour-intensive activity, it seems. *Mr W Binnington*

Figure 8. A furniture van of c1930 pictured in the yard of Sheard, Binnington's of Doncaster (Frederick Binnington is in the coat). The van, which appears to belong to William Rhodes Ltd of Nottingham and Leeds, may have been making a delivery or alternatively it may just have been purchased second-hand by Sheard Binnington. *Mr W Binnington*

cases buying up surplus military vehicles. Doncaster had its share of these small firms but there were a few older established ones. The removal firm W Westfield & Sons Ltd of York Road, Doncaster began as a family outfit 101 years ago, in 1896, and still exists, though for the last few years the family has had no involvement with it. At first horses pulled the waggons, but in 1905 steam traction engines were put into service, operating at eight miles per hour on coke (even, *in extremis* and illegally, on coal). Every ten miles a stop had to be made for water which is about as often as horses would have had to be changed. This is one of the few instances I have discovered in Doncaster and district where steam traction was used for transport as against road rolling and farm and fairground work. There must however have been some more of this haulage as the Town Council from time to time considered the loads each engine might haul. As far back as 1862 B D Taplin & Co of Lincoln had advertised in the Doncaster press new patent prize traction engines for drawing heavy loads. Steam lorries were used around the time of the Great War, the Corporation's Gas Undertaking purchasing one in June 1914 for £570. Darley's, the Thorne brewers, also used them. Westfields incidentally had faith in the internal combustion engine and before 1914 owned the first petrol-engined removal vehicle in town. Another old established firm was Sheard Binnington, furniture dealers and furniture removers; they, too, progressed from horse to motor traction (Figures 7–9), around 1914. It is impossible to track down the numbers of post-1918 motor haulage firms in the Doncaster district, but one can find advertisements for some of the most significant of them in the local newspapers of that time: Kemp & Jepson, Morris, J L Dickinson and Don Transport Company of Balby Road who advertised furniture removal and general haulage with two or three ton lorries. Firms like these gradually extended their field of operations and in 1937 Rawson's of Edenthorpe were advertising a regular York–London 'truck transport service'. Postal deliveries and collections by motor came along in the early twenties and gradually horsedrawn freight vehicles were squeezed out, although much less quickly than had been the case with passenger vehicles and numbers of them survived until the Second World War. Leading undertaker Steadman & Sons used motor hearses (are hearses freight or passenger vehicles?) from 1924 but did not phase out their horsed hearses until 1935. It was not until September 1932 that the London & North Eastern Railway used a motor horsebox to bring racehorses to the St Leger meeting; prior to that time horseboxes were horsedrawn – in the early days the racing steeds probably had to reach the course on their own four legs.[5]

Doncaster expertise had a part to play in the motor revolution. In that same month, September 1932, Harold Wilkinson of Carr Grange Works built for Redline Glico a petrol tanker of 2500 gallons capacity, 27'6" long and 8'6" wide on a Mammoth Major AEC chassis, five times the capacity of a tanker lorry Wilkinson had built for Redline in 1928 (Wilkinson's still exist but do not now build lorry bodies). The building of larger and larger lorry bodies was to be a factor in the post-war success of road freight trans-

Figure 9. Grey horse with Sheard Binnington container van, c1900–10. Henry Binnington, founder of the furniture/removals firm in 1885 (its headquarters was at 44 High Street), appears centre (in the frock coat). Furniture was often packed in containers for transport by rail to more distant destinations. *Mr W Binnington*

port, allied to more reliable engines using diesel fuel and the decline of the railways as bulk carriers. This is as true of Doncaster as anywhere else, for all that the place remains in important railway centre. But Doncaster is an important road centre, too, with north–south and east–west motorways passing close to the town centre, the former by-pass dating from the 1960s, the latter from the 1970s. As early as 1971 the railway trunk line serving the Wheatley Industrial Estate to the north-east of the town centre, put in by the LNER in the 1930s, was closed, the major industrial firms on that Estate finding it more convenient to use road haulage entirely for raw materials in and finished products out. It is arguable that geography, quite as much as technology, has played its part in ensuring that Doncaster, in common with so many other places, now relies so heavily on its roads for the carriage of freight. The road indeed now carries a larger **proportion** of goods traffic, to, from and through Doncaster, than it did even in the heyday of the stage-waggons, for practically no freight now goes by the Navigation, much less, both proportionally and absolutely, than in the century after 1740. With the railways struggling to keep what freight business they still have, the road is now very clearly the dominant means of transport.

Notes and References

1. On packhorses and carriers generally, see David Hey, *Packmen, Carriers and Packhorse Roads: Trade and Communications in North Derbyshire and South Yorkshire* (Leicester, 1980).
2. For examples see my 'Packet Boats From Thorne 1809–1860', *Thorne Local History Society Publications*, 1995, pp 6–12, also my 'Nineteenth Century Stage-Coaches and Carriers in Thorne', *Thorne Local History Society Publications*, 1966, pp 8–12.
3. See 'Packet Boats, etc' p 8.
4. *Doncaster Gazette*.
5. The motor horsebox is illustrated in the *Doncaster Chronicle*, 8 September 1932.

Acknowledgement

I am indebted to Mr Laurie Thorp for the map and the drawing of the stage-waggon.

2. HISTORICAL NOTICES OF THE DEMAULEY FAMILY: MEDIEVAL LORDS OF DONCASTER

by Brian Sprakes

IN THE YEARS FOLLOWING the Norman Conquest, William the Conqueror set about reorganising and redistributing lands formerly belonging to the Saxon earls amongst his own followers (Figure 1). Robert, Count of Mortain, the half-brother of William, was granted great tracts of land in Yorkshire amounting to some 180 manors which he in turn granted to two tenants-in-chief: Nigel Fossard (or Fozzard) who with 91 manors got the lion's share, and Richard Surdeval who received 55 manors.[1] The rest were granted to lesser tenants.

The chief estate acquired by Nigel Fossard was the late Earl Tostig's manor at Estorp (Hexthorpe) which included Doncaster, Wheatley, Sandal, and Barnby Dun to the east, and Rotherham and Clifton to the west.[2] In mid-Yorkshire he held Bramham and Clifford; in the East

Figure 1. Feudal Families of Yorkshire following the Norman Conquest.

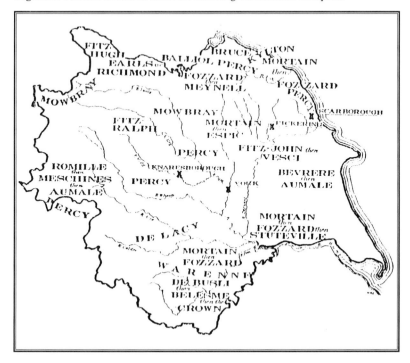

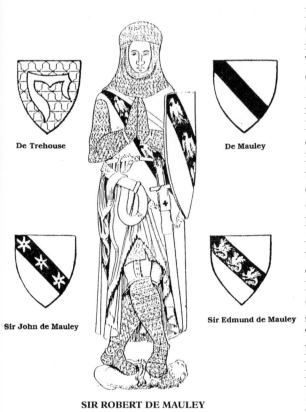

De Trehouse

De Mauley

Sir John de Mauley

Sir Edmund de Mauley

SIR ROBERT DE MAULEY

Figure 2. Aspects of the de Mauley heraldry.
Brian Sprakes

Riding, Lockington, Hotham, Cave, and SouthDuffield; and in Cleveland, lands around Whitby, at Ayton, Mulgrave, Goldsborough and Egton. Many of the place-names mentioned in the Domesday Book have disappeared or changed beyond recognition. In York, Nigel had two houses that formerly belonged to Godfrey, Bishop of Coutances. The family were liberal benefactors to St Mary's Abbey, York, and to it they gave the advowsons of the churches of Doncaster, Houghton, Bainton and St Crux in York, together with sixteen houses in Doncaster.[3] To defend these holdings Nigel built several castles: Birdsall (Montferrant Castle), Lockington and Aughton (fortified manor house) in the East Riding; Mulgrave, north of Whitby and Langthwaite (Castle Hills, north of Doncaster), and in Doncaster itself on the site formerly occupied by the Roman fort, now under the parish church of St George. Most of these fortified sites were of the motte and bailey type, and in some cases earthworks remain. Only at Mulgrave was there subsequent building in stone. The majority of these holdings were eventually inherited by the de Mauleys.

About the year 1135 heraldry evolved throughout Europe, and the Fossards adopted the arms or a bend sable – that is to say a gold shield with a black diagonal stripe upon it. This shield was also to be the basis of the later de Mauley heraldry (Figure 2).

As we can see from the pedigree, (Figure 3), the male line ended with William Fossard II. Joan, his daughter, married Robert de Turnham and so the barony passed to him in right of his wife. Robert de Turnham was the younger son of Robert de Turnham, founder of

PROVISIONAL PEDIGREE of DE MAULEY

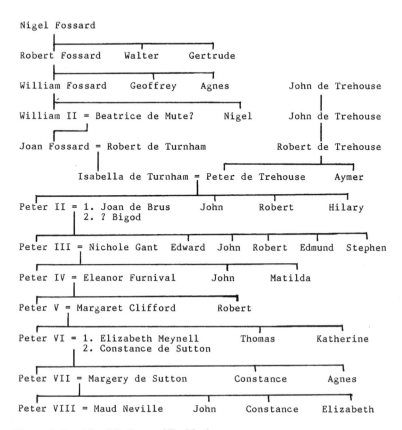

Figure 3. Provisional Pedigree of De Mauley.

Combwell Priory in Kent, and together with his brother Stephen took part in the Third Crusade, and in May 1191 was in command of half of King Richard's fleet which captured enemy galleys in the waters around Cyprus. He remained in Cyprus as Justicar until returning to England in 1193 when Richard rewarded him with the hand of Joan Fossard. In 1193 Turnham was Senechal of Anjou, and on Richard's death in that year surrendered the castles of Chinon and Saumur together with the treasure there to King John, and at once became a faithful adherent of the new king.[4]

In 1201 John sent Turnham to suppress the revolt in Poitou, and for the next four years he was Senechal of Poitou and Gascony. Poitou was captured by Phillip Augustus in 1205 and Turnham taken prisoner. No doubt a ransom was paid, for Turnham was back in England with the king in January 1206. Robert died in 1211, leaving his wife Joan and daughter Isabella who was born after 1200.[5] It seems that Joan spent most of her married life at Turnham Castle near Maidstone, though she did found a priory at Grosmont near her castle at Mulgrave in 1202.

Peter de Mauley I

Peter de Mauley I, alias Petrus de Malo Lacu, alias de Trehouse was the son of a Poitevin noble whose family had possessions in England near the Fossard holdings in the East Riding. Before King Richard's death, Prince John, then Earl of Moreton, had met the young Peter de Mauley and persuaded his widowed mother to let him accompany him back to England. Peter left his inheritance in Poitou in the care of his brother Almeric (or Aymer).[6] According to legend, Peter was employed by John to murder Prince Arthur of Brittany, but this is unlikely, and indeed the only contemporary writer of note – Ralph of Coggleshall says that Arthur was drowned.[7]

Following John's accession to the throne in 1199 (Figure 4), Peter remained a favourite and in 1202 was given lands in Normandy upon reaching his eighteenth birthday and is thereafter mentioned in many Close and Patent Rolls as being in the King's service. Peter stood by King John during his defiance of the Pope together with Robert de Turnham, thus provoking Matthew Paris to brand them 'the king's evil counsellors'.[8] By this time, Peter had acquired lands in Bedfordshire, Wiltshire, Leicestershire and Surrey. As we have seen, Robert de Turnham died in 1211 leaving the young heiress Isabella as a ward of the Crown. Three years later, on 25 April 1214, King John gave her in marriage to Peter de Mauley, together with all her lands and titles, on payment of the enormous sum of 7,000 marks, to be paid at the rate of 1,000 marks per year.[9] The following individuals gave sureties for Peter: Ranulf, Earl of Chester; Reginald de Pontibus; William, Earl Ferrers; Savary de Mauleon; William, Earl of Salisbury; Hugo de Burgo; Arnold de Avelant; and Peter, Bishop of

Figure 4. King John, who reigned 1199–1216.

Figure 5. Corfe Castle, Dorset, King John's 'treasure house'.

Winchester.[10]

Peter saw military service with King John in the expedition to Poitou in 1214, and in the following year was given his most important post – Castellan of Corfe Castle in Dorset (Figure 5).[11] He was now in high favour with King John and stood alongside men such as Peter des Roches, Bishop of Winchester and Chief Justicar of England, and Fawkes de Breaute, Castellan of Windsor. These men stood squarely with John against the barons in the months that led to Magna Carta. This is illustrated by the fact that John issued an order in Nottingham on 30 March 1215 commanding the bailifs of Peter de Mauley to enclose the town of Doncaster with a palisade and ditch, and to build a barbican upon the bridge to defend the town (Figure 6).[12]

The importance of Corfe Castle is explained by the fact that it was King John's principal treasure house. Here were hoarded 40,000 marks, 15 gold cups, and the crown and state regalia. Corfe was also a sort of 'state prison' where important guests were kept in protective custody. These 'guests' included Margaret and Isabel, the daughters

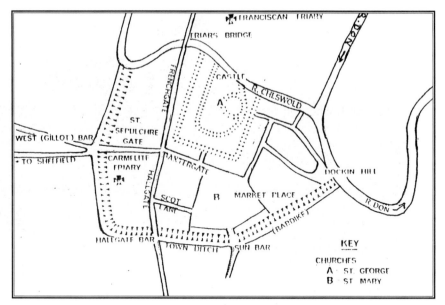

Figure 6. Medieval Doncaster and its defences.

of the rebellious King Alexander of Scotland, and the Demoiselle of Brittany, sister of Arthur. It was to Corfe that John sent the young prince Richard, Earl of Cornwall (later to become King of the Romans) to act as page to Peter de Mauley and the Demoiselle.[13]

The war with the barons continued. On 12 October 1216 John left Wisbech to go to Swineshead Abbey, and it was while crossing the Wellstream (river Nene) that John lost some of his treasure, not all of it, as legend would have it, for the bulk was still with Peter de Mauley at Corfe. John, however, was ill and he rested at Sleaford for two days, and thence to Newark where he died on 18 October 1216, having made a brief but dignified will directing that the young prince Henry was to be under the protection of the much respected William le Marshall, while Prince Richard was to stay with Peter de Mauley at Corfe. He also appointed Savary de Mauleon and Fawkes de Breaute to act as executors.

Three months earlier, on 26 June, John had appointed Peter de Mauley to be sheriff of the counties of Somerset and Dorset, a post which he retained during the first years of the reign of Henry III. Because he was a minor, Henry was not crowned until the fourth year of his reign.

On 7 May 1220 Peter de Mauley was summoned to Westminster Abbey for the coronation of King Henry III (Figure 7), and was instructed to bring with him the king's brother, Prince Richard, and the state regalia.[14] Young king Henry was very much under the influence of the new Chief Justicar, Hubert de Burgh, who had been created Earl of Kent and had also married Princess Margaret of Scotland, who had formerly been in Peter's care at Corfe. Hubert was regarded as an upstart by the barons. He removed de Breaute from Windsor and occupied it himself. His next move was against Peter de Mauley who was arrested in 1221 on a charge of treason. The charge being that he had promised to hand over the Demoiselle Eleanor to the king of France.[15] Peter was forced to resign all his offices. He handed over to the king the castle at Corfe, the Demoiselle, Princess

Figure 7. The Great Seal (reverse) of King Henry III, 1270. *Durham Dean & Chapter*

Isabella of Scotland, together with all the jewels, 'military engines' and ammunition there. The charge does not seem to have had much substance, for the following year Peter was back in royal favour, being granted the castle at Sherborne.

In 1221 Peter and Isabella were granted lands in Rossington to the south of Doncaster, together with a wood and fishery there. Here they erected a fortified manor house at a place called Draw Dykes which lay between Hunster Wood and Rossington village. The park around it was said to be a thousand acres. The antiquary, Dugdale, wrongly stated that Peter died in 1222. This unfortunate error confused later historians and as a result many of the de Mauley pedigrees drawn up before 1896 – when Kingsford noted the error – are incorrect.[16]

Throughout the whole of this period, Peter and Isabella were gradually fortifying their castle at Mulgrave. Robert de Turnham had begun building a stone castle immediately adjacent to the old motte and bailey he had inherited from the Fossards (Figure 8). To

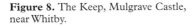

Figure 8. The Keep, Mulgrave Castle, near Whitby.

Turnham's rectangular keep Peter now added circular turrets on each corner, thus the keep assumed a plan unique in this country.

In 1233 Henry III dispossessed Gilbert Basset of the manor of Nether-Haven, in Wiltshire, which he then granted to Peter de Mauley, and the following year Peter was given custody of the royal castle of Devises. Peter promptly installed Sir Robert de Thweng, who seems to have been a personal friend, as Constable of the Castle, a post which he held for three years. Two years later, in 1236, Peter was appointed Sheriff of Northamptonshire.

Peter's wife, Isabella, died on 8 June 1238 and was buried in the newly completed chapter house in the Cistercian Abbey at Meaux where her kinsman Michael de Bruno was abbot and also one of the executors of her will. The following extract shows the provision that Peter made for her burial and for the endowment of the chantry chapel there:

> ... to the monks of Meaux Abbey in Holderness, with the body of Isabell de Turnham his wife, to be there buried, the homage and rent of sixty shillings per annum, of six ox-gangs of land in Ake, also two ox-gangs with the tofts in Wharrum. Likewise two mills, with the tofts and crofts in Lockynton; and one mill, with the holme in Briddeshull, and the suit thereto; for the perpetual maintenance of the two secular priests, and two clerks; one of the priests to sing in the Chapel of Our Lady near the Bridge in the Wood, for the souls deceased; and for the celebration of the Anniversary of the said Issabell, in that Abbey of Meaux upon the eighth calends of June for ever; and for the maintenance of five wax tapers, at the said Mass of Our Lady.[17]

On a happier note, Peter stood as a godfather at the christening of the king's son, Edward (later King Edward I), in 1239.

In 1240 Isabell Marshall, wife of Richard, Earl of Cornwall and King of the Romans, died in childbirth, a heavy blow for Richard who decided to go on the crusade with William de Fortibus, Earl of Abermarle. Included in Richard's party were William Longspee, Earl of Salisbury and his old mentor, Peter de Mauley. Seventy knights bachelor went with them, but not Simon de Montfort who had intended to go. Fate had another role for him to play in England. As Peter's eldest son, Peter II was still a minor and had to leave his lands in the care of other members of his family. Doncaster was left under the supervision of his steward, Reginald de Ketelbergh.

This was the last successful Christian Crusade, the Kingdom of Jerusalem was once more under christian rule, but sadly Peter de Mauley died of old age in 1241, and his heart and bones were brought back in a trunk which acted as a coffin. According to Joinville, 'Each man was allowed a long box to serve as a trunk, a small barrel of fresh water, a chamber pot and a lantern'. Peter and Isabella left four children that are known to us: Peter II (eldest son and heir), John, Robert and Hillary. There were also several brothers, namely, John, Edmund and Andrew – a rather shadowy figure.

Peter de Mauley II, c1226–79

As Peter was a minor at the time of his father's death he became a ward of the king who let out his lands to Gerard la Grue at an annual rent of 500 marks, and he had to keep up the castle at Mulgrave at his own expense.[18] This seems to have been beyond his means for the following year a similar lease was granted to Guido de Russlim who continued to hold the lands until Peter came of age.

The marriage of Peter II to Joan de Brus took place when he was very young, as the *Inquisition Post Mortem* of Peter de Brus informs us:

On 27th September 1237, the king, then at York, was pleased to approve of a marriage which had been contracted between Peter, son and heir of Peter de Brus and Hillary, eldest daughter of Peter de Mauley [I] and also of one between Peter son and heir of the said Peter de Mauley and Joan, eldest daughter of the said Peter de Brus.

It seems that Joan was older than Peter and she died in 1243 seemingly without issue. Peter, despite the fact that he had been married for six years was still a minor! He eventually married again some time before 1249 when his son and heir, Peter III, was born. The name of his second wife is uncertain but she is thought to be of the Bigod family.

Like his father, Peter II was a military man, and he often had to lease out his lands when he was away of military duty. For instance, Doncaster was leased out to Simon de Montfort for ten years in 1252, and the following year he was fighting in Gascony.[19] Two years later he was in Wales with the king. In 1258 the Scots made their own king, Alexander III, a prisoner, and Peter de Mauley was summoned, together with other northern barons

to prepare himself with horse and arms for the rescue of that king, being then under the protection of the king [Henry III] whose daughter [Margaret] he had married.

In 1277 Peter II was in dispute with the Abbot of Whitby with regard to his manors to the north and 100 tofts of land in the town itself. The litigation was still going on at the time of his death in Pontigny, in 1279, where he was again on military service. An extensive *Inquisition*

Post Mortem was subsequently drawn up at Windsor, dated 16 July 1279. The sum of knight's fees held by him was thirty-three, and he held the advowsons of four churches and over 42,000 acres of land.[20]

We have already noted that Hillary was named as his eldest sister, so there must have been others. Several brothers are mentioned, notably John who seems to have been the second son of Peter I and who received his paternal estates at Hotham, and thereafter he and his descendants are known by the surname 'de Hotham'; but to confuse the issue further, there was an Andrew de Mauley and family also living in Hotham. Peter II received his mother's more important estates at Mulgrave and Doncaster. Another brother, named Robert, died in 1252, leaving a young son, also named John.

Peter II left issue: Peter III, the eldest son and heir; Edward; John; Edmund; Stephen and Robert whose son, also named Robert, held Hexthorpe and Rossington and lived in the manor house there.

Peter de Mauley III, 1248–1309, 1st Lord Mauley.

Peter III was aged thirty-one when his father died. By 1273 he was already married to Nichole de Gant, sister and co-heir of Gilbert de Gant, son of Gilbert de Gant, Earl of Lincoln and Folkingham, and indeed Peter was named as one of his heirs in the *Inquisition Post Mortem* of Gilbert de Gant dated 26 January 1273–4. As a result of this Peter inherited lands at Iwardby in Lincolnshire in right of his wife.

In 1280 the family was again in conflict with the Abbot of Whitby when Peter claimed lands on his side of the river Esk for his parish of Lythe. The case grew to such proportions that it was eventually taken to Rome for a decision of the Pope, who found in favour of the Abbot.

Peter III was, like his father and grandfather, a military man. He had taken part in the first Welsh invasion of 1277 when his father was still alive. He was summoned to the muster at Worcester in May 1282, and again at Rhuddlan later in the same year. The following year found him at the muster at Montgomery and from there he was summoned to the Parliament at Shrewsbury on 30 September for the trial of David, the brother of Llewelyn.

Peter III was summoned to appear *equis et armis* (equipped with horses and arms) at a military council at Gloucester in July 1287 before Edmund, Earl of Cornwall. Following this, Sir Edmund de Mortimer was ordered to march against Rhys ad Meredydd in South Wales. Peter was to go with him and provide ten horses *cooperti*, that is to say completely armed in mail. These horses were individually valued, the best (Peter's) worth sixty marks. The reason for this was that if the horse was killed in battle, its value was to be paid to its owner or his next of kin.[21]

Military service continued, to muster at Portsmouth in September 1294 for service in Gascony the following year. All this service at last brought its rewards, for in 1295, the Barony of Mulgrave was confirmed by writ – so Peter became the first legal Baron (Lord) de Mauley. This was the moment when the old arms of de Trehouse (*Vair a mauche gules*) was abandoned and the ancient arms of the Fossards (*or a bend sable*) assumed.

Peter's wife, Nichole, died in 1297 and was buried in the newly completed chapel of the Vavasours at Hazelwood Castle, near Tadcaster. The Vavasours were related to the

Figure 9. Seal of Peter de Mauley III.

de Mauleys by marriage, and they also held some of their lands of the Mauleys formerly belonging to the Fossards.

Once more, Peter was called upon for military service, fighting at the Battle of Falkirk, on 22 July 1298. Though not summoned to the Parliament at Lincoln, he did sign the famous barons' letter to Pope Boniface (12 February 1300/1) protesting against certain practices in relation to the Church of England, and attached his seal, Figure 9, with the others. The reverse side of the seal shows his shield with lion supporters and crest, and is considered to be an early example of true supporters. Peter was ordered, on 20 January 1303, to place himself, together with all his men equipped with horses and arms, under the command of John Segrave, the king's lieutenant in Scotland. This army was defeated on 24 February at the Battle of Rosslyn, near Edinburgh.

Peter evidently survived the battle for, on 18 January 1307/8, he was summoned to attend the coronation of Edward II at Westminster Abbey on 25 February following. Two years later he was dead. A writ of *diem clausit extremum* was issued at Langley, dated 25 August 1309.[22]

Peter III and Nichole had two children known to us: Peter IV, the eldest son and heir, and John. There were also several brothers, Edward and John who served with Peter in Gascony during 1294/5. and Robert, Edmund and Stephen. Edward attended the York Parliament later that year. It must be remembered that Edward I made York his headquarters during the war with the Scots. A grant from the

Figure 10. De Mauley shields, South aisle of York Minster.

king to the Abbey of St Mary there bears the signature of Edward de Mauley *senescallo domini Regis*, Steward of the king's Household, a position still held in 1313 when he was granted letters of protection when going beyond the seas, together with others on the king's service.[23]

Robert was granted lands at Rossington, though his brother, Peter III, retained the advowson of the church there. He was knighted in 1301, and was appointed Sheriff of Roxburgh and Keeper of Bolsover Castle in 1312.[24] He married Joan (? Colvile) and they had at least two children: Robert and Isabell who married Sir Thomas Thweng of Sheriff Hutton. Sir Robert died in 1330 and was buried in York Minster (Figure 10). His tomb was destroyed by fire in 1829.

Sir Edmund de Mauley served in Scotland in 1301 and became a close friend of the future king Edward II and his unpopular favourite Piers Gaveston. In 1308 Sir Edmund was excommunicated for laying violent hands on Robert Hardy 'to the shedding of blood' in the church at Misterton, Nottinghamshire, for which he did penance and was absolved in 1309. He was made Steward of the Royal Household by Edward II and Governor of the castles of Bridgenorth and Bristol in 1312, and also the castle

Figure 11. Robert the Bruce, victor at Bannockburn, 1314.

of Cockermouth in early 1314. This was the year of his death, for he was with the king at the Battle of Bannockburn, 25 June, drowned on the flight that followed that defeat (Figure 11). In the words of a chronicler, 'he for dread [fear] went and drenched himself in a fresh ryver that is called Bannockesburne'.[25] He is buried against the south wall of Bainton church where his effigy (Figure 12) shows a man in full coat armour, but with a tonsure showing that he was in Minor Orders – probably an acolyte. His *Inquisition Post Mortem* was held the following August, and shows that he was unmarried, and that his nephew, Peter de Mauley IV, was the heir to his lands at Southburn, Latton and Whitby.

Stephen pursued a career in the church, and on 26 April 1270 was presented by his father to the family church at Bainton, then he was appointed rector of Lockington, again by his father, in 1279, despite the fact that he was only a sub-deacon. Letters of Attorney were granted to him in 1286 when going to study at the University of Paris.[26] In 1288, Sir Stephen, as he was then styled, was presented to the church of Lythe by his brother, Peter III. His appointment as Archdeacon of Cleveland (though still not an ordained priest) came in 1289 and he was duly installed on 17 July. He retained the archdeaconry until his death. On 21 May 1291, Stephen, described as Deacon and Papal Chaplain, received a dispensation from Pope Nicholas IV to hold the churches of Bainton and Lythe, and the Archdeaconry of Cleveland hitherto held by him without dispensation.[27] On the same day he obtained an indult to receive the fruits of his archdeaconry and benefices for five years, without residing or being an ordained priest, as he proposed to go on a Crusade with the king, Edward I (Figure 13).

It is not known whether or not Stephen went to the Holy Land, but the next notice of him is five years later when he was presented by the Prior and Convent of Newburgh to the church of Owston in the Isle of Axholme, void by the death of John Clarell, and was instituted on 15 March 1296, he resigning

Figure 12. The de Mauley tomb in Bainton Church.

Figure 13. Edward I on horseback, the 'Warrior King', who reigned 1272–1307. He was also a great sponsor of tournaments and enjoyed hunting.

the church of Lythe in accordance with the above dispensation. On 23 November 1299 he was collated to the Prebend of Bugthorp (and thus became a Canon of York Minster).[28]

As we have seen, Stephen's brother, Peter III, had married Nichole de Gant, a relative of Anthony Bek, Bishop of Durham (1284–1311) and Canon of York, and he, supported by archdeacon Stephen financed the translation of the bones of St William of York to a new shrine in the Minster on the day of his consecration. Bishop Bek heaped offices on archdeacon Stephen, he was appointed Bek's vicar-general, Dean of Auckland, and senechal of his castle there.[29] As Palatine bishop, Bek had to defend the north of England against the Scots, and was in command of his forces at the Seige of Caerlaverock.

About this time, stained glass windows were being inserted in the newly-built nave of York Minster, and Stephen was the donor of the de Mauley window in the south aisle, c1315 (Figures 14–15). This window shows members of the family kneeling in full armour and holding aloft their shields of arms. As one of the figures depicted is that of his brother, Sir Edmund, who was killed at Bannockburn, it may be regarded as a memorial window.

In 1215 Stephen was appointed Dean of Wimborne, two years later he was dead, the exact date is given in Archbishop William de Melton's Register: 'the Archdaconry [of Cleveland] has been vacant since the Friday after St. Laurance [12 August

Figure 14. The de Mauley window in York Minster, c1315.

1317] by the death of Sir Stephen de Mauley'.[30]According to Sir Richard de Thweng of Mikelby, near Mulgrave, Peter de Mauley was born about the hour of cock crowing (*circa hora gallicantus*) on 10 March 1279, following a night of great storms of unusual violence. He also says that he was baptised on the ninth day after his birth in the chapel of Mulgrave Castle by the Prior of Grosmont, and that Peter de Rothersfield and William de Roseles were his godfathers, and Maud, the wife of Robert de Acclom was his godmother. This information was given at an *Inquisition* or 'Proof of Age' held before the king (Edward I) on 8 July 1300 when Peter IV claimed lands at Iwardby left to him by his mother's brother, Gilbert de Gant.[31] Peter paid homage for these lands on 20 July 1302. The Inquisition also tells us that Peter is married 'by his father, who is still living (to Eleanor Furnival, daughter of Thomas, Lord Furnival, and sister of Alianora, the wife of Walter, second Lord Vavasour) by whom he had a son and heir, Peter V, born c1300'.

Lucia Thweng married Sir William Latimer at the age of fifteen, and in 1304 when her husband was away fighting in Scotland, Lucia fled from his family home at Brunne to Mulgrave Castle and became the mistress of Nicholas, Baron

Figure 15. De Mauley window in York Minster, detail of Archdeacon Stephen with Peter de Trehouse, founder of the family.

de Meynell of Whorlton who later married her.[32] Peter received his knighthood on Whit Sunday 1306, at Westminster on the same day as the Prince of Wales, and was first summoned to Parliament on 26 October 1309, two months after his father's death.[33]

Peter IV was a notorious character in Yorkshire. On 11 April 1310 he appeared before the Chapter of Beverley Minster as a supplicant, praying that his servants, who were charged with breaking the Peace of St John, might be absolved from excommunication. Peter de Mauley, with John Hotham and Geoffrey Hotham, knights, and others of Sir Peter's council, were required to ask 'upon their bended knees' absolution – for communicating with the servants when excommunicate. After a psalm, miserere, and other prayers, satisfaction was given 'by stroke of rods'.

On another occasion Peter and 'his council' were accused of carrying off a wagon load of nuns (seven in all) belonging to the Prioress of Whatton. Two other carts were also taken 'containing divers kind of gear, goods and chattels, deeds and writings, which together with ten horses they carried off in triumph'.[34]

York Minster benefited greatly from fines levied upon Peter after several amorous exploits, one of these included absolution for incest with his sister-in-law in 1313. This was probably Alianora Furnival, wife of Walter Vavasour who seems to have died that year. The conjecture is that Alianora had gone to live with her sister at Mulgrave, and had a child to Peter. It is interesting to note that Sir Robert de Mauley, the bastard, claimed lands of Peter in Hexthorpe and Balby when he came of age in 1335!

On the credit side, Peter served on the Priory Council in 1312, and was appointed one of the Wardens of the Northern Ports beyond the Trent in 1314. On 13 April 1315 a Mandate was issued by Archbishop Greenfield (then at Scrooby) to his officials at York:

> A Council against the Scots to be held in Doncaster on the Monday after Accession Day – summon all the clergy, they are either to send proctors or to attend in person.

A similar summons was sent to others, including Peter de Malo Lacu (Mauley) and John de Doncaster. As a result of this Council, Peter saw military service in Scotland.

1315 was also the year that Peter IV granted land to the Franciscan Friary at Doncaster. The area is still marked by the name Greyfriars Road, situated behind St George's Church. More land was added to the de Mauley holdings, for in 1318, he inherited the lordship of Ascot in Oxfordshire (presumably Ascot-under-Wychwood). 1322 saw him again on military service in Scotland.

In 1323 Peter was granted a licence for the foundation of a chantry chapel dedicated to St Nicholas in St George's Church, Doncaster. In the same year he was in trouble again, accused of adultery with Alice Deyvill, and then with Sara de London in 1327. Meanwhile, in June 1325 Warin de Eglemercher of the County of Cornwall was mainpernor, together with Peter de Mauley the younger, Robert Hilton, knight and others for Peter de Mauley the elder, outlawed in Essex. In 1322 Edward II granted a licence to Peter to grant the Manor and Town of Doncaster, together with the advowson of the church at

Rossington to John de Warren, Earl of Surrey, for his lifetime only, thereafter reverting to the heirs of de Mauley. The Earl paid £100 for the privilege. Peter IV died after 21 January, and before 24 August 1336 when his son, Peter V, was summoned to Parliament.

As we have seen, John, his brother, succeeded Archdeacon Stephen at Bainton, he also held Mulgrave Castle and had a grant of the fisheries at Doncaster and Rossington for his maintenance, and Robert his half-brother and Johanna his wife were living in the manor house there. There were also two sisters: Matilda, who married Thomas, Lord Multon of Gillsand, and another (name unknown) who may have been the wife of William de Roos – according to Dodsworth, who saw their shields impaled in the east window of Bainton church.

Peter V, Third Lord Mauley, c1300–55

Peter V was married to Margaret, the daughter of Robert, Lord Clifford III in 1322. He was described as a 'man-at-arms' in 1324, and knighted the following year; and summoned to Parliament several times between August 1336 and March 1354. He also held the position of Commissioner of Array in the North Riding of Yorkshire.

He was at the Seige of Calais in 1345, and fought at the Battle of Crecy in 1346 where his half-brother, Robert was knighted.[35] Later that same year he fought at the Battle of Nevilles Cross.

The alliance with the powerful Percy family was strengthened by the marriage of Lord Henry Percy to Ida Clifford, sister of Margaret, the wife of Peter V.

Peter died on 31 July 1355, leaving Peter VI, his eldest son and heir, Thomas and a daughter, Katherine who married Sir Thomas Ughtred of Kexby. Peter V made ample provision for the maintenance of his widow, leaving her the manors of Hexthorpe, Balby, Sandal, Bramham and Lockington until the day of her death when they were to revert back to their grandson, Peter VII and Margery Sutton, his wife and the heirs of their bodies. Peter VI retained the manors of Doncaster and Bainton.[36] Margaret eventually took the veil in the Abbey of Denny in Cambridgeshire where she died as late as 1382.

Peter VI, Fourth Lord Mauley, 1331–83

Peter VI fought at the Battle of Poitiers in 1356 and was knighted in 1357, the year that he married his first wife, Elizabeth Meynell, widow of Lord Darcy of Knaith, a marriage that had not been approved by the king (Henry III, Figure 16) and for which they were fined £100. Elizabeth died childless in 1367. His second wife was Constance, daughter of Sir Thomas Sutton of Branscombe by whom he had issue:

Figure 16. The lifelike monumental sculpture of Henry III in Westminster Abbey.

Peter VII and two daughters – Constance who married Robert Hilton, Lord of Swine, and Agnes who married Sir Thomas de St Quentin of Harpham. They are shown together on a brass (Figure 17) in Harpham church, dated 1418. In 1368 Peter VI was appointed Warden of the Eastern Marches, an appointment that was enewed in 1370 when he was to serve with the Bishop of Durham, and again in 1380 when he was to serve with the Earl of Northumberland. He was also Commissioner of Array in the East Riding of Yorkshire. He was appointed Governor of Berwick in 1368.[37] He attended Parliament between 1355 and 1383, the year of his death. He was buried in the Franciscan Friary at Doncaster. His will is dated 8 March 1381, he bequeathed £5 and his best beast of burden as his mortuary.[38] The witnesses were Lord Henry Percy, Lord Roger Clifford and Sir John Goddard and he had issue.

Peter VII c1359–80

Peter VII died two years before his father and therefore was never styled Lord Mauley. He married Margery Sutton, the youngest sister of his father's second wife, by whom he had issue: Peter VIII, John, Constance and Elizabeth.

Peter VIII, Fifth Lord Mauley, c1377–1415

Peter VIII succeeded his grandfather as the 5th Lord Mauley in 1383, and as he was a minor his inheritance was administered by the Crown until he came of age. The Crown appointed Sir Thomas Percy, long time ally of the family, to act for them. In 1399 Peter inherited lands at Iburnside left to him by his uncle Thomas. Also in that year he was created Knight of the Bath at the coronation of king Henry IV. He is also shown on a roll of arms to be a Knight of the Golden Fleece, where he appears alongside Lord Lumley and Lord Scrope.[39] He was called to Parliament between 1399 and 1415. He married Maud, daughter of Ralph Neville, 1st Earl of Northumberland. Unfortunately the marriage was childless. Peter died in 1415 and his will directed that he was to be buried in the church of St John, Bridlington (now under the sea).[40] Maud died in 1438 and was buried in the church of the Friars Preachers, Scarborough. Because the marriage was childless the land and titles devolved on Peter VIII's brother and sisters. Unfortunately Peter's only brother, John, died young, so there was no male heir and the titles became extinct. The lands were divided

Figure 17. Monumental brass to Agnes de Mauley and her husband, Sir Thomas de St Quintin, c1420, in Harpham Church.

between the two daughters: Constance, heiress of Mulgrave, who married, first, William Fairfax of Walton, and secondly, Sir John Bigod of Settringham; Elizabeth, heiress of Doncaster, who married John (George) Salveyn of Newbiggin and Kilham. Their descendants held the Manor of Doncaster until 1622 when the Corporation paid them £3,000 to quit all claim to the Lordship of Doncaster.

Notes and References

1. For an account of the Fossard family see *Yorkshire Archaeological Society Journal* (YASJ), No. V, pp 314–17.
2. J Hunter, *South Yorkshire*, I, 1828, p 9.
3. *ibid.*
4. Dugdale, *The Baronage*, p 662; see also *Dictionary of National Biography* (DNB), p 370.
5. *Chronicon de Melsa*, i, p 106.
6. DNB, pp 90–91.
7. Walter of Hemmingburgh, i, pp 232–33; DNB, p 90.
8. Matthew Paris, ii, p 531; DNB, p 90.
9. A mark was a metal unit of currency worth 13s. 4d., two third of a pound.
10. *Excerpta e Rot. Finium*, i, p 54.
11. *Rot. Litt. Patt.*, p 128; DNB, p 90.
12. Calendar of Close Rolls 16 John. m. 16(1); E Miller, *History and Antiquities of Doncaster*, 1804, p 40.
13. T W E Roche, *The King of Almayne*, p 16–17.
14. *Rot. Litt. Claus*, i, 417b.
15. Walter of Coventry, *Memoriale*, ii, p 260; DNB, p 91.
16. C L Kingsford. 'The Barons de Mauley', *English Historical Review*, Vol. XI, pp 515–20, July 1896.
17. *Monasticon Anglicanum*, Vol 1, p 800 n 20/30.
18. *Excepta e Rot. Finium*, i, p 364; Kingsford, *op cit*, 517.
19. Michel's *Roles Gascons*, i, 2090, 2151–2, 2342–3, 3598.
20. Yorks Inquisitions, i, pp 191–200. Vol XXI, *Yorkshire Archaeological Society Record Series* (YASRS).
21. Sir Samuel Meyrick, 'Observations on the Monumental Effigy of De Mauley', *Archaeologia*, Vol XXXI, p 234.
22. Palgrave *Parliamentary Writs*, iv, p 1154.
23. Cal. Pat. Rolls, 1307–13, p 582; YASJ, Vol XXVII, p 246.
24. Cal Close Rolls, Edw. II, 1307–13, p 230 and 313–18; Kingsford, *op cit*, p 519.
25. Chron. Edw. I & Edw. II, i, p 215, pp 272–3, ii, 42, 183.
26. Cal. Pat. Rolls, 1281–92, p 261; Reg. Wickwane, p 109 n. 26.
27. Reg. Romeyn, *Surtees Society*, i, p 378.
28. *Le Neve*, York Minster Fasti, iii, p 178.
29. *Registrum Palatinum Dunelmense*, i, p 107; Kingsford, *op cit*, p 520.
30. YAS, Vol LXI, *Miscellanea*, i, p 141.
31. YASJ, *Yorkshire Inquisitions*, p 5.
32. YASJ, Vol XXII, p 87.
33. Palgrave, *op cit*, p 1154.
34. Meyrick, *op cit*, p 248.
35. Barnes, *History of Edward III, p 355;* Kingsford, *op cit*, p 518.
36. Lists & Indexes, Vol 17, Inq. Ad. Quod. Damnum, ii, p 576.
37. Kingsford, *op cit*, p 518.
38. YASJ, Vol XXXII, 1934–36, p 300.
39. *Biblioteque De L'Arsenal*, MS 4790.
40. *Testamenta Eboracensia*, i, pp 379–81.

3. AN ABBOT IN RETIREMENT

by Tom W Beastall

THE FINAL WILL AND TESTAMENT of Henry Cundall the last abbot of Roche Abbey came to light in 1986.[1] It illuminates not only the life of a local sixteenth century dignitary in retirement after the dissolution of the Abbey in 1538 but also the Church life of the nearby parish of Tickhill (Figure 1). Little is known of those whose world collapsed with the dissolution once they had left their monastic houses so this document is especially welcome to local historians. Henry Cundall's election as abbot was probably not long before the dissolution though it seems he was there three years earlier in 1535.[2] Roche, founded in 1147 by Richard Fitz-Turgis and Richard de Busli was a Cistercian house, the home of 'White Monks' so called because of

Figure 1. Oral tradition has long held that this oak chest with five locks belonged to the Abbot of Roche and that it came to Tickhill at the dissolution. Evidence of Henry Cundall's retirement to the parish gives weight to this belief. *The Author*

their white habit worn beneath a black gown (Figure 2). Roche's annual income had fallen in a year from £222 to £170 and debts of £20 had accumulated. This decline put the Abbey within the terms of the Act for the suppression of the lesser monasteries and soon it was subjected to a visitation by Dr Leigh and Dr Layton the Crown's commissioners. The Founder or Patron of the Abbey was recorded as Henry Clifford, Earl of Cumberland whose family had held this position since 1446. Five monks were accused of crime, one was suspected of treason and the site itself was condemned as being a place of superstition as pilgrimages were made there to venerate an image of the Crucifix in the rock face of Roche Abbey valley. Such accusations were usual before the commissioners began their work.

Figure 2. Cistercian monk in white habit. *Brian Elliott*

Little is known of Henry Cundall's background. His surname suggests a family origin in North Yorkshire from the village of that name near Ripon. His will, however, indicates a clear family association with Crowle near Thorne and Scunthorpe. The surname appears in many nineteenth century Lincolnshire directories for Crowle. Pigot's 1828 publication has a Joseph Cundall gentleman, a Robert Cundall and William Cundall listed as an ironmonger. White's directories of 1856 and 1872 have Cundalls as a butcher, an innkeeper and a solicitor's clerk. In Kelly's directory of 1885 William Cundall appears as a farmer at Ealand. Henry Cundall's time as Abbot if short was not without domestic trouble as he had at least one difficult monk in his community to disturb the peace in the beautiful valley between Maltby and Stone (Figure 3).

The abbot wrote a hasty and exasperated letter to the Earl of Cumberland as Founder of the Abbey and Lord of the Manor of

Figure 3. Roche Abbey in the Magnesian Limestone valley between Maltby and Stone. *The Author*

Maltby about Thomas Acworth one of his brothers. Acworth had made complaints about his treatment at Roche to the Patron or Founder at Tuxford as the Earl made his way through the village on his journey to London. The Abbot, who had heard about Acworth's letter from the Earl's bailiff of Maltby, wrote with all speed to challenge the accusations and to inform the Earl of the complainant's reputation. Brother Thomas Acworth had been given responsibility for the general management of the House as sub-prior but under his administration it had declined. When the Abbot had spoken to him about his work, 'he did allwaiez lightly regarde it'. He would, '. . . take no payne', but would make trouble amongst the other brothers. When the visitor from the Order came to look at affairs at the Abbey he too met with unsatisfactory responses from Thomas Acworth who was then demoted to Kitchener; a good office the Abbot contended if it were properly managed. As with his other work this fell to '. . . ruyn and decay under his hands . . .' What the outcome was of the correspondence we do not know but Thomas Acworth was still at Roche in 1538 when he signed the deed of surrender to the Crown in the Chapter House on 23 June. He had not regained his office as sub-prior for one Thomas Twell signed as such and Thomas Acworth's signature is entered at eleventh place in a list of eighteen.[3]

Although the dissolution involved not only the activity of the workmen who accompanied or quickly followed the commissioners and the subsequent pillaging of the site by local people the settlement for the inmates suggests that they gave little trouble. The Abbot's provision could be called generous. He was given a pension of £33. 6s. 8d. a year, his books, a quarter of the plate, the cattle, household stuff, a chalice and vestments, a lump sum of £30 in cash and a portion of corn. Each monk received half a year's portion and twenty shillings for clothing; and the Crown was to clear the £20 debt outstanding. Servants were to have half a year's wages. Some fifteen years later twelve of the eighteen who signed the deed of surrender were still receiving their pensions including Henry Cundall and Thomas Twell the former sub-prior but not Thomas Acworth.

James Aveling in his history of the Abbey, written in 1870, suggests that like other abbots Henry Cundall may have made preparation for the dissolution by pawning a tabernacle noted at the visitation as being 'in pledge' in the commissioner's inventory and that the small amount of plate listed points to some presumptive action by the Abbot. At all events he seems to have lived in some style and comfort in his retirement home shared with Robert Stanley, the vicar of Tickhill. The Vicarage was probably on the site of the present *Darfield House* or 'Old

Vicarage' given that the parish tithe barn approached by Tithes Lane lay behind it. This house is a rebuilt property of 1785. We do know that the sixteenth century vicarage was a large dwelling for George Aislaby, the first Anglican incumbent appealed to the Archdeacon of Doncaster to have it reduced and the building materials so made available used to repair the rest of the structure which was in a state of decay.[4]

Why did Henry Cundall choose Tickhill as his retirement home? He had personal property, friends and perhaps relations in Crowle. Tickhill's proximity to Roche with all its associations may have drawn him there. It seems to have been a conservative parish in ecclesiastical terms for one of the Abbot's brothers from Roche, Nicholas Collys became chaplain in the chantry chapel of the Holy and Blessed Trinity within St Mary's parish church.

Figure 4. A piscina in the south aisle wall of Tickhill Parish Church marks the site of the chantry chapel dedicated to Our Lady. William Marshe was chantry priest here. *The Author*

There were other chantry priests there too who were to be mentioned in Henry Cundall's will. John Knaggs, who signed the will in October 1554 held the chaplaincy of the chantry of the Holy Rood and Crucifix. William Marshe who was to hold a dinner for mourners after the Abbot's funeral was chaplain of Our Lady's chantry in the parish church (Figure 4). It seems then that Tickhill afforded not only ample living accommodation but congenial company for a retired abbot. The chantries, not dissolved until 1547, were seen perhaps as a link with the old ways. Did this exile from Roche entertain hopes of an eventual return? Tickhill was to remain something of a centre for traditional practices for as late as 1569 Mass was still being said in the chapel of the *Maison Dieu* almshouses on the south side of the parish church. A stone altar was there, it was alleged before the High Commission court and local people on hearing a bell rung for Mass went there rather than to the parish church.[5]

Not just Tickhill but the Doncaster area generally has been described as a 'staunchly traditionalist district'.[6] It was the home of Richard Rolle of Hampole (Figure 5), the fourteenth century mystic

Figure 5. Richard Rolle of Hampole.

whose life and writing had an influence well beyond Doncaster. In the upheavals of the mid-sixteenth century Robert Parkyn, parish priest of Adwick-le-Street wrote about the abandonment of traditional practices with all the disapproval of one steeped in the Catholic tradition to the extent that he has been called the last Medieval Englishman.[7] Though he conformed reluctantly under Henry VIII and Edward VI and was to do so again under Elizabeth, he reported that under Mary many local clergy were ready to follow the lead given by Catholic gentry to sing Mass again as soon as a new law or statute allowed it.[8]

Henry Cundall was to live long enough to see Mary Tudor succeed her half-brother Edward VI in July 1553. In many parts of England a Catholic reaction started before the Queen made public in August her desire for a return to Catholicism. We do not know when or to what extent Tickhill returned openly to Catholic ceremonies but Henry Cundall's will has a preamble and contents which affirm a traditional, Catholic belief. Indeed it has features in common with the traditional, pre-Reformation will of Alexander Leeson of 1497.[9]

After stating his clerical order, his being in Tickhill and claiming soundness of mind and memory his will goes on to thank God for his condition considering the 'manyfold danngere and evill of this fowll world and the disseses and sekness where with & am and oftymes hath been greved with'. He mentioned the vanity of this mortal life and went on to bequeath his '. . . soul to almighty god my maker redeemer and saviour through whome and by whome I trust faithfully to be partaker and inheritor of the kingdome of heaven with our blessed ladie marie and the celestial company . . .' His body was to be buried in the 'high quire' or chancel of the parish church (Figure 6) if '. . . it fates me in Tickhill to depart'. This suggests, and later provisions of his will confirm that even in advancing years and with indifferent health he moved about, at least between Tickhill and Crowle. His will, dated 18 October 1554, would be made after the Queen's marriage to Philip of Spain and the start of their joint reign, on 25 July 1554 after which it was hoped the Queen would give birth to an heir who would secure a Catholic succession. Though this was not to be, nevertheless, the last months of Henry Cundall's life may well have passed in an atmosphere of traditionalist confidence and expectancy. So he willed that his corpse bearers were to have eight pence each and for Mass and Dirge said or sung, every priest was to be paid six pence and the parish clerk four pence and the 'syninge' boys two pence each.

Figure 6. Tickhill Parish Church. *The Author*

Here were obvious preparations for a traditional Catholic funeral. The inmates of the *Maison Dieu* almshouses received eleven pence and the poor of the town the same. The vicar of Tickhill received a number of personal bequests including a worsted tippet, a black felt hat, a large chair and a cushion. John Emerie, priest, received a worsted jacket and John Yates, priest, a doublet with a pair of hose sewn into it. Evidently the Abbot could afford to employ a servant for John Blaxton was rewarded with a feather bed, a mattress, bed coverings, two coverlets, a pair of blankets, a pair of sheets, a bolster, a pillow and a chamlet doublet with a pair of hose sewn to it, twenty pence in money and a tin basin. The Vicarage servant, Anne Smith, was given five shillings and a kerchief. Another servant received three shillings and four pence and George Wilkinson the Vicar's manservant, was to be given eight pence and John Smith, probably husband to Anne Smith, was to have four pence. No doubt these bequests acknowledged the extra work made by the Abbot's residence at the Vicarage. They indicate that the household was, if not an opulent one, then at least one that provided a well-serviced home for the Vicar and the retired Abbot.

Henry Cundall was active in spite of ill health in the last year of his life for his executors were to sell twenty gallons of honey '. . . which I ma'd at Crowle this year'. Twenty shillings from the sale were to be given to the poor of Crowle and the rest of the sale return was to be used for payment of legacies. Clearly he expected a good return on his honey! Katherine Moore's daughter at Crowle received a mattress, two coverlets, a pair of sheets, a bolster and twenty pence. Godchildren at Tickhill and Crowle were to have six pence each in addition to the six pence he had already given them. William Marshe, priest at Tickhill, was to have the Abbot's finest gown which he had from brother Nicholas Collys and articles of bed covering and hangings. The 'wife of the house' at William Marshe's residence was to be paid ten pence for her work and that of a maid in providing a dinner after the funeral. William Marshe occupied a chamber and a parlour in the house of William and Joan Hall from September 1546. He had leased the property, a 'mansion house' belonging to the Chantry of Our Lady where he had been chaplain, to the Halls reserving for his personal use the two rooms, one a bedroom, the other a reception room.[10]

Katherine Clewe, Robert Clewe's daughter at Crowle was given bed coverings, bees and a pewter dish and ten pence. It appears that Henry Cundall had a mill at Crowle for he bequeathed it with its tolls to George Curtis who also received twenty pence, 'of Thomas Frost bond', a loan on which interest to the Abbot '. . . should have been paid long since'. He also gave him a feather bed and half the coverings of a bed '. . . like to the other half which I have at Tickhill'. References to bed coverings and hangings suggest a high degree of comfort and decoration in the sleeping quarters both at Crowle and Tickhill. A mention of what appears to be the 'founders bed' suggests that perhaps the Earl of Cumberland as Patron of the Abbey had a bed there set aside for him when he stayed at Roche on his journeys in the district and within the lordship of Maltby. Some bed hangings seem to have been painted suggesting that they took the form of screens or similar draught-excluding furnishings.

John Curtis, a godson at Crowle, was given a swarm of bees and twelve pence. Henry Clewe, another godson, had a swarm and ten pence and the other children of Robert Clewe, a family friend it would seem, were to have six pence each. Thomas Willis and Katherine Moore were his joint executors to dispose of his estate '. . . for the health of my soule. . .'; another traditional reference to good works towards his soul's repose. George Curtis and Robert Clewe of Crowle and William Marshe and Robert Woodruff of Tickhill were to be supervisors of his will. They were to be paid three shillings and four pence, each it seems, and their costs. If any of the executors were not present at his burial then the Vicar of Tickhill and William Marshe, with Robert Woodruff were to supervise at Tickhill.

Witnesses were Robert Stanley, Vicar, John Knaggs, priest, William Marshe, priest, Robert Woodruff, Robert Eston and John Burton, all of Tickhill. The will was proved before the Archdeacon of Doncaster, James Box, on 4 May 1555. Henry Cundall was buried at Tickhill on 14 December 1554 and registered in the parish burial volume as 'Sir Henry Cundall Clark' on folio 138.

So ended the life of Henry Cundall. He was surrounded by a circle of friends, clerical and lay, godchildren, neighbours and servants. Dividing his time between Tickhill and Crowle, keeping bees, making honey, attending to godchildren, associating with chantry priests and living in some comfort, outwardly at least his must have been a relatively acceptable retirement. Whether he lived on regretting his life at Roche and hoping for a restoration, if not of the monastic life then of the Catholic order in parish churches, we do not know. Before his death the ecclesiastical practices and beliefs he had known were for a short time put in place once more before the Church in England moved on yet again to the Elizabethan settlement and a new Anglican tradition came into being.

Notes and References

1. Borthwick Institute of Historical Research (BIHR). Prob. Reg. 14. p. 78v.
2. Clifford Letters of the Sixteenth Century; 11, p. 75, Henry, Abbot of Roche to the first Earl of Cumberland [undated; c.1535].
3. James W. Aveling, *The History of Roche Abbey*, 1870, pp. 86–7.
4. BIHR, Court Book 1, 1567, V1567/8/cb/1.
5. BIHR, Act Book 4, f89–92.
6. Eaman Duffy, *Stripping of the Altars*, 1992, pp. 462–3, 527.
7. *ibid.*
8. *ibid.* p. 527.
9. Surtees Society, vol. IV, 1869, p. 132.
10. Foljambe Papers, Nottinghamshire Records, DDFJ/7/80/11.

Acknowledgements

I thank Elizabeth Atkinson and Malcolm Dolby for all their help in the identification and interpretation of Henry Cundall's will. The staff of the Borthwick Institute of Historical Research in York and the staff of the Local Studies section of the Central Library in Doncaster as well as Doncaster Archives staff have been of real assistance in the production of this chapter. To Colin Webb, Carol Hill and Brian Barber I offer my thanks.

4. THE LANDED GENTRY OF THE DONCASTER DISTRICT

by Brian Barber

VISITORS TO THE DONCASTER DISTRICT, even those from other parts of Yorkshire, are routinely and pleasantly surprised by its rural aspect. Images of coal mining and railway engineering and their environmental consequences have created an impression which, to the outsider, characterise the entire area. At the end of the twentieth century, those influences are in headlong decline and, indeed, in reverse. Railway engineering is a vestige of its Victorian self and coal has gone into precipitate, politically motivated, decline. Economically, the Doncaster district is now in a period of change as striking, but far less certain, than any in the last century and a half. Despite the changes in the local economy since the 1850s, the Doncaster area remains substantially rural. Apart from the town of Doncaster itself, the area has mostly small and medium-sized communities surrounded by swathes of fields and woodland. Ribbon development disguises this from the motorist along some roads, but the principal through routes, the M1 and M18 and, outside Doncaster itself, the main east-coast railway line, pass almost entirely through rural areas.

The rural features of the Doncaster area are the focus of this chapter, which surveys some aspects of the history of the landed gentry from the seventeenth to the twentieth century. Using the records of the landed families which have been gradually accumulating in local archive departments over the previous fifty years, it would now be possible to write a study of the local gentry at some length. This, however, is not possible in the confines of the present chapter. Here, the aim is only to make a preliminary review of some of the broad themes, for the most part using published works rather than archives, and draw attention to the records which are now available, in the hope that it will stimulate some of the readers of this chapter to take the research further themselves. To help this hope towards realisation, the reader will find at the end of this chapter a brief guide of the records of the landed gentry which can be found in local repositories, and in particular in Doncaster Archives. No doubt the commonest way in which those travelling around the area become aware of the former presence of the landed gentry is through the phys-

Figure 1. The gatehouse at Hooton Pagnell, which Pevsner dates as fourteenth century although the medieval core of the Hall was much 'restored' by Mrs Julia Warde-Aldam at the end of the nineteenth century. The Hall was extended by St Andrew Warde in the 1780s to a design by William Lindley. The house is still the seat of their descendants, now the Warde-Norbury family. *Brian Elliott*

ical evidence of their existence, most notably by the presence in the landscape of country houses. These are synonymous with the lifestyle of the leisured rural class of earlier centuries, although those which now survive are all of the eighteenth and nineteenth century.[1] Most survive in a guise which would have surprised their builders. One has become the property of English Heritage: Brodsworth Hall, the mid-

Figure 2 Warmsworth Hall, said to have been built in 1702, was the seat of the Battie family from 1668 until the marriage of John Battie with Isobel Wrightson, the heiress of the nearby Cusworth estate. The Hall and grounds were sold by the estate in 1945 and in 1960 were purchased by British Ropes for the site of their group headquarters, designed by T H Johnson and Son of Doncaster. The company vacated the premises in 1985 and the Hall and the new buildings are now a hotel. *Brian Elliott*

Figure 3. Owston Hall was the seat of the Davies-Cooke family of Doncaster from 1698. They were one of several branches of the Cooke family of Doncaster to establish themselves amongst the local landed gentry. Brian Cooke married a Welsh heiress in 1786, and their descendants took the surname of her uncle and benefactor, John Davies, in addition to their own. In the twentieth century, the Davies-Cookes came to prefer their Flintshire estates and the family sold Owston in 1980. *Brian Elliott*

nineteenth century Italianate home of the Thellussons (see chapter 5), but several remain in private hands. At Hooton Pagnell, where a medieval gateway set back from the road (Figure 1) alerts the visitor to what in the turbulent border regions of Northumberland would be called a peel tower, the house is occupied by the descendants of the family which purchased it in the early eighteenth century and nearby, Frickley Hall, also visible from the road, has been in the ownership of the same family since the 1840s. Cantley Hall, disposed of a century ago by the family who built it, remains a private house. However, Warmsworth Hall (Figure 2) is hidden in the grounds of a hotel converted from twentieth century office buildings. High Melton Hall, with incongruous additions, is concealed at the centre of a modern college development. At Cusworth Hall, the change is internal, as the house holds a museum of Yorkshire social history and Wadworth Hall has housed first a county council home for the elderly and then private businesses for the last thirty years. Burghwallis Hall has been a rest home run by nuns since the 1940s, perhaps the most apt successors of the Catholic recusant family which owned it for generations and Owston Hall (Figure 3) has been converted into flats. The remains of Edenthorpe Hall have been incorporated into a school and Wilsic Hall is also a school. Some houses are no longer standing, victims of the changing circumstances of their owners in recent times. In Campsall, both Campsmount and Campsall Hall have gone, as have Skellow Grange, Crookhill Hall and, perhaps the most serious architectural

Figure 4. Sprotbrough Hall, the former mansion of the Copley and Bewicke-Copley family. *Brian Elliott Collection*

loss to the area, Sprotbrough Hall (Figure 4).

The starting point for this present survey must be to define the term 'landed gentry'. One definition lies readily to hand, at least for the nineteenth century. This is to be found in John Bateman's gazeteer, *The Great Landowners of Great Britain and Ireland,* published originally in 1876. His work was a refinement of the information which appeared in a Parliamentary Paper of 1874, which printed the results of a nationwide return of land ownership. The return had been undertaken at the prompting of Lord Derby, in the confident belief that it would refute the assertion of radicals that the country was in the ownership of a mere thirty thousand individuals. However, when completed, the return dealt a severe blow to Lord Derby's expectation. Whilst it showed that more than a million people had a stake, however small, in the land of the United Kingdom, it revealed that eighty per cent of the country was in the hands of only seven thousand owners.

Bateman defined as landed gentry all those who owned at least three thousand acres of land and an estimated gross income of at least three thousand pounds a year from it. This, as Bateman stressed, was gross estimated income, and the net income of the landowner would invariably be significantly less. Taxes and other estate expenses, and inherited obligations to other members of the family (which, if in the form of annuities bequeathed under the wills of one's predecessors, were not optional payments and ended only with the death of the beneficiary) have to be taken into account. A local, although perhaps extreme, example is provided by the Sprotbrough estate in the early-eighteenth century. A statement of income and expenditure shows that the Yorkshire and Nottinghamshire estates of the Copleys were producing a handsome annual income of £1,731. But out of this, the estate had to provide payments totalling £1,240 to other members of the family, £100 in tithes and a further £360 in interest payments, leaving the net income of the estate at £507, or well under one third of the gross.[2]

Below the gentry in Bateman's classification were the squirearchy, the country landowners with between one and three thousand acres or under £3,000 a year gross income from land. Above the gentry were the major landowners, mostly but far from exclusively, the nobility, with broader acres and greater income. A local example would be the Earl of Scarbrough, whose estates covered over 21,000 acres and produced a gross estimated rental of over £31,000 a year.[3] The boundaries between nobility and gentry were, of course, fluid and there are a number of local examples to illustrate this. The Woods of Hickleton (Figure 5) moved into the aristocracy in 1866 with a title taken from Sir Charles Wood's House of Commons constituency of Halifax: his grandson became Foreign Secretary in Neville Chamberlain's Conservative government of 1937 to 1940. In the early twentieth century, the Copleys of Sprotbrough acquired a title of nobility through the lengthy and expensive pursuit of a claim (on grounds so

Figure 5. Hickleton Hall was purchased by the Wood family of Hemsworth from the Wentworth family of Woolley [West Yorkshire] in 1828. The political career of Sir Charles Wood [1800–1885] turned a baronetcy into a peerage; that of his grandson, foreign secretary in Neville Chamberlain's government from 1935 to 1940, turned a viscountcy into an earldom. Like the Davies-Cookes, the family came to prefer their other home, and the house is now occupied as a nursing home by the Sue Rider Foundation. *Brian Elliott*

tenuous that claims of the same type were made impossible in 1927) to the long-dormant medieval barony of Cromwell, an enterprise which ultimately cost them more than £4,500.[4] In another sense also, the boundaries between aristocracy and gentry were fluid, for the possession of a title alone was not an automatic indicator of wealth.

The Streetthorpe estate, for example, was sold by one of the branches of the Cooke family on inheriting the Yarborough estates to the north of Doncaster from spinster aunts in 1802. This relatively modest estate was later purchased by a peer, Lord Auckland, one of the gentry family of Eden of County Durham, in 1871 (perhaps on account of its proximity to the Cantley estate owned by the family of his first wife), but even after being enlarged by further purchases in 1872 and 1874, it still comprised only 868 acres.[5] But if Lord Auckland (who renamed his estate 'Edenthorpe' to commemorate his family name), was of relatively modest means, another landowner in the area rejoiced in the description of the 'wealthiest commoner in England'. Andrew Montagu could have had a title if he had so wished, and for political services which were, in their unique way, of a remarkable nature. In 1862, Montagu offered to help the Conservative cause, and found himself providing personal financial help to Benjamin Disraeli. At the discreet suggestion of the party managers, he bought up Disraeli's substantial debts – estimated at some £60,000 – from moneylenders and substituted a three-percent mortgage on Hughenden, Disraeli's Buckinghamshire country home, for the usurious rates of interest the party leader had been paying. In return, a grateful if incautious Disraeli, when prime minister, tried to make Montagu a peer. Fortunately for Disraeli, he declined the offer for, had the reason for it become public knowledge 'there might have been an uproar which would have even put the Honours Scandal of 1922 in the shade.'[6]

Bateman's work identified eleven local landowners as landed gentry, with a further two who, although technically 'under the line' by one of his criteria, clearly qualify. For an updated version see Table 1, page 70. Several issues need immediate comment. One, the fluid line separating the gentry from the peerage has already been mentioned. Another is a matter of definition: clearly, some of these local gentry can only be regarded as 'local' in a limited sense: the Childers, Davies-Cookes, Franks, Montagus and Wrightsons had landed estates outside the area, and, indeed, some may have looked upon their other estates as their principal residence. This, of course, became a significant issue when the Doncaster area became more industrial in character. A study of the map (Figure 6) shows that there is a remarkable concentration of gentry and squirearchy in the west of the district, specifically along the limestone ridge. From Wadworth, to the south of the river Don, through High Melton, Sprotbrough, Cusworth, Hickleton, Brodsworth, Hooton Pagnell, Frickley, Owston, Bughwallis, Skelbrooke and Campsall and continuing beyond the district to Womersley, the line of landed estates runs almost seamlessly from one to another. Only the estates of the Cookes of Wheatley and those of the Childers at Cantley and the Edens at Edenthorpe lie further to the east. Bateman's major survey gives us an indispensable but necessarily static picture of a group at one point

Figure 6. This extract from Thomas Jeffreys' *Map of Yorkshire*, published in 1772, shows most, but not all, of the seats of the gentry in the Doncaster district. Owston has been omitted and Brodsworth has become 'Broadsworth'. Owston was not by-passed by what is now the Doncaster to Selby road until the construction of the turnpike road following the Act of 1832.

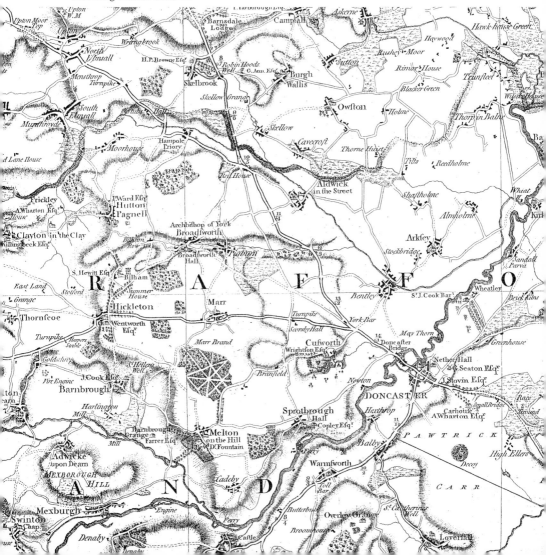

in time, the late nineteenth century, but to gain some insight into the historical circumstances which led up to these statistics and, indeed, which led away from them, we need to look to other sources.

The gentry was not a caste – a fixed social group – and its membership changed for a variety of reasons over the centuries. Some of the families who appear in Bateman were only recently arrived in the district. Most recent of these were the Woods of Hickleton who had moved into the district only in 1828 from nearby Hemsworth, when Sir Francis Lindley Wood purchased the estate from the Wentworths of Woolley. Others, like the Annes of Burghwallis, could trace their local ancestors back to the early fourteenth century. Others, such as the Aldams of Frickley, were, as we will see, new recruits to the gentry. It is clearly not possible to trace the fortunes of local gentry families over several centuries in the scope of this chapter, but the sources for doing this are not difficult to find. Generations of readers interested in local history have turned to Joseph Hunter's *South Yorkshire*, which, in the absence of a modern *Victoria County History*, remains, despite its great age, the only substantial survey of the area. Its primary interests, as befits its period, are in the genealogy of gentry families, the ownership of landed estates, and ecclesiastical matters. To the local historian of Hunter's generation, 'the history of a district is very much the history of the property of that district', as he wrote in the preface to his own work. Given the resources at his disposal, no researcher can fail to be respectful of Hunter's achievement, and what would now be regarded as the narrow focus of his interests is no disadvantage in the present context.[7] Even a casual reading of his genealogies reveals several facts of importance to our survey. One is the degree of change amongst the gentry families over the centuries. As Hunter observed of the Anne family:

> it is a remarkable fact that this Catholic family is the single instance of the male line being maintained in its ancient port and rank out of all the gentry of this deanery summoned to appear before the heralds in 1584.

Hunter's choice of the Anne family is significant for another reason also. Although he asserts that the family is a

> singular instance of a family in this deanery continuing from the reign of Edward II to the present time in the possession of considerable estates within its limits

it is significant that he notices the family in his chapter on Frickley with Clayton. Yet by the time of his writing, the family had sold its Frickley estate to the Wardes of Hooton Pagnell and had taken up residence at Burghwallis.[8] If the ownership of gentry estates could change, so could the estates themselves: some increased in size, some shrank. How and why this took place (was it by buying out the small owner-occupiers or, as in the case of Frickley, by one gentry family purchasing the estates of another? Had, for instance, estates elsewhere been told to purchase others in lieu, or was there an actual increase in the size of the estate?) would be a theme which a detailed study of the gentry would need to explore. One factor which could be crucial to the survival of an estate was the continuity of the male line. Sometimes this continuity was more apparent than real. The failure of a direct male heir was often remedied by settling the inheritance of the estate on a relation, near or distant, and stipulating that he assume the surname of the benefactor and so give a continuity at least to the family name. Henry Browne of Skelbrooke, for example, arranged for his estate to pass to the younger sons of one of his sisters and, in the event of a failure of male heirs, to the younger sons of his other sister, and expressed the hope that the grateful recipient would take the surname of Browne. In the event, the two families produced only one such heir, and the estate passed instead to Henry's cousins, the Neviles.[9]

Besides obscuring discontinuities of inheritance by direct heirs, the practice of changing surnames in recognition of inheritance could introduce apparent discontinuities. Thus Hunter's instance of the Anne family ancient name is in a sense ironic, for in 1810, Michael Anne changed his name to Tasburgh in acknowledgement of his wife's inheritance of the Norfolk estates of George Tasburgh, her mother's first husband. (It is a quaint complication of the story that the second husband, the father of the bride, had himself changed his name from Crawthorne to Tasburgh when he married the widow.) At Burghwallis, the next generation reverted to the Anne surname, but at Owston, the children of Brian Cooke (died 1821) bore the surname of Davies-Cooke in acknowledgement of their mother's inheritance of a Welsh estate from her bachelor uncle, John Davies, and future generations continue to do so. More drastic was the decision of the Wilson family of High Melton to adopt the surname of Montagu, in recognition of an inheritance from a relative.

The failure of the male line might lead to the dissolution of the estate. The handsome Wadworth Hall (Figure 7) stands as a memorial to the founding and foundering of a family aspiring to the gentry. The Wordsworth family originated some twenty miles to the east in Penistone, but migration to the City of London and success in foreign trade brought substantial wealth to Josias Wordsworth. In 1748, the fortunes of the family were seemingly sealed with the marriage of Josias junior to Ann Robinson of Hull, the daughter and grand-daughter of collectors of customs. The proud father settled a large estate on the thirty-year-old couple, and at Wadworth, commissioned them a fine house, completed if not begun, by James Paine, then the favoured architect of the local gentry, and bought them the advowson of the parish. All seemed set fair for a new dynasty, but by the time of the son's death in 1780, these hopes had vanished. The marriage had produced two daughters. Unlike the spinster sisters of Campsmount, they had both married, and married social superiors, and neither of the husbands gained sufficient from the alliance to be induced to change their surname on inheriting their share of the property. (Daughters inherited equal shares of an estate, in the absence of sons.) In the decade after the death of the nonagenarian widow in 1814, the daughters' husbands retained some property, but the house and most of the estate was sold by auction.[10]

The aspirations of the Wordsworths were far from unusual, and they differed from some of the Doncaster gentry only by their failure to establish a male line. Fortunes made in business and the professions were the source of the prosperity of many landed families, although generations of living as landowners sometimes appears to disguise the origins of their wealth. The wealth transferred from commerce or the professions into land originated from both local and more exotic sources. Doncaster and Pontefract, the two corporate boroughs in the

Figure 7. Wadworth Hall, a small, elegant house completed by James Paine for Josias Wordsworth, a merchant whose son's marriage failed to produce the male heir which would have transformed a mercantile fortune into a landed dynasty. In the 1930s, the Hall became the home of the Cooke-Yarboroughs after the sale of Campsmount, and subsequently an old people's home and then business premises. *Brian Elliott*

area, were small market towns, and in comparison with other West Riding towns of the early modern period, something of backwaters.[11] It seems, however, that the opportunities for enterprise which they provided led to the accumulation of the wealth which enabled several of their townsmen to launch themselves into the local landed gentry. The Cooke family traced its origins to Edward Cooke, mayor of Doncaster for four years in a row in 1504 to 1508. Edward was the father of the two sons. One of these was Lawrence, who became prior of the Carmelite priory of Doncaster, and who was executed in 1540, after protesting against the dissolution of his priory two years earlier and the other was William, from whom the prolific family descended. However, the first member of the family to be documented in its pedigree is Brian (Figure 8), mayor of Doncaster in 1630, who married the daughter of Henry Riley, another mayor of the borough. It was his third son, George, who inherited an estate at Wheatley from his childless elder barrister brother Brian purchasing the manor of Bentley in 1655, and who, by virtue of the family's exertions in the royalist cause in the civil wars, was created baronet in 1661. The Childers family of Cantley also had its origins in the urban elite of Doncaster, and married into the elites of more important towns. Hugh Childers, mayor of Doncaster in 1604, was married to the daughter of alderman Hardy of Newcastle-upon-Tyne and built Carr House, on the southern outskirts of the town, in the early seventeenth century. He also purchased some manorial rights in Cantley in 1610, and his son, Francis, acquired the manor of Brampton in the parish of Cantley in 1667. Thomas, son of Francis, married one of the heirs of the lord mayor of York. The family moved from Carr House to Cantley, building a new home there, in the late eighteenth century, completing their domain with the purchase of the rectory and advowson in 1784.

Two other local gentry families originated in Pontefract, although one of them arrived at gentry status through an infusion of metropolitan merchant wealth. The Frank brothers, John (an alderman of the borough of Pontefract) and Henry, began to acquire property in the area a few miles south-east of the town in 1606, with the purchase of the manor of Trumfleet. By the time a marriage settlement for Richard's son John and his wife Ann Ellis was being drawn up in 1619, the brothers possessed property in a dozen townships round about. Henry died unmarried, and the estate of both brothers descended to John's son, Richard. The property then passed to the children of Richard's daughter, first to Edward and then to his brother Matthew, who was thus at the end of the seventeenth century rescued from his life as a cloth merchant of precarious solvency in Hamburg. Each

Figure 8. The funeral monument of Brian Cooke of Doncaster, who died 27 December 1653 in his eightieth year. The carving of the founder of the fortunes of the Cooke family is to be found in the Lincolnshire church of St Edith, Coates by Stowe. *The Author*

changed his surname from Ashton to Frank on inheriting their grand-father's estates and it was through Matthew's family that the Campsall estate descended. The Wardes of Hooton Pagnell also originated from Pontefract, but their ascent into the landed gentry was financed through the City of London.

It was there that Sir Patience Warde (1629–1696), sprung from a prosperous Pontefract family, gained the opportunity to make his fortune. Besides success in commerce, he achieved prominence in other spheres, and as Lord Mayor of London and MP for his native borough he robustly exposed himself to the turbulence of contemporary politics, which culminated in a period of prudently self-imposed exile in Holland. He was childless and willed his substantial resources in trust for his nephew, Patience Warde of Pontefract, with the proviso that the money should be used to acquire 'lands of inheritance so near as might be convenient to his (that is, his heir's) own paternal estate' at Tanshelf, Pontefract. The Cattal Hall estate, near York, was offered and rejected, but in 1704, Colonel Byerley, the inheritor by marriage of the Hutton of Goldsbrough estates, was looking to sell the manor of Hooton Pagnell, a few miles south of Pontefract, 'if he can meet with a good chapman [or 'middleman']', as his agent reported. This was the opportunity the Wardes had been waiting for, and six months later the estate was purchased for Patience by his uncles. The inheritance settled on his male heirs, who continued in succession until the mid-twentieth century.[12] Heredity as well as inheritance in the Warde family was influenced by the London career of Sir Patience. One of his merchant colleagues was Tobiah Harvey, and when he came to find his own country estate, his choice fell upon Womersley, a few miles from both Pontefract and Hooton Pagnell. The acquaintance which Warde and Harvey shared was made stronger by the proximity of their families in subsequent generations. Tobiah Harvey the younger had three daughters, and two of these married their neighbours, Patience Warde of Hooton Pagnell and Thomas Yarborough of Campsmount in Campsall. The ties of family were renewed in the next generation but one, when St Andrew married his cousin Maria Josepha Harvey.

Wealth generated in business, but this time in the Yorkshire woollen trade in Leeds, was the foundation of the Frickley estate of the Aldam family. Here again, the failure of the male line (the Aldam family of Warmsworth, a yeoman, rather than a gentry family, and one which had close links with the Society of Friends) led to the adoption of a relative to take on the family line. This was the Quaker William Pease of Leeds, in origin a member of the Pease family of Darlington (instigators of the Stockton and Darlington railway, who had originated at Fishlake), who became, by royal licence, William Aldam. The wealth of the newly-dubbed Aldams derived from Aldam, Pease and Co, woollen merchants of Leeds.[13] In the early nineteenth century, the profits of the firm were providing the Aldams with a very substantial income. The career of William Aldam the younger (1814–1890), exemplified that of many offspring of the successful business men of the age, with the adoption of the characteristics of the established leaders of society in place of those of their forebears. Instead of a life bounded by the counting house and meeting house, there was higher education (Trinity College, Cambridge, where he gained a first in mathematics), membership of an established profession (he was called to the bar and was a member of the Middle Temple), conformity in religion (he became an Anglican), and a political career, as Member of Parliament for Leeds from 1840 until he fell foul of the Leeds nonconformists in 1847.[14] This was followed by entry into the landed gentry, with his father's purchase of the Frickley estate as a wedding present in 1845. Although not directly involved in the business which had produced the family's prosperity, Aldam did not, however, disengage from commerce, and numbered amongst his activities directorships on the boards of the Leeds and Liverpool Canal Co and the Aire and Calder Navigation Co, of which he was chairman from 1853 until his death.

However, the most spectacular example of the transition from business to the landed classes was another nineteenth century recruit to the Doncaster gentry, the Thellusson family of Brodsworth. In its origins, the family was French-Swiss and it became involved in banking in the mid-eighteenth century. George Thellusson was in partnership with Jacques Necker, remembered to history as the last of a succession of royal ministers of finance to grapple with intractable financial problems of France on the eve of the Revolution; his brother, Peter, migrated to England in 1762, where he remained and became naturalised. He died in 1796, and his posthumous fame arose from the provisions of his will, which bequeathed the greater part of his large fortune made in the West Indies not immediately to his own sons, but in trust to accumulate until his grandsons should be of age to inherit. This remarkable condition caused national consternation. It was found to be entirely legal, and an Act of Parliament had to be passed in 1800 – the 'Thellusson Act' – to prevent any such eccentricities in the future.[15] Litigation was relentlessly pursued by the relations, and not resolved until 1859. The similarity to the long-running Chancery suit in Dickens' *Bleak House* did not, however, extend to the outcome. A substantial estate remained to be divided between Lord Rendlesham, the head of the senior branch of the family (founded by Peter Thellusson the younger, who used his banking wealth to acquire an estate in Suffolk and buy an Irish peerage from Pitt the younger) and the cadet branch.

The junior branch also inherited the estate at Brodsworth which the Thellusson trustees had bought from the earls of Kinnoul some fifty years earlier. The existing Georgian house was demolished and an unusual but opulent house took its place. Its owner, C S Thellusson seemed to have provided splendidly for posterity in other ways as well, fathering four sons, seemingly more than enough to ensure the inheritance. As events turned out, his fecundity was futile. The estate passed to his son Peter, then in 1899 to Herbert, to Charles in 1903 and finally to the fourth son Augustus in 1919. With the death of Augustus in 1931, the direct male line was exhausted. The estate then passed to Charles Grant-Dalton, whose title to it derived from his mother, the sister of the four sons. He predeceased his wife, Sylvia, who then married the next heir, his cousin Eustace, whom she also survived. It was her solicitude for the future of the house which led ultimately to its transfer to English Heritage in 1990.

Given the uncertainties of succession, which have been amply illustrated here, it is natural that gentry families would take special care to provide for the inheritance of the family estate. The means by which this was achieved was through deeds of settlement which, over the centuries, the lawyers acting for landed families brought to a high degree of legal sophistication. The deed of settlement was not only a means of establishing the succession to the estate, but a tried and tested device for ensuring, as far as humanly possible, the integrity of the estates from generation to generation. Any survey of the history of the gentry can produce instances of families which disappeared from its ranks as a result of improvidence. In the Doncaster area, we can cite the examples of Sir John Jackson of Hickleton, penniless at his death aged twenty-seven in 1679, or the last two John Adams of Owston, 'said to have been wild extravagant men' according to Hunter, from the younger of whom their Owston estate passed into the hands of a branch of the Cooke family. To prevent the breaking up of an estate by a spendthrift heir, to arrange the descent of the estate from one generation to the next, and to make provision should there be no direct male heir, and other subsidiary needs, led lawyers to devise means to limit the control in law which anyone coming into possession of an estate could have over its future.

Essentially the aim was to make the possessor not the outright owner but little more than the tenant for life, receiving the income but denied control of the capital. The estate was vested in trustees – other members of the gentry, neighbours and often relations – whose duty it was to ensure (on the advice of the family attorney) that the often complicated provisions of the deed of the settlement were observed.

Thus in 1817, the reaction of George Pate Nevile, the heir to the Skelbrooke estate, to the recklessly improvident behaviour of his eldest son, was to instruct his lawyers to draw up a will to create a trust which would prevent George junior squandering his inheritance. The trust they created, and the intransigence of the trustees in the face of George's importuning, ensured the survival of the estate in the hands of his children.[16] Deeds of settlement needed regular revision: the arrangement of dowries for daughters, portions for younger sons, allowances for widows, the exchange of properties within the settlement and the like had to be negotiated. Consequently, settlement business bulks large in the archives of many of the gentry: the marriage settlement which Anne and Tasbugh family lawyers agreed in 1813 was the subject of two deeds which together comprised nineteen sheets of parchment, each over two-feet square and the archives of Hooton Pagnell include no less than fifty-two deeds which arranged and rearranged the various settlements of family affairs between 1651 and 1864.[17]

Besides being an important factor in the local economy, the landed gentry played an important role in other spheres. Since the government of the country was dependent on the great landowners, it was natural that the smaller landowners would be important at the local level. Members of parliament were recruited, although not, of course, exclusively, from the gentry: as we have seen, Sir Patience Warde and William Aldam and both served as MPs whilst outside their ranks. The gentry were ubiquitous in local government and in particular dominated the magistracy, represented by the court of quarter sessions. The justices of the peace were (as they were up to 1973) appointed by a royal commission of the peace – issued for each county (and for each of the Ridings of Yorkshire) and exercised their powers in petty sessions, where they tried minor criminal cases, and in quarter sessions (which, as their title implied, met four times a year) where they tried the more serious criminal cases not grave enough to be heard by the royal judges on the assize circuit. In addition to their criminal jurisdiction, quarter sessions also transacted a wide range of administrative business, maintaining county bridges, providing lunatic asylums, prisons and the police, and hearing appeals from petty sessions about poor law business. Furthermore, individual magistrates were *ex officio* members of highway boards and boards of poor law guardians. The magistrates in quarter sessions were, in effect, 'a rural House of Lords', an unelected institution responsible for both criminal justice and important local government functions, although losing the latter to the newly-created county council in 1889.

Membership of the county (or West Riding) bench was something which any reputable member of the gentry could expect if he wished, and was able to, join. Thus it was thought necessary in one obituary to explain that the appointment of Sir Alington Bewick-Copley as magistrate had been delayed until his fiftieth year because his military career had prevented him from spending much time at Sprotbrough before his retirement. Some of the gentry became heavily involved in the work of the magistracy. Godfrey Higgins of Skellow was active in promoting the care of the mentally ill through the building of the first West Riding pauper lunatic asylum. William Aldam found it yet another outlet for his exceptional abilities, and in a career on the bench which began in 1842 and ended only with his death nearly fifty years later, he was at various times, chairman of the finance committee of quarter sessions, chairman of quarter sessions, and chairman of the Doncaster division of petty sessions. Likewise, G B Cooke-Yarborough of Campsmount (Figure 9) served as a county magistrate from 1871 until his death in 1915, having been chairman of both quarter sessions and of his local petty sessions court. By the later nine-

Figure 9. George Cooke-Yarborough of Campsmount, Campsall. He was the son of John Cooke of Streetthorpe [now Edenthorpe], who had taken the surname of Cooke-Yarborough on inheriting the Yarborough estates from his spinster aunts. *Doncaster Archives, DZ/MZ/30/ZI*

teenth century, the West Riding magistracy was no longer dominated by the gentry, as urban and industrial development had ensured that other social groups were represented in areas around the major towns, but in the rural districts of the Riding, like Doncaster, the gentry still held sway, as it had done for centuries before. A revealing late-eighteenth century draft of an advertisement amongst the Hooton Pagnell archives alerted newspaper readers to the advertiser's need for

A Butler and Justice's Clerk

Wanted a Man to serve both Capacities, he must write a good hand and have a good Character from his last place, if he has acted Clerk to a Justice before, it will be a recommendation to preference.[18]

The gentry can, of course, also be found filling other local offices, such as deputy lieutenancies, commissions in the militia and taking their annual turn as high sheriff (Figure 10).

By the early twentieth century, the world of the gentry was increasingly under threat. Much of the information about the succession to the Brodsworth estate used earlier derives from the inheritance-tax returns following the deaths of each of the Thellusson brothers.[19] Lady Bracknell's words in *The Importance of Being Earnest* were becoming increasingly true: 'What with duties expected of one during one's life and the duties exacted of one after one's death, land gives one a position and prevents one from keeping it up'. There were other, probably more significant, financial pressures on the gentry as well. The most important was the impact of the fall in agricultural prices which came in the late nineteenth century. On the Frickley estate, for example,

Figure 10. Col. St A Warde-Aldam as High Sheriff with his retinue outside Leeds Town Hall, 1940. His great grandfather and namesake, St Andrew Warde, had manoeuvred to avoid the position in 1798, arguing that it cost its holder at least £1,000 for his year of office and that his net income was only £1,600. *Doncaster Archives, DD/WN/B4/6*

there were reductions in rents which caused a fall in rental income from £1,920 to £1,388, or over a quarter in the five years from 1879 and 1884.[20] Yet for some, this period was one of new financial opportunities. The landed classes were not necessarily wholly dependent upon agriculture as their sole source of income. The Wardes, for instance, in the eighteenth century had supplemented their revenue from rents with income made from legal fees through the leasing of the manorial courts of Tanshelf from the Duchy of Lancaster and from taxing their tenants and neighbours by leasing the right to gather tithes at Clayton and Hooton Pagnell from the Crown.[21]

Rents from tenants other than agricultural ones provided alternative sources of income. The expansion of towns allowed some landowners to profit from ground rents and leases on urban and suburban housing. The Earl of Scarbrough, for example, was able to benefit from the development of Skegness as a holiday resort. In an area like Doncaster, there was little scope for profiting from urban development, although a number managed to take advantage of the high price for land compulsorily-purchased by railway companies. But one of the gentry was well-placed to take advantage of both. Sir William Cooke owned estates in Wheatley and Bentley, on the northern and eastern outskirts of Doncaster. In the five years between 1907 and 1911, his agent recorded sales of slightly more than 120 acres of land for a remarkable sum of £19,400.[22] A quarter of this came from three private developers, and a further thirty per cent was raised from purchases by the Great Northern and Great Central Railway Companies. The largest single purchaser, however, was Barber Walker and Co, the Nottinghamshire-based colliery company who were buying land at Bentley for their new colliery village. For the Cookes as for some other local landowners, it was coal which brought a bonanza at the end of the nineteenth and in the early decades of the twentieth century (Figure 11).

The exploitation of the Yorkshire coalfield was moving eastward in the later nineteenth century, as the technology which allowed its increasingly deep seams advanced. Denaby Main, sunk in 1864, remained a solitary local venture until the same company began sinking its Cadeby shaft a short distance away in 1889. Over the next thirty years, other new collieries came into being, including Frickley (sinking begun in 1905), Bullcroft (1908), Brodsworth (1905) and Bentley (1905–1908).[23] Some of the gentry began to receive income from mining royalties, paid by the colliery companies for the right to mine coal which lay under the lands which the gentry owned. In some cases royalties became a substantial part of their income. On the

Figure 11. The growth of coal mining had political as well as economic and environmental implications for the Doncaster district. In the general election of 1922, Sir Alington Bewicke-Copley of Sprotbrough, the Conservative candidate for the Doncaster parliamentary division, was defeated by Wilfred Paling, the Labour candidate and checkweighman from Bentley. *Doncaster Archives, DD/WN/B3/2*

Burghwallis estate, for example, where the income from agricultural rents was around £2,800 a year in the early 1880s, coal royalties from Bullcroft Main Collieries Ltd were yielding an average of £1,600 a year in 1909–1914. At the same period, the Frickley and Hickleton Main collieries were paying £2,500 a year to the Hooton Pagnell estate when the net rental from the estate was £1,600.[24]

This was not, however, sufficient to guarantee the future of the landed gentry as a presence in the Doncaster district and, indeed, the rising income which they received from coal working was itself indicative of the increasing unattractiveness of the area as a place for some of them to live. The High Melton estate, for example, looked down onto the Denaby and Cadeby Main collieries in the Don valley and at Owston the Davies-Cookes were the all-too-close neighbours of Bullcroft Colliery. Consequently, the twentieth century witnessed the gradual disappearance of most of the gentry families resident in the area. Cantley had been sold by the Childers to a colliery company as early as 1901,[25] but after the 1914–18 war, the exodus gathered momentum. The next to go were the Copleys, now barons Cromwell, of Sprotbrough. In 1925, the entire estate was put up for sale by auction. The contents of the library alone raised over £10,000 and the property, including the hall itself (although with a number of initially unsold lots), a further £80,000.[26] In the following decade, the Cookes

Figure 12. The seventeenth century staircase of Wheatley Hall, now at the Royal Observatory, Herstmonceux. The hall was leased to various tenants by the Cooke family from the mid-nineteenth century, and finally sold with its park to Doncaster corporation as the site for an industrial estate in 1933 for £60,000. This, and four other photographs of the interior, were taken in 1930. *Doncaster Archives, DY/DAW/87*

TABLE 1: MAJOR LANDOWNERS IN THE DONCASTER AREA IN 1873

Name and Estate	Landownership (acres)		Rental (gross est.)
ALDAM,William of Frickley Hall	Yorks,WR	4,579	£7,403
	Lincs	365	
	Total	4,944	
ANNE,George of Burghwallis		2,473	£3,745
BROWN,James of Rossington*	Yorks,WR	8,563	£11,388
CHADWICK,William of Arksey*	Yorks,WR	1,229	£1,270
CHILDERS,John Walbank of Cantley	Cambs	7,402	£18,769
	Yorks,WR	5,709	
	Lincs	222	
	Total	13,333	
COOKE,Sir William Ridley Charles Bt. of Wheatley Hall	Yorks,WR	3,368	£6,228
COOKE-YARBOROUGH,George Bryan of Campsmount and Lincs	Yorks,	2,894	£4,240
COPLEY,Sir Joseph William Bt. of Sprotbrough	Yorks,WR,	3,783	£7,620
DAVIES-COOKE,Philip Bryan of Owston	Yorks,WR,	3,379	£12,740
	Flint	3,379	
	Denbigh	86	
	Total	6,862	
DONCASTER CORPORATION*	Yorks,WR	2,045	£6,187
DURHAM,Makin of Thorne*	Yorks,WR	1,323	£1,930
FRANK,Frederick Bacon of Campsall	Yorks,WR	2,232	£5,761
	Norfolk	1,777	
	Total	4,009	
HALIFAX,Viscount of Hickleton Hall etc	Yorks,ER	10,142	£12,169
HATFIELD,Mrs of Skellow*	Yorks,WR	1,247	£1,752
MONTAGU.Andrew of Ingmanthorpe	Yorks,WR	20,700	£53,034
	Notts	3,354	
	Cornwall	2,657	
	Northum	648	
	Devon	6	
	Total	27,265	
NEVILE,Percy Sandford of Skelbrooke*	Yorks,WR	977	£1,445
THELLUSSON,Charles Sabine Augustas of Brodsworth	Wilts	419	£14,064
	Yorks	7,875	
	Northants	2	
	Herts	400	
	Total	8,891	
WARD,Rev William,of Hooton Pagnell*, executors of	Yorks,WR	1,482	£1,950
WRIGHTSON,Richard Heber of Cusworth	Yorks	7,771	£10,610
	Northum	1,158	
	Durham	486	
	Total	6,260	

Sources: John Bateman, *The Great Landowners of Great Britain and Ireland*, (4th edition,1883,reprinted by Leicester U.P.(1971), and *Return of Owners of Land,1872-3*,Parliamentary Papers,1874,LXXII,Parts I and II.A copy of the return for the West Riding only is available in the Library of the Headquarters of the West Yorkshire Archive Service,Wakefield.
The symbol * against an entry indicates that it does not appear in Bateman and has been taken from the Return.

completed their retreat from Doncaster by disposing of Wheatley Hall (Figure 12) to Doncaster Corporation as a site for an industrial estate and Campsmount was sold to the West Riding County Council, which at first intended to use the estate as a 'colony' for twenty thousand of the mentally handicapped.[27]

Over the next thirty years, the Annes sold Burghwallis to the Roman Catholic diocese of Leeds, the Earl of Halifax disposed of Hickleton in preference to Garrowby, the Davies-Cookes came permanently to prefer their Welsh estate to Owston, and Cusworth was sold off to the Doncaster Rural District Council in 1952. This process of divesting culminated with the transfer of Brodsworth Hall to English Heritage in 1990, to be preserved as 'an outstanding example of a Victorian country house'. But a few miles away, a radically different scenario was in evidence. Cantley Hall, having passed through several hands since the Childers had disposed of it, came into the ownership of Sir Graham Kirkham in 1990. He was, in the words of an *Independent* journalist, one of the 'coal miners' sons who struck a rich seam', a successful businessman whose origins were to be found in the local mining community rather than amongst the colliery owners and the receivers of coal royalties. Like Andrew Montagu a century earlier, he has used his wealth to help the Conservative Party, but in most other ways there could not be a more significant symbol of social and economic change in twentieth century Britain.[28]

Printed Sources

The greater part of this chapter has been written from published sources for, as I wrote at the beginning, the detailed archival research on the subject has yet to be done. There is not space here, even if it were necessary, to produce a full bibliography of works on the local landed gentry, and I confine myself to books and articles which have been particularly useful to the writing of this chapter. Like many before me, I have drawn extensively on Joseph Hunter, *South Yorkshire: The History and Topography of the Deanery of Doncaster* (two volumes, London, 1828 and 1831, reprinted by E P Publishing Ltd, East Ardsley, 1974), with occasional reference to Edward Miller, *The History and Antiquities of Doncaster* (Doncaster, undated, but 1804). Genealogical information may be found in John Burke, *A Genealogical and Heraldic History of the Commoners of Great Britain and Ireland* (London, 1836–8). In these chaotically arranged volumes, there are, in volume one, entries for Higgins of Skellow Grange (pp 155–7), Walbanke-Childers of Cantley (pp 229–30), Coke of Owston and Gwysaney (pp 276–278), Fountayne-Wilson of Melton (pp 268–70) and Frank of Campsal [sic] (pp 575–77); in volume two, Wrightson of Cusworth (pp 184–5); in volume three, More of Barnburgh [sic] appears on pages 449 to 453 and Yarburgh of Heslington on pages 661 to 665, and in volume four, Woodyeare of Crookhill on page 361. Joseph Foster, *Pedigrees of the County Families of Yorkshire, volume I, The West Riding* (London, 1874) contains genealogies of more recent date than available in Hunter. The various editions of *Kelly's Handbook to the Titles, Landed and Official Classes* are always useful; that for 1916 (the 42nd annual edition) was used here.

Biographical information on the more prominent members of the gentry or their relatives may be found in the *Dictionary of National Biography*. There are entries for Thomas Aldam of Warmsworth (volume 1, 1885), H C E Childers (*Supplement*, volume 1, 1901), Sir Godfrey Copley (volume 12, 1887), John Fountaine and John Fountayne [sic] of Melton (volume 20, 1889), Godfrey Higgins (volume 26, 1891), Peter Thellusson (volume 56, 1898), Sir Patience Ward (volume 59, 1899), and Sir Charles Wood (volume 62, 1900). There is also C E Whiting, 'Sir Patience Warde of Tanshelf, lord mayor of London', *Yorkshire Archaeological Journal*, volume xxiv, 1938–39, and by the same author, 'The Huttons of Hooton Pagnell', *Transactions of the Hunter Archaeological Society*, volume iv (1950). On William Aldam, there is an article by J T Ward, 'Squire as Businessman: William Aldam of Frickley Hall', *Transactions of the Hunter Archaeological Society*, volume viii (1963). The landed gentry are viewed in the national context in G E Mingay, *The Gentry: the rise and fall of a ruling class* (London, 1976), in the same author's *English Landed Society in the Eighteenth Century* (London, 1963) and in F M L Thompson, *English Landed Society in the Nineteenth Century* (London, 1963). The process of settlement is succinctly explained in B English and J Saville, *Strict Settlement: a Guide for Historians*, University of Hull, Occasional Papers in Economic and Social History, no. 10 (Hull, 1983).

   Local works of importance include David Hey, *The Making of South Yorkshire* (Ashbourne, 1979), and Derek Holland, *Changing Landscapes in South Yorkshire* (Doncaster, 1980). On local government and the role of the landed gentry within it in a national context there is Esther Moir, *The Justice of the Peace* (Harmondsworth, 1969) and for the West Riding in the nineteenth century, B J Barber and M W Beresford, *The West Riding County Council 1889–1974*, chapter one. On specific families and estates, there are English Heritage, *Brodsworth Hall* (London, 1995), Gordon Smith, *Cusworth Hall and the Battie-Wrightson Family* (Doncaster, 1990), and P Skidmore, M J Dolby and M D Hooper, *Thomas Tofield of Wilsic: Botanist and Civil Engineer* (Doncaster, undated, 1970s?).

Location Guide to the Archives

The archival sources for a detailed history of the Doncaster gentry are to be found in a number of Yorkshire record offices. This is not the place to explain why these archives have found so many different homes, but the potential researcher deserves some guidance on where to find them. Some basic information can be found in published guides. Those mentioned below are: *Guide to the Doncaster Archives Department*, 2nd edition, (Doncaster, 1981); *Leeds Archives, 1939–1988* (Wakefield, 1988); *Guide to the Manuscript Collections in the Sheffield City Libraries* (Sheffield, 1956), and R Meredith, *Sheffield City Libraries: Guide to the Manuscript Collections Supplement 1956–1976*, (Sheffield, 1977); and S Thomas, *Guide to the Archive Collections of the Yorkshire Archaeological Society 1931–1983 and to the Collections Deposited with the Society* (Wakefield, 1985).

Anne of Burghwallis   There are deposits of records at the Yorkshire Archaeological Society (*Guide*, pp 42–3), and at Doncaster Archives. By far the greater part of both comprise title deeds. In addition, there are records relating to the family and estate in the archives of Baxter and Somerville of Doncaster, solicitors, held at Doncaster Archives.

Battie-Wrightson of Cusworth and Warmsworth   The greater part of the archives are now to be found at Doncaster Archives.

Childers of Cantley   There is a small number of deeds in the records of Baxter and Somerville, solicitors, at Doncaster Archives and other archives are held at the Cambridgeshire Record Office.

Cooke of Wheatley   The records, which consist almost exclusively of title deeds, are held by Sheffield Archives: see *Guide Supplement*, 1977, pages 8–9. Doncaster Archives holds the records of J Dawson and Sons of Doncaster, estate agents, which include the records of the firm's agency business for the Cooke estate in the twentieth century.

Cooke-Yarborough of Campsmount   Most of the original records are held privately, but a catalogue of them, some of the originals (mostly maps and plans), and microfilms of the remainder (with the exception of the title deeds) are available at Doncaster Archives.

Copley of Sprotbrough   The records are to be found divided between Doncaster Archives, Sheffield Archives (*Guide Supplement*, 1977, page 9) and the Yorkshire Archaeological Society (*Guide*, page 6).

Davies-Cooke of Owston   The records of the Yorkshire estates are deposited at Doncaster Archives: see *Guide*, page 45.

Frank of Campsall   The records are held by Sheffield Archives: see *Guide*, 1956, pages 31–33.

Montagu of High Melton   Title deeds of some of the properties of the High Melton estate are on deposit at Sheffield Archives (*Guide Supplement*, 1977, pages 15–16).

Nevile of Skelbrooke   No family records are on deposit with any local record office, but Doncaster Archives holds some miscellaneous items relating to the estate. Additionally, the estate was administered on behalf of its absentee owners from 1770 to 1824 by Doncaster solicitors whose records subsequently became part of those of Baxter and Somerville, now held at Doncaster Archives.

Thellusson of Brodsworth   The greater part of the archives, including those of the estate, are held by Doncaster Archives. Those held by the Yorkshire Archaeological Society (*Guide*, 1985, pp 22–23 and 28) mostly comprise the title deeds and some personal papers.

Warde-Aldam (formerly Aldam) of Frickley   The greater part of the papers of William Aldam are held by Doncaster Archives (*Guide*, pp 46–47), with some material in the Goodchild Collection at the John Goodchild Local History Study Centre, Wakefield, formerly at the Wakefield Department of Local Studies (see Royal Commission on Historical Manuscripts, *Papers of British Politicians 1782–1900* (London, 1989), page 3.

Warde-Norbury (formerly Warde) of Hooton Pagnell   The title deeds and earlier estate and personal records (17 to early 19 century) are held at Hooton Pagnell, although there is a catalogue, and copies of a part of the archives available at Doncaster Archives. Later nineteenth century and twentieth century estate and personal records are held at Doncaster Archives.

Wood (subsequently Halifax) of Hickleton   The archives of the family are held at the Borthwick Institute of Historical Research, York (see *Royal Commission on Historical Manuscripts, Papers of British Politicians, 1782–1900* (London, 1989), page 113.

No records have been traced for other gentry families. In addition to the records of specific families, there are two general archival sources which are of great importance here. The first is the West Riding Registry of Deeds. The registry, established in 1704 and functioning until 1970, was an institution which, by virtue of a local Act of Parliament, established a public register of deeds relating to freehold land. Registration was never compulsory, but it was widely observed, particularly in the case of larger estates, and thus the records of the registry are a major source of information about land transactions from the early eighteenth century. The second source is the records of the West Riding Court of Quarter Sessions. Most relevant to the present theme has been the records relating to the magistrates themselves, in particular the obituaries filed by the clerk of the peace in the printed annual lists of magistrates in the later nineteenth and early twentieth century. Both the records of the Registry of Deeds and the Court of Quarter Sessions are available for research at the Wakefield Headquarters office of the West Yorkshire Archive Service. Information on both is to be found in B J Barber, *Guide to the Quarter Sessions of the West Riding of Yorkshire 1631–1971* (Wakefield, 1984).

Notes and References

1. Some of the earlier houses are illustrated in *Samuel Buck's Yorkshire Sketchbook* (Wakefield, 1979), pp 64–73 and 76.
2. Doncaster Archives, reference DD/CROM/6/23.
3. On the Scarbrough estates, see T W Beastall, *A North Country Estate: The Lumleys and Saundersons as Landowners, 1600–1900* (London, 1975).
4. Doncaster Archives. DD/CROM/8/3 and /6.
5. West Yorkshire Archive Service Headquarters, West Riding Registry of Deeds, 668/136/151, 734/580/651, 842/452/537 and 1903/30/869/403.
6. Robert Blake, *Disraeli* (London, 1966), p 424.
7. Much of the information in this chapter is derived from reading Hunter's *South Yorkshire*, and page references will not be given where readers can readily turn up reference by referring to Hunter themselves. Other published sources of information are given at the end of the chapter.
8. Hooton Pagnell Archives, HP/4/5.
9. Doncaster Archives, DZMD/453/2.
10. In addition to the account in Hunter, see Doncaster Archives, P/21/3/D7; Sheffield Archives, LD 1355; and Peter Leach, *James Paine* (London, 1988), pp 54, 154–55 and 212.
11. See G H Martin and others, *Doncaster: A Borough and Its Charters* (Doncaster, 1994), p 10 and chapter four.
12. Hooton Pagnell Archives, HP/1/28 and 10/1. Hunter's statement (*South Yorkshire*, volume 2, p 143) that Sir Patience himself was the purchaser of the Hooton Pagnell estate is incorrect.

13. The business records of the firm, 1738–1839, are amongst the Warde-Aldam archives at Doncaster Archives, DDWA/B/1–28.

14. For William Aldam's parliamentary papers, see Doncaster Archives, DDWA/P/1–31.

15. The Act of Parliament is the *Restraint on Accumulations Act*, 39 and 40 Geo. 3. chapter 98.

16. Doncaster Archives, DX/BAX/S/61602/5 and DZMZ/453/2.

17. Doncaster Archives, DD/ANNE/1 and Hooton Pagnell Archives, HP/2.

18. Hooton Pagnell Archives, HP/27/28.

19. Doncaster Archives, DD/BROD/3/34–65.

20. Hooton Pagnell Archives, HP/17/25.

21. Hooton Pagnell Archives, HP/7 and HP/22.

22. Doncaster Archives, DY/DAW/12/45.

23. The Midland Institute of Mining Engineers, *Sections of Strata of the Coal Measures of Yorkshire* (Sheffield, 1927 edition).

24. Doncaster Archives, DD/ANNE/4/6–7 and DD/WN/A1/4. See also DD/CROM/4.

25. West Yorkshire Archive Service Headquarters, West Riding Registry of Deeds, 1901/22/852/432 and 1901/22/872/433.

26. Doncaster Archives, DD/CROM/13/1–11.

27. B J Barber and M W Beresford, *The West Riding County Council, 1889–1974: Historical Studies* (Wakefield, 1979), p 67.

28. 'Coal miners' sons who struck a rich seam', *Independent on Sunday*, 3 November 1996, p 8, and 'In the Hot Seat: The astonishing story of sofa mogul Graham Kirkham, *that* Tory party loan and *that* knighthood', [*Daily*] *Telegraph Magazine*, 14 September 1995, pp 20–28.

Figure 13. A procession in South Elmsall in 1914, perhaps on St George's Day, led by parish clergy of the recently-built St Mary's church. Coal owners in the Doncaster area funded the building of three churches in new colliery villages: Lord Halifax at Goldthorpe, Charles Thellusson at Woodlands and Mrs Warde-Aldam at South Elmsall. The first and last were served by the clergy of the 'High Church' persuasion in the Church of England, as can be seen in this photograph. *Doncaster Archives, DD/WN/B8/14*

5. CHARLES SABINE AUGUSTUS THELLUSSON AND ITALIANATE BUILDINGS ON THE BRODSWORTH ESTATE

by Peter Gordon Smith

WHEN CHARLES SABINE AUGUSTUS THELLUSSON was born, in Florence, Tuscany, on 5 March 1822, quite an assembly was present at the birth. These included Lord Rendlesham, Mr Dawkins the British Charge d'Affairs, the Reverend Dr Trevor and three Italians, a lawyer, a notary, and a scribe. In a letter to his own mother the proud father wrote that all was well with mother and child and that 'he had taken every precaution as to the Registry.'[1] As this was no royal birth, albeit the Duke of Sussex was subsequently to stand as God parent, one might wonder what all the fuss was about. Contemporaries who read the news sheets of the age would have understood and perhaps would have raised an eyebrow, for the baby Charles Sabine Augustus was born not so much with a silver spoon in his mouth as with a golden spade encrusted with diamonds hanging tantalisingly over it. The new born child was, among other potential claimants, an heir apparent to the magnificent fortune left under the infamous terms of the will of his great-grandfather, Peter Thellusson.

At his death in 1797 this immensely wealthy City merchant had left £700,000 (around fifty million pounds today) in trust to accumulate at compound interest during the lives of his sons and grandsons alive at the time of his death, and only on the death of the last of these was the eventual estate to be divided between the eldest male lineal descendants of his three sons then living. It was computed that the capital would grow into a fabulous fortune over the intervening generations and that the trustees would be able to exercise an undue influence on the commerce of the day. Indeed the extraordinary terms of the will, apart from prompting the *Accumulations Act* of 1800 (also known as the *Thellusson Act*, which contrived to limit the time that any testator's estate could be left to accumulate), led to a protracted course of litigation waged by the family against the terms of the will and its later administration, which was to be pursued intermittently through the Courts of Chancery for over half a century.[2] A curious public was even reminded of the frustrating circumstances by Charles Dickens' oblique reference to it in his introduction to *Bleak House* which featured the interminable case of Jarndyce v Jarndyce.

IN MEMORY
OF
CHARLES THELLUSSON ESQ.RE
ELDEST SON OF CHARLES THELLUSSON ESQ.RE
THIRD AND YOUNGEST SON OF
PETER THELLUSSON ESQ.RE
FORMERLY OF BRODSWORTH.
BORN 31ST JANY 1797. DIED 5TH FEBY 1856.

Figure 1. When Charles Thellusson died in 1856, his son Charles Sabine ensured that his claim to his great grandfather's estate was set in stone. *Brodsworth church yard*

One might be forgiven for wondering at this point where this is leading us, but the circumstances of the birth were to be of the greatest importance to the future of Brodsworth, a village lying a little to the north west of Doncaster in the County of Yorkshire. Charles Sabine's father, also a Charles Thellusson, was the last grandson born to Peter Thellusson in his lifetime; hence Charles Sabine would have to wait at least until his father's death before he could lay claim to any of the accumulating fortune which had been laid down in 1797. By taking 'every precaution with the Registry', Charles Thellusson was acting solicitously on his heir's behalf, which is just as well as he seems to have spent freely himself, perhaps in the knowledge of his son's assured future. He appears to have lived life to the full, maintaining his growing young family abroad in Italy and France before returning to settle in England in the 1840s. Whilst he was resident at *The Casino*, Worthing, his surviving diaries record a sociable life spent dining out, playing billiards and, all too often, running up debts at race meetings. As a young man Charles Sabine seems to have had little option but to bide his time and pursue a traditional career for himself in the army. By 1848 he was a captain in the 12th Lancers (there is a gallant equestrian portrait of him at this time hanging in Brodsworth Hall) and he only resigned his commission prior to marrying Georgiana Theobald in 1850. It was a good match. Georgiana brought a handsome settlement with which they established themselves in Brighton and began their family which was to grow to include six children.

Then in 1856 Charles Thellusson died (Figure 1). It should have meant that the time had come at last for the resolution of the will made back in 1797, but in fact it took another three years and a further protracted Case in Chancery before Charles Sabine was to come into his great-grandfather's fortune which it was decreed he was to share with his second cousin, the fourth Lord Rendlesham. Alas, the fabulous fortune failed to materialise as the costs of all the litigation compounded by mismanagement by the trustees had consumed much of the anticipated growth; they actually shared a sum little greater than the original capital investment of £700,000. So much for over half a century of anguished anticipation and family strife! Notwithstanding in 1859 it was still a significant amount of money, tens of millions of pounds by today's standards. Charles Sabine's portion included the Brodsworth Estate, which Peter Thellusson had purchased shortly before his death, plus still ample funds to satisfy his amibitions. Foremost among these was his wish to establish Brodsworth as his principal country residence and he set about planning a splendid new mansion and expanding and improving the Estate with immediate effect. It might be worth mentioning at this point that the other great interest of his that we know of lay in the construction and sailing of racing yachts, of which he was to commission some of the finest and fastest examples of the age. This is a subject of current research by others and it is planned to mount a special exhibition on this interesting subject in Brodsworth Hall in 1998.

With regard to his ideas for Brodsworth we shall never know exactly what Charles Sabine (Figure 2) had in mind, or how readily or otherwise his thoughts came together. Estate records tend to deal in the particulars and in their consequent financial detail rather than in the thoughts and designs behind them but the built evidence does suggest that he wished to mark his new domain with a decidedly Italianate stamp. Whilst it was by no means uncommon at the time to desire an Italianate house – such architects as Sir Charles Barry had been designing country houses in that style for years, and the Queen herself together with Prince

Figure 2. Charles Sabine Augustus Thellusson as Victorian paterfamilias. *Brodsworth Hall Photograph (English Heritage)*

Figure 3. The eighteenth century Brodsworth Hall, photographed in the 1850s before the building was demolished to make way for the present hall. *Brodsworth Hall Photograph (English Heritage)*

Albert had commissioned *Osborne House* back in the 1840s which in turn had spawned countless imitation Victorian Italianate villas across the country – what was to make Brodsworth unusual was that the house was inspired by a design from an Italian architect and the Italian style was carried further in the construction of some substantial farm buildings across the estate. Was Charles Sabine intent on creating a Tuscan architectural landscape, an image of the land of his birth, in his now adopted home in the County of Yorkshire?

Turning our attention first to the house, Charles Sabine inherited a substantial eighteenth century mansion that stood on the site of the earlier manors of Brodsworth, which in turn date back to the Domesday Book. Fortunately several early photographs of this house survive (Figure 3). It had formerly been the country home of Robert Hay Drummond, Archbishop of York, prior to its purchase by Peter Thellusson.[3] The house, however, must have been considered inconvenient and unsuitable for a young family, as Charles Sabine decided to have it demolished and to build a new house, a little to the south of it, commanding an improved aspect. Two original design elevations of the proposed new house survive and are signed by 'Chevalier Casentini', architect and sculptor.[4] The Chevalier G M Casentini, of Lucca, Tuscany, remains a somewhat mysterious figure. He would appear to be more of a dilettante than a practising architect and something of a dealer in the sculpture trade of the time. Other than these two drawings there is no further trace of, or reference to him, until several years later, after the new house was completed, when he evidently exercised his hand in the design of the formal gardens. How Charles Sabine knew him is a mystery, perhaps they were old friends who had shared some of the Italian *La Dolce Vita* together, though one has to admit that the apparent formality of their brief correspondence does little to support this view. Notwithstanding Casentini's design for the new house was certainly impressive, a palazzo to be proud of.

Figure 4. Design elevation of Brodsworth Hall signed by Chevalier Casentini. *Ink Drawing at Brodsworth Hall (English Heritage)*

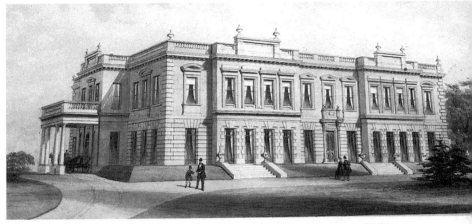

Figure 5. Unsigned drawing of Brodsworth Hall, nearly as executed, perhaps by Philip Wilkinson. *Watercolour at Brodsworth Hall*

Charles Sabine must have been impressed by it as it was to be built in its essentials under the direction of an architect from London, Philip Wilkinson. Comparison of the Casentini drawing with the watercolour (Figures 4 & 5 respectively) shows that some simplifications were introduced however. The proposed statues on top of the ballustrade were deleted in favour of finial urns and the sculpture filled pediments deleted in favour of simpler stepped parapets. Whether the client got cold feet at the cost of this riot of sculpture or perhaps he was advised, correctly as it turned out, that such detail would result in onerous future maintenance, we shall never know. Neither was the rather grand conservatory executed, more's the pity.

The design is somewhat atypical of its type as befits its unusual origin. English Italianate houses of the period had a more deliberately picturesque aspect by the asymmetrical placing of wings and towers, in contrast Brodsworth Hall is frankly symmetrical on each elevation. The noble proportions of the structure are superb and can be enjoyed afresh from whatever angle it is viewed from. Only two storeys high, with the roof hidden below the balustrade, it nevertheless contrives a lofty appearance, despite the long thirteen bays of its garden facade. Superbly proportioned, it owes its ancestry to the lofty town palaces of Italy. It is conventional in its use of architectural detail with abundant rustication on the ground floor and with emphatic architraves and pediments over first floor windows. The *porte cochere* over the principal entrance adds a note bravura to the whole. Less conventional, indeed rarely if ever seen on other English country houses, are the patent revolving shutters which when down protect the large French

Figure 6. The house after its recent restoration. *English Heritage Photographic Library*

windows which open on three sides onto the terrace; designed to combat a hot sun they seem more appropriate to the continent than to Yorkshire, though they do serve a useful conservation purpose today by controlling light levels inside the house.

The new house was built in 1861–2 and happily the building contract survives, it being a model of its kind:

> *Specification of Works required to be done in pulling down and rebuilding the Mansion known as Brodsworth Hall near Doncaster, Yorkshire for Captain Thellusson agreeably to the accompanying Drawings prepared by Philip Wilkinson, Architect and such further Drawings as may be from time to time supplied*[5]

Dated February 1861 the contract specification details in less than fifty pages of foolscap, in neat copper plate writing, every aspect of the required construction right down to the supply of an ebony boss at the bottom of the turned mahogany handrail of the principal staircase (which exists). It ended with a penalty clause which doubtless helped the contractor, Longmire & Burge, to complete the construction within only eighteen months. A curious feature of the house is the large number of false windows, there are no less than seventeen of them, this presumably came about as Philip Wilkinson was obliged to fit his interior within the external elevations designed by Casentini. By using

Figure 7. The flower garden with fountain supplied by Casentini. *English Heritage Photographic Library*

the local magnesian limestone quarried on the Estate and carefully reusing materials from the old house, as specified in the contract, the building costs were kept down to around £20,000.

Charles Sabine was evidently prudent with his new wealth. The interior, beyond the scope of this essay, was to be finished with extensive painted marbling of superb quality and the house was furnished in 1863 and practically ready for the family to move into (Figure 6).

Early in 1866 Charles Sabine was considering further plans supplied by Casentini for the ornamentation of the gardens in the Italian style. In a letter from Lucca, Casentini incidently sheds an interesting light on production costs of the time:

He describes the pieces as 'very superialy [sic] executed', a fact that can be readily appreciated to this day.[6] These excellent quality marble statues, vases, dolphin fountain and architectural embellishments are beautifully laid out around the terrace and along the paths leading from the house. The recent restoration of the gardens has if anything enhanced their visual value (Figure 7).

During the time that the new Brodsworth Hall was being planned and built, Charles Sabine had by no means ignored the Estate. His solicitors, Reyroux & Bromehead, acted as agents and there are

Figure 8. Aerial view of Elm farm buildings. *Courtesy of Geoff Morrell*

records of a significant amount of building activity whilst the Estate grew to encompass some 5,000 acres. Numerous new houses were constructed and cottages repaired. The heart of the village of Brodsworth was changed significantly when the Head Gardener's house and the kitchen gardens were laid out. The adjoining village of Pickburn took on its present appearance of an estate village with the building of a row of neat semi-detached stone houses of a particular character. A number of substantial farm buildings also date from this time and they share some interesting architectural features. Changes in agricultural practices in the course of the twentieth century have however forced some adaptation and modifications on these buildings, indeed have been demolished altogether, but two excellent examples survive, one at Pickburn and the other at Marr.

At Elm Farm, Pickburn (Figure 8), stands what must be accounted one of the most remarkable farm buildings in Yorkshire. In size and scale it stands comparison with Brodsworth Hall itself and it dwarfs its adjacent farm house. The building has considerable architectural style and an emphatic Italian flavour. The exterior is liberally embellished, for what is basically a barn, with traditional Italianate detailing and its arched open ranges are supported on large solid limestone columns which are a particular feature on the Estate. Above the largest entrance, opening into a cavernous barn, is a small stone plaque which is carved with the initials C.S.A.T. AD1864 (Figure 9). There can be no doubt that Charles Sabine was proud of this splendid construction. Unfortunately we do not know who was responsible for the design. A privileged guided tour of this country house among barns revealed it to have been an exemplar of its age. Within it comprises of a rational arrangement of cattle byres, stabling, with farm vehicle storage below and grain and hay storage above together with pigeon lofts (Figures 10–11). Geoffrey Morrell, whose

Figure 9. Stone plaque over entrance to the barn at Elm Farm. *Geoff Morrell*

family have farmed Elm Farm for the greater part of this century, recalls that on several occasions drivers who have delivered agricultural produce to Italy have remarked that they have seen 'just the same' form of buildings there. Given a few pine trees dotted around

Figure 10. East elevation of Elm Farm buildings. *Courtesy of Geoff Morrell*

Figure 11. North-west angle of Elm Farm buildings showing architectural embellishments and false opening.

and on a hot afternoon, gazing at the decaying rendering, one could be transported to Tuscany.

Another interesting set of farm buildings, once part of the Brodsworth Estate, can be found at Marr Hall Farm, a mile or two south of the village of Brodsworth. Here there is a striking range of no less than fourteen arched openings supported on solid stone piers, which once would have offered protection to drays, carts and miscellaneous farm machinery (Figure 12). Leading off this range on the

Figure 12. The colonnaded range at Marr Hall Farm has something of the flavour of antiquity about it. *Courtesy of John Harrison*

opposite side are three shortened wings which offer winter protection for cattle (Figure 13). It is a remarkable building and elegantly fit for its purpose.

A number of other lesser examples of these columned farm build-

Figure 13. The three wings on the opposite side of the colonnaded range form two courtyards which house contented cattle. *Courtesy of John Harrison*

ings survive to a greater or lesser extent on the Estate and in their heyday, when complete and well maintained, must have given the impression of well ordered efficiency and well-being. This seems to fit with what little we can glean from the character of Charles Sabine Augustus Thellusson who, when he died in 1885, left behind him a little of the spirit of Italy, set in stone, for the enjoyment of future generations.

Notes and References

The greater part of the Brodsworth archive and the related Thellusson papers are held either by the West Yorkshire Archives Service at the Yorkshire Archaeological Society in Leeds (YAS) or by Doncaster MBC Archives Department, in Doncaster. A comprehensive hand list and index has been compiled for English Heritage and is available at both locations.

1. Copy of Thellusson family letter, courtesy of Mrs Penley.
2. The will of Peter Thellusson has given rise to volumes of court proceedings and a number of learned commentaries and articles over many years. 'The Most Famous Will In the World' by A G Salmon in *The Solicitors' Journal*, Volume 118 is among the most lucid.
3. Horace Walpole, the eighteenth century author and gossip, refers to the Archbishop as a 'sensible, worldly man, but much addicted to his bottle'. Mrs Hay Drummond lies buried in Brodsworth church as indeed does Peter Thellusson.
4. The original Casentini drawings are in Brodsworth Hall.
5. YAS ref DD168/2.
6. YAS DD168/7/1/15.

Acknowledgements

I am indebted to Caroline Carr-Whitworth, Art Curator for English Heritage, Historic Properties North, for her industry in first exposing the extensive archive whilst researching for the Brodsworth Hall guidebook; to Geoffrey Morrell and his family at Elm Farm for the enthusiastic sharing of their knowledge and giving up their valuable time; likewise to the family of John Harrison at Marr Hall Farm; and lastly to Ronald Williams, the present owner of the Brodsworth Estate for his helpful observations.

6. OPEN FIELD FARMING IN FISHLAKE AND HATFIELD: THE EVIDENCE OF THE COURT BOOKS, 1582–1808

by Dan Byford

BECAUSE THE VILLAGES OF THE MANOR of Hatfield were at the centre of the first major drainage scheme to be carried out in England, a very distorted view of their nature and activities has arisen. In 1626 the drainage of the wetter parts of Hatfield Chase, north Nottinghamshire and the Isle of Axholme in Lincolnshire was started by a largely Dutch consortium of which Cornelius Vermuyden, a Dutch immigrant settled in London, was the figure-head. The drainage agreement made with Charles I (Figure 1), the owner of Hatfield Chase (a royal forest) and Lord of the very large Manor of Hatfield, was the result of long pressure from the Dutch colony in London and the financial problems of the first two Stuart kings. The main object of the scheme was, of course, to make money for the entrepreneurs who were behind it and to turn land which brought almost no income for the Crown into a source of profit. It was presented as a boon to the nation and to the impoverished fen dwellers of the area. As a consequence of the need to justify the drainage, the wetness and

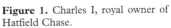

Figure 1. Charles I, royal owner of Hatfield Chase.

uselessness of the region was greatly exaggerated and the area was represented, along with the similar area in East Anglia, as the home of the 'fen slodger' who was 'neither an agriculturalist nor a shepherd' but 'a fisherman of sorts, a wild fowler and a gatherer of natural resources such as berries and reeds'. Darby claimed that this view and many others produced a 'distorted picture of life in the fens'.[1] Later Hoskins wrote 'It is one of the commonest delusions that the Fens were little more than swamps before Vermuyden arrived in the seventeenth century'.[2] These historians and others were attempting to correct a view of the East Anglian fenland and fenlander largely created by enthusiasts for drainage, but their arguments apply equally to Hatfield Chase.[3]

Figure 2. Hatfield and neighbourhood: an extract from J Alexander's 'Map of the Deanery of Doncaster' printed in volume I of Joseph Hunter's *South Yorkshire* (1828).

At Domesday the villages of what became the Manor of Hatfield were part of the Warenne fee of Conisbrough. When the Manor was created is unknown though its first court roll dates from 1324–25. The series continues until the parliamentary enclosure of the Manor of 1811–25.[4] Whilst matters of main interest to the lord such as transfer of the copyhold land, disputes between himself and the tenants or between tenants, law and order and breaches of his rights as owner of the Chase, were dealt with in the Manor Court, matters which affected the smooth running of the townships, especially of the farming system, were dealt with by the villagers in their own court, though in theory decisions had to be ratified by the Manor Court.[5] The Manor of Hatfield consisted of three parishes: Hatfield, Fishlake and Thorne (Figure 2). In Hatfield parish were the settlements of Hatfield Woodhouse, Tudworth, Dunscroft (Figure 3) and Stainforth which had its own chapel. Fishlake parish, like its chapelry, Sykehouse (earlier Dowsthorp), was made up of many small settlements. Thorne had no separate parts until after the drainage when Thorne Waterside and Moorends developed. The Manor Court was held at Hatfield and it seems that there were four subsidiary or byelaw courts at Hatfield, Fishlake, Sykehouse and Thorne.

The Manor was approximately 38,500 acres in extent. It is not easy

Figure 3. The Grange at Dunscroft had the initials 'H L' and the date 1611 carved on a beam (information from Ben Brown). Dunscroft Grange was possibly built in the early seventeenth century by Henry Lee, son of Sir Henry Lee of Quarrendon, Bucks who had been given the tithes of Hatfield by Elizabeth I. Among the outbuildings was the Tithe Barn. The house was demolished in 1965–6.

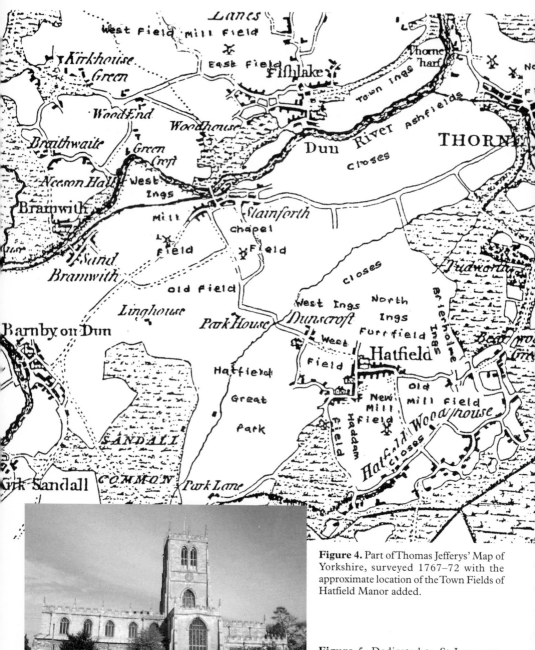

Figure 4. Part of Thomas Jefferys' Map of Yorkshire, surveyed 1767–72 with the approximate location of the Town Fields of Hatfield Manor added.

Figure 5. Dedicated to St Lawrence, Hatfield is a large cruciform church with a splendid crossing tower. *The Author.*

to work out the area requiring drainage. The figures used by contemporaries suggest 60,000 and 70,000 acres but only a minority of this was within the manor. A 1693 list of lands in the Manor liable to scotts (drainage rates) totalled 13,891 acres although some of the acreage belongs to other manors on the Hatfield boundaries.[6] There was also a huge area of peat moor which was not part of the seventeenth century drainage. Thorne Waste, the general name for all the peat moor of Thorne, Cowick, Rawcliffe, Goole and Crowle, was estimated at over 4,000 hectares (c10,000 acres).[7] Roughly a third of it was in the Manor and there was a similar acreage in Hatfield Moor. All the Manor townships had peat moor allocated to them though for most of them it was a long distance away. The exception was Thorne which had a thriving river trade in turves into the eighteenth century. It can be assumed, therefore, that approximately half of this very large manorial acreage was available for agriculture in some way. Some of the townland was susceptible to winter flooding adjacent to the rivers Don and Went but this was usually on the ings which relied on winter floods to maintain their fertility. Much of the townland in Hatfield itself was poor sand but the soil quality in Stainforth, Fishlake and Sykehouse was better. Thorne was short of townland, though the clearance of peat from the moorends through several centuries exposed clay land which, according to the map of 1669 by Nicholas Prole, 'lies for Meadowes or Corne'.[8] Thorne also had arable and pasture in the former park of Ashfields which had been disparked in the fourteenth century.[9] Until the pre-enclosure maps of the early nineteenth century almost nothing of this is shown on maps. The map of the Isle of Axholme before the Drainage which appeared in Read's *History of the Isle of Axholme* (1858) was a reconstruction, as it says, 'From Domesday Book, Saxton, Leland and other Ancient Authorities'. Hatfield is the only fen edge village shown and the townland is represented by a few trees to indicate the position of the Great Park. Two maps were produced immediately after the drainage and both are, naturally enough, only concerned to show details of the drained land although they indicate the position of the villages.[10] Thomas Jeffreys' Map of Yorkshire (Figure 4), 1767–72, shows the baulk which went from Hatfield church (Figure 5) to Dunscroft through the middle of the West Field, which Read's cartographer copied, also common land and rough pasture but no fields or closes. The only one to show fields is Prole who marks three fields in Stainforth and Mill Field in Hatfield, but no others.

Apart from the misunderstanding surrounding the area in predrainage times, the nature of its agriculture has been further distorted by the fact that the private Chase of the de Warenne's had become a royal forest. Forest Law had been extremely strict in medieval times but it had moderated over the centuries and its administration was lax by the sixteenth century, especially far from London. In any case the aim of the Forest Law had not been to prevent the economic development of a forest area but to preserve the game. Protecting the game could, and did, affect some agricultural activities; for instance, the keeping of sheep or goats was prohibited as they competed with deer for the shorter grasses. Many activities developed in royal forests and 'there was a complete range of land uses including extensive arable and even towns'.[11] However, in very severe winters or bad flooding, deer could be forced from their pastures on the wet lands onto the townlands where they broke into the arable in spite of the fences which surrounded the open fields and closes, and stole hay from the farmers' stacks. Being part of a royal forest could, therefore, be a nuisance, especially as there were huge numbers of deer in the Chase.[12] However, the 1626 agreement also included the dischasing of the area and the deer did not survive the drainage. It is not known what happened to them, although in April 1629 the King promised to 'use his best endeavours to remove the deer before November 1 next'.[13]

When the drainage of the Levels started (Figure 6), the townland of the Manor had been organised into traditional open fields for a very long time; there is, for example, a mention in the Court Rolls of the 'south field' of Hatfield in 1342.[14] In 1634 Hatfield had four fields; Stainforth and Fishlake had three; Thorne had two; Tudworth had one divided into three sections. Sykehouse also had one small field and several closes with 'field' names. Dunscroft and Hatfield Woodhouse shared the open fields of Hatfield. In addition to the open fields, the townships, with the exception of Thorne, had the advantage of a large number of closes which allowed farmers to avoid the restrictions and traditionalism of open field farming. In 1634 a new, and very short-lived, Lord of the Manor, Sir Edward Osborne, Vice-President of the Council of the North, commissioned a survey of all the townlands. This huge document gives details of all the houses, cottages and open field selions (strips of arable). It also gives the acreage of hundreds of closes. Hatfield had 322 closes amounting to 670 acres. Fishlake had 420 amounting to 1,226 acres, Sykehouse 408 amounting to 1,488 acres and Stainforth had 254 amounting to 728 acres. Thorne, reflecting once again the smallness of its townland, only had 91 totalling 140 acres. In every township there were a number of closes where the acreage was not given, especially in Thorne where the

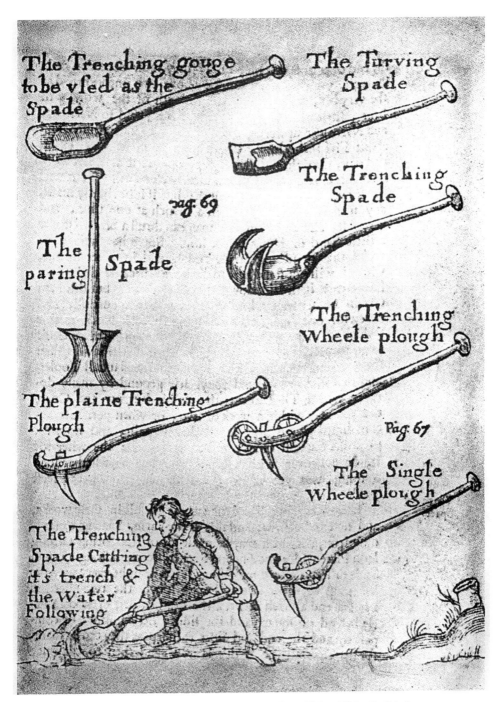

The Trenching gouge to be vsed as the Spade

The Turving Spade

pag. 69

The Trenching Spade

The paring Spade

The Trenching Wheele plough

The plaine Trenching Plough

Pag. 67

The Single Wheele plough

The Trenching Spade Cutting it's trench & the Water Following

Figure 6. Seventeenth century draining tools. From Walter Blith, *English Improver Improved*, 3rd. ed., 1653.

number was quite large, possibly representing half the close acreage.[15]
The townships also had extensive commons both on the townland and
on the Levels; Thorne even had copyhold pasture at Midlings and
Severals in the High Levels, the latter name indicating that parts of
this supposedly useless land was fenced.[16] There is no doubt, therefore, that the inhabitants of the Manor had all that was needed to be
agriculturalists with the added advantages presented by the fenland.
The villages could all be described as fen edge villages, with the
possible exception of Thorne, which was barely on the edge. The
description, 'fen edge villages' has been used with reference to similar
villages in Cambridgeshire where it was claimed that they

> seem to be in many ways endowed for sustaining peasant communities.
> In each case the arable base was well matched by ample pastures and
> hay for winter feed. By its return in manure, this abundance of fodder
> gave field systems of the Midlands type a much better chance than
> average to work well.[17]

The non-agricultural advantages of fishing, fowling and reed gathering were a bonus to the inhabitants not a rival to their main
agricultural activities, thus making nonsense of a recently expressed
view that the inhabitants of the Chase were 'transformed . . . from
marshmen into farmers' by the drainage.[18]

Two sources have survived which illuminate the work of the township or village courts of the Manor. The two volumes of the Fishlake
Bye-Law Book cover the period 1582–1674 and 1680–1808 (Figure
7); the two volumes of the Hatfield Town Book deal with the years
1691–1717 and 1713–55.[19] The two sets of volumes are very different
in arrangement and coverage, though the central concern with the
farming of the ancient village lands is the same. The Hatfield Town
Court was a vestry court, though the term is not used in the books. It
met much more frequently than the Fishlake Court and the two
volumes are a disorganised mixture of lists of expenditure produced
by the poor law guardians and the constable, which the court ratified,
and the minutes of the meetings of the Court which were sometimes
entered at the front, sometimes at the back, and occasionally upside
down. Much of the business was the same as the Fishlake Court such
as the appointment and oversight of the grassmen but attendance at
meetings, judging from the signatures appended to the minutes, was
very haphazard with only the few men who controlled affairs being
there regularly except when matters of great importance were being
decided. The problem of nonattendance at meetings experienced by
the Fishlake Court in its later years suggests that the elected bye-law

Figure 7. 'Title page' from Fishlake Bye Law Book for 1680, *Courtesy of Doncaster Archives/Fishlake Parish Council*

Figure 8. The quality and detail of Norman carving can be seen on this engraving of the south doorway at Fishlake church, reproduced from the second volume of Joseph Hunter's *South Yorkshire* (1828)

men would have preferred a more open system of attendance.[20] The Bye-Law Court books cover a long period and return frequently to the same problems but it is fortunate that nearly fifty years of the first volume deal with the pre-drainage period, likewise, although the period covered by the Hatfield Books is much shorter, it is similarly fortunate that the second volume is largely concerned with the attempt to bring the latest ideas in agriculture into the open field farming of the village.

Fishlake is a parish of small settlements which is reflected in the organisation of the Bye-Law Court. Every year representatives were chosen from all the settlements. The main settlement around the church (Figures 8 & 9), referred to as Kirktown, had four representatives:Thorninghurst, Fosterhouse(s), Fleethouse and Westend, which was sometimes called Morehouse and Westend, had two each. Also chosen yearly were three grassmen and four banksmen. The duties of the grassmen were to oversee the grazing of the commons, especially the control of illegal grazing and the collection of fees from outsiders who sent animals to be pastured. The banksmen inspected and maintained the low bank which kept the high waters of the Don to the south and Turnbridge Dyke to the east off the townlands. Fishlake (and Sykehouse), unlike most other settlements of the Manor, were on alluvium; the other townlands were on islands which raised them above normal flooding. The court also appointed a paid 'pynder and nowter' (a herdsman or neatherd) who protected the animals grazing on the commons (Figure 10). At various times the Court reiterated that the pinder should remove both stray and tethered animals from the fields and fine their owners fourpence and also 'kepp the wheat and peys fields'. In 1610 and 1611 the offices of the pinder and herdsman were separated and their duties laid down in detail giving a good idea of the effort required to make an open field system work:

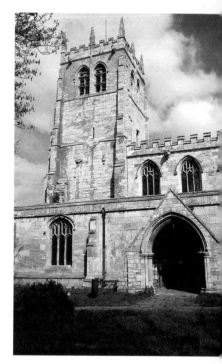

Figure 9. Fishlake's church (St Cuthbert's) is also large and impressive with an exceptionally fine Norman south doorway. *The Author*

> . . . *the saide Pynder* . . . *shall walke and viewe the 2 sowne feilds twice and the said by laweYnge evry daye once betwixt lady day* [25 March] *and michallms* [29 September] *and when he findeth defalte in the fences or gates he shall give warning to the p[ar]ty to make and rep[ai]r the same presently* . . . [he] *shall suffer none to get pescale but the owner The Newteherd for this yeare shall* [take?] *from May day till the usall tyme daly to and from the pasture such kine as shalbe put thither and shall allso tak notice of and look into all such geiste* [joyste, gist or

Figure 10. Fishlake pinfold. A surprising number of village pounds and pinfolds have survived (in various states of restoration) in the Doncaster area, most of them now protected as 'listed buildings'. *Brian Elliott*

gisted] *horses or cattle as shall* [be] *taken by the grassmen the yeare pylt and flay* [skin] *all morte falling in the Common for the year and be at all dryftes both at home and abroad as nede shall require*

The agisting (pasturing at a cost) of animals on Fishlake commons from outside the township indicated that the commons in the pre-drainage period were more than the local graziers needed. They were an important source of village income. In 1591 'gyst' money was 36s. 0d, in 1610 it was 54s. 6d. In the latter year the outsiders paying for grazing included Watson of Wadworth 6s. 0d for three foals and Cocker of Rotherham for a grey nag 2s. 6d. The following year Mr Godfrey Copley of 'Sprotburghe' paid 3s. 4d for three sows and four swine and George Byngley, also of Sprotbrough, paid 21s. 0d for four beasts, two horses and fourteen swine. Animals from as far away as Carlton and Wakefield were also agisted. Parts of the commons were also let to inhabitants and others for their sole use. The income was used for many purposes: repairing the town boat and replacing its ropes, repairing bridges over dykes and paying the pinder and herds-dman. Once the poor law had become a parish responsibility by the Acts of 1598 and 1601 the income from the commons was used to reduce the poor rate although it had been used to help the poor before 1598. Another form of income from the commons raised by the Bye-Law Court involved the granting of common rights to the builders of new houses:

> *The townshippe doe agree . . . that Thomas Wayte of ffosterhouses and those who sall* [sic] *have right after him in one new builded house whereon he now dwelleth or which shall hereafter dwelleth on the same shal for ever . . . have free ab*[ili]*ty to put their goods . . . upon the common . . . without paying giste for which he is contented to pay to the use of the towne XXs.*

Robert Bladworth paid 6s. 8d for a similar right on the same date, 18 September 1615.

The regulation of the open fields produced constant problems for the Court. Individuals who wished to ignore the fallowing routine or to put their animals onto stubble before others had finished reaping created situations which it was the Court's job to prevent. In 1603 the bye-lawmen agreed that 'no man shall gyve leave to anye to gleane ye corne of anye land before such tyme as the corne be l[ea]d away of it'. A century later gleaning was still creating problems and more detailed orders were issued to regulate it:

> *. . . Yt is unanimously agreed and Allso a By law made by us whose names are hereunto subscribed that noe pson shall glean or gather Corn as gleaners Except any pson tolerate or Give leave to them in ye time of Shearing Untill such time as the white corn be all led away out of the Common ffields and the ye ffields of ye white corn be kept unbroken for the gleaners 12 days.*

It is clear from these examples that before the drainage Fishlake was an agricultural community with many similarities to the Midland open field villages with the addition of commons so extensive that they could be used to contribute to village expenses. One of the problems of Midlands open field farming was a tendency to a shortage of pasture.

The drainage and the subsequent drowning of Fishlake produced a five year gap in the Bye-Law Court records. It was not until 1630 that normal Court business was resumed. The drainers caused a great increase in the chances of flooding on the northern bank of the Don by raising Ashfields bank on the south side and by cutting off the southern arm of the two courses of the river which encircled Ashfields.

This forced all the flow into the northern arm against the Fishlake bank. More seriously, by cutting off the Don completely from its ancient tortuous route through the Levels at Thorne and forcing its total flow into the medieval Turnbridge Dyke, it produced a situation with which neither the Dyke nor the ancient low bank of Fishlake could cope. A long legal struggle ensued to force the drainers to open a channel to the Ouse (the Dutch River) and to raise the Fishlake bank to an adequate height. The latter struggle went on for much of the seventeenth century before the Participants (the financiers of the drainage and their successors) were forced to raise the bank. Even then the inhabitants of Fishlake had to pay annually for its maintenance. The origin of Turnbridge Dyke is not known but it was not a broad channel and it was probably only made to relieve the flow into the Levels. The problems caused by these drainage errors were not really cured until the middle of this century. Although they must have been in the forefront of the minds of the bye-lawmen until the record ends, there is no indication of the increased flooding risks in the Bye-Law Court minutes except for more references to the maintenance of internal dykes and of the cloughs or sluices linking them to the river. In 1667 the Court agreed that John Goodridge should have a piece of the common between Double Dyke and the meadows for 'dicking the dubell dike betwixt the clawe [clough] and the 2 inges' and for maintaining Blacksike 'clawe'. The Double Dyke was so warped up that the Court sent labourers to speed up the scouring and assessed all 'dwelling places' in Fishlake twopence to pay them. In the same year a system of fines was introduced for failure to maintain fences to the common and between fields and 'any common wather cowerses'. Later, several other members of the Goodridge family were paid in cash for maintaining drainage channels, and not by use of the common. In 1692 George Goodridge was elected ferryman on condition that he provided a lock for Black Sike clough and 'lett no tides in without the Town's consent'. Three years later he was re-elected on the same conditions.

The ferry was of great importance to the Fishlake people as they were cut off from the rest of the Manor and from their Dykesmarsh pasture by the river. The way into Hatfield was by the ford at Stainforth until the 1740s when a timber bridge was built.[21] The ferry, at Hangmans Hill near the site of the modern Jubilee Bridge, would be used for animals as well as people. In 1671 when John Carter was elected ferryman an attempt was made to improve the service. He was told that he was:

to kepe ye bote at ye partings of ye river at Hangmans Hill and . . . to

> *cast a bancke for people to get dry to ye bote and . . . to have for his*
> *pains 1s. and . . . to loocke well to drawing up ye blaxed clow shutes*
> [shutters] *and putting them downe a gayne in time ye water day*
> *flowin and he shall for his wages 3s. 4d.*[22]

Thomas Stappelton was elected as Carter's successor the following year on condition 'that he is not to kepe any ale to sell'!

Throughout the period covered by the two volumes there was concern about illegal grazing on the commons and drifts were regularly organized to check the right of an animal to graze. This involved the corraling of all the animals on the common and it was the duty of the inhabitants to assist the herdsman in checking their ownership. In 1610 'at Thorne drifte' four shillings was taken in fines. Fishlake Common in Dykesmarsh was more convenient to Thorne graziers than it was to those of Fishlake. In the later years of the seventeenth century the problem of illegal grazing appears to have grown as more drifts were organised but this may have been a result of the petty corruption which the accounts show to be increasing.

In 1689 the sum of £1. 8s. 0d. was 'disburst at the drift' and five shillings was 'Recievd of John Scoley for bease that was driven'. In 1690 the disbursement was clarified 'at a drifte in ale and meate to men that helped us up with Drift 12/-' and 'Disburst at Drift £1. 1s. 6d.' The sums taken in fines were less than this. Over several decades this pattern continued despite a memorandum at a meeting in 1698,

> *yt ye Bylawmen shall not spend any of ye money yt they receive for*
> *Incomes, but shall be Laid out upon necessary Repaires*

The memorandum had no effect and there are increasing signs of Bye-Law Courts themselves turning into social occasions: 'ale and meate' at bye-law meetings in 1710 cost £2. 1s. 2d. It was possibly to try to correct this trend that from 1680 a respected (usually richer) member of the community began to be appointed as 'foreman' of the bye-law men. It did not stop it, however, as a memorandum of 1718 shows,

> *there was Severall psons of Thorne Dikesmarsh and Moor Ends pd for*
> *Trespasses on Dikesmarsh & c wch was spent at Meetings.*

It is also possible that the increasing sociability of meetings was an attempt to counter some reluctance to serve the community indicated by the unwillingness of bye-lawmen to attend meetings and of others to do their share of the occasional duties required to keep the open field system working. On 1 January 1711 a list was made in the book of 'Defaults in pforming ye Bylaw Comon-day Works at ye rate of 3d p day for Poor Men and 6d p day for others'. Some missed the odd day; others missed up to four. Several bye-lawmen missed days and all were fined sixpence. Several could or would not pay and were distrained: 'Matt Wilkinson a tankard for three days, Richard Forster a dish and a swingletree for four days and Richard Crabtree a bible'.

An apparent disenchantment with communal effort might have been a foreshadowing of the pressure for enclosure but in the early eighteenth century there was still a great deal for the bye-lawmen to do in the management of the bye-law fields and commons. There was, for instance, much concern about the wetness of the open fields. The Court book in 1712 included a list of fines on

> *Persons who had not well and sufficiently Gripped or Goyted their severall lands in ye West and East fields . . . ye Defaults being viewed by all ye Bylawmen and finding Abundance of Water Stand* [illegible] *doe the same Vizt 6 men and such as would not pay we distrained on and made Pay for doeing the same and allsoe two pence for every Rood as a Penalty for their Neglect, According to ye By Law in this book and sett downe each flatt and quantity of land in default.*

This was strong action and a possible reflection of the growing impatience of the better (ie bigger) farmers to improve farming conditions. Evidence of the desire of larger farmers to limit the rights of the smaller comes in a declaration of 1735 by the 'owners and possessors of Lands in the Town Ings' to stint or restrict the grazing of the fogg or aftermath there according to the number of acres occupied. 'To Witt for every acre we possess four Beasts or two Horses, and so on in proportion'. Within a few years of the declaration the Bye-Law Court was introducing new courses for the open fields in an attempt to modernise their agriculture.

The Hatfield Town books contain a great deal of the social history of the village during the first half of the eighteenth century. In addi-

Figure 11. Hatfield Workhouse. Erected c1734 after a decision at a Town Meeting to borrow £120 from Henry Casson of Thorne for the purpose. After the 1834 Poor Law Amendment Act the poor were moved to the Union Workhouse at Thorne. *Brian Elliott*

tion to the Overseers' and the Constables' lists of payments the books show the Court attempting to deal with felons; to arrange the take over of a farm mortgage held by a soldier serving abroad; to support orphaned children and arrange apprenticeships; to maintain the pond for the ducking stool; to borrow money to build a workhouse (Figure 11); and other topics, too many to cover in this study.

The meetings were often concerned, as they were in Fishlake, with the state of the field and common drains and with fences, gates and hedges in need of repair, but there was no mention of agistment fees collected or drifts being arranged. There were, however, details of agreements to lease parts of the common land. In 1707 the town could not pay its debts and borrowed £50 from a Mr Whitaker. The debt problems were still pressing in 1714 when Cornelius Dickinson, a large Hatfield farmer, was allowed to rent the 'common called Lawne Hill for 20/-'. A year later it was decided to try

> to lett the turbary near Epworth, Belton and other Isle towns . . . for the benefit of the parish and towards the payment of the debts . . . Mr Woodcock clerk Thos Eldwick Gent John Hatfield Junr Gent and John Cook to be trustees . . . Mr Prim be assistant to 'em to lett the said turf graft to the best advantage.

Such decisions could obviously be the cause of great dissension within the parish. Another agreement of 1714 let the use of the area called Clownes to a Mr Scholey but when he came to reap the crop he was 'hindered by severall of the neighbours'. He issued a writ against the grassmen who were sent to Leeds to make the best agreement they could with him, any costs to be met 'by ye Town out ye Constable Assessment'.

Financial support was usual for town officials engaged in tasks which resulted in legal action, or were likely to do so. Although the Court did not appear to be concerned with minor abuses of common rights, it was sometimes constrained to take action:

> to prevent abuses on our commons for ye future from any persons and especially Nicholas Kirke Senr of Hatfield Woodhouse who has now commenced an action of Comon Law against Wm Moore Richard Walton John Nicholson and Thomas Dearman and Christopher Sutcliffe present Grassmen and others and which is now in all likely-hood to be tryed this assias [assizes] at York. That ye said defendants have all their reasonable cost and charges of suit paid and allowed to them by and at ye publick charge and expense of ye parish.

Rejection of their authority does not appear to have been a problem for Fishlake officials even though they were forced to distrain goods for non-payment of fines for breach of bye-laws, but even trivial cases could bring threats of legal action in Hatfield. In 1728 William Flather broke a bye-law of 1724 on the repair of his fences and was distrained 'one pewter dish' by the pinder against whom he brought an 'action at Law'. The Town meeting responded in support of the pinder:

> *We the owners and occupiers of ye Townfeilds and Ings . . . agree and consent to vindicate ye byelawmen . . . against ye Action . . . and we do hereby binde ourselves to defray all reasonable charges in the management of the suite.*

It is possibly the increase in the risk of being involved in litigation which explains alterations in the terms of service for grassmen. An entry for 1715 shows that until then the office of had stayed in the same hands for several years but in that year 'for better regulating the office of Grassmen for the future', they were to be elected annually. Three were named for Hatfield, two for Woodhouse and one for Stainforth. In 1735 the period of service was increased to three years. The reduction to one year had come very shortly after a great change in the running of the Town fields brought a considerable increase in the grassmen's work. There is no sign in the Town Book before 1713 that revolutionary changes to the open field agriculture of the village were imminent. Indeed only fifteen years earlier a decision had been made to reduce the fallowing period to one year and to fallow the fields in sequence which does not suggest that Hatfield farmers were on the brink of modernisation. However, there is some indication in probate inventories of the new crops coming into use. At his death in 1691 Robert Moore of Hatfield Woodhouse had 'Certain rye and turneps on ye ground', but there are only four other inventory references to turnips in the next forty years and no inventory mention of clover until 1719.[23] Yet the evidence arising from the tithe dispute shows both crops to be an established part of the open field cropping course by 1729–34 and a very important crop in the closes. Presumably the new crops had proved their value in the closes before the decision to introduce them to the open fields was made in 1713–14.

The meeting which approved the decision was well attended with thirty seven townsmen signifying their agreement to several proposals. The most important was that

> *. . . the West Feild and Hundoake feild be sown with Turnipps and ye same be sufficiently fenced in before ye first day of July noe seed sowne before ye 25th day of . . . July by each owner or occupier in ye said Fields.*[24]

Haddam Field was to be fenced in the Autumn in preparation for turnips and the other fields in succession. The change was necessary, according to the introduction to the decision, for

> *. . . ye better management of our Town fields for destroying of tares go [missing] and Other pernicious Weeds subject tu ye sd Land and for ye better Encouragement of Husbandry and Good of ye publique.*

The agreement also controlled the eating of the turnips. Entry to the turnip field was confined to the occupiers of the land and carefully stinted according to every half acre cultivated. No animals were to be allowed in until 1 November. On this day cattle to be admitted were to be brought to

> *ye Lords folde . . . to have ye feild Brand sett upon them which shall be a Staggs* [Head?] *and when so branded to be admitted into ye feild by ye Bylawmen paying them the summe of sixpence for every acre and rateably for a lesser quantity which said summe ye said bylawmen shall Imploy as shall be directed at some towns meeting towards ye charge of scouring ye said feild and turnipps ye keeper of ye . . . feild to be at the By lawmens choice.*

As the new system was so open to fraud, a system of fines was devised for smuggling in unbranded animals and for pulling turnips for sale or feeding to pigs. Occupiers were allowed to pull them for their 'own boyling' or for 'setting for seed' but had to pay sixpence a peck. The work involved for the bye-lawmen was recognised by the payment of half the two shilling fine paid for every unbranded animal found in the field in addition to being allowed to put one animal into the field above their stint. In an attempt to anticipate the objections of those who lost fallow grazing the turnip field was to be opened up on 1 March and no occupier was to begin ploughing until 2 February. This was poor compensation and undoubtedly encouraged the illegal grazing of animals and theft of turnips which bedevilled the change. To assist the project the Hatfield men who farmed the tithes from the Duke of Devonshire, William, Thomas and Henry Moore and Cornelius Dickinson, 'promised to give up all their right of tythe of Turnips in ye said Feilds'. A decision of some importance when the Duke sold the tithes in 1729.

At a meeting in January 1720 the important decision was made to divide the Mill Field into two parts. The new boundary was to be fenced and hedged with quicksett, the eastern part to be called Old Mill Field and the western part New Mill Field. The division of the field indicates that the new cropping pattern could not be accommodated within the existing four fields. A course was laid down as part of this agreement which included barley in two fields every year, a choice of clover or peas and rye and turnips in the other fields. In 1722 the course was amended and clover was not mentioned but clearly it remained an alternative to peas. By the time of the tithe dispute, of which clover and turnips were at the centre, clover had ousted peas from the course and in 1736 a Town meeting agreed 'yt ye Clover field should not be broken as usual but be eaten by horses belonging to ye owners of the Lands in ye said Clover feild'. Clover had become a very important crop as an undated letter of c.1741 from Frank Moore to Lord Irwin's Steward at Temple Newsam illustrates. Moore, who claimed to have introduced clover to the common fields, wrote that its spread had been rapid because clover produced two to three times as much fodder as 'nathural' hay and it allowed more corn to be grown because 'The Parishioners Lettin no more Land Ly for Hay than is absolutely necessary to Keepe a stock sufficient to manidge their Husbandry', used the former meadow land for corn.[25]

The leading members of the community, judging from their constant attempts to make the new husbandry work, agreed with Frank Moore but it was not easy to make it acceptable to everybody. The exploitation of the new crops by some of those with land in the fields by pasturing animals beyond their stint and pulling turnips beyond their allowance caused problems in the Town Meeting for many years. In 1714 the right of occupiers to pull turnips was limited o a peck an acre. Abuse attracted the very large fine of a shilling. In 1748 attempts were made to stop occupiers from selling their turnip grazing rights outside the parish. There was even more trouble from those who were now excluded from the fields. Those who drove their swine into the turnip fields were threatened with presentation at the

Manor Court in 1721, but by 1746 the Town Meeting was outraged that 'some had dar'd to turn in their cattle [to the fields] in the night'. The meeting went on to complain of the lowness of the fines for trespass on grass, clover or corn which were 'too light' and made trespassing worthwhile. They demanded an increase from 1d. for a horse and a halfpenny for a beast. There were also constant attempts to make the grassmen more effective in policing the fields by reiterating offers of a share of the fines and protection against legal action.

The commoners' objections to the changes since 1713 are easy to understand and so are the reasons for a lack of enthusiasm by some of the farmers. Firstly, it was realised,

Figure 12. Arthur Young (1741–1820), the leading agricultural writer and journalist.

Figure 13. The Manor of Hatfield Court House c1740. *Brian Elliott*

as early as 1714, that the hope that turnip growing would eradicate weeds was false. This is not surprising as it appears that turnips in Hatfield were never hoed. Both Arthur Young (Figure 12) in the 1770s and Robert Brown in the 1790s were very rude about turnip cultivation in Hatfield.[26] Secondly, it proved very difficult to find a regular course of cropping which worked to the satisfaction of the meeting. Experiments were still being tried in the 1750s. Thirdly, it was an expensive system to maintain. The fees for the entry of branded animals to the turnip field had to be increased in 1714 and the meeting was frequently looking for ways of reducing the costs. Fourthly, the changes caused increased tension in the village which is seen not only in the breaches of the fields by the poor, but the resentment of the bigger farmers at the use of resources by small men. This is clearly expressed in a letter, probably written by John Hatfield, the chief figure in the decisions of the Town Meeting (Figures 13 & 14),

Figure 14. Barn built by the fourth and last John Hatfield in 1789. Next to it is one built by John Hatfield III in 1755. Both were adjacent to *Hatfield House* which had grounds encroaching into the West Field. All four John Hatfields were important figures in the history of the village. The first, who settled in the village after the Civil War was a Parliamentary officer. The second and third were very powerful in the Town Meetings covered in the Hatfield volumes of 1692–1755.

to the Lord's Steward. He wrote,

> *our commons* [are] *very large and great quantities of sheepe kepte as many as actually are some dry years pyned.* [The farmers are] *oblidged to milk their cows and have their horses for bit* [and are] *oblidged to Sumer ym out which is commonly done a boute thorne Moore for 2s. 6d. to 3s. 0d. for a grown beas . . . in some other pastures we can have yt at 1s. 6d. a gate a grown beast at Barnby Dun a boute 2 miles from us. Our own neighbours yt have not common right usually pays about 4d. or 6d. and seldom ever a shilling for a grown beas somring to ye gras man.*[27]

At the time this was written, in the early 1740s, the Hatfield farmers were presenting their case for the tithing of turnips and clover as fodder which was, in Hatfield, a traditional modus of one penny per acre instead of a tenth of the crop which the tithe owner, Lord Portmore, demanded. The tithe case and the agricultural changes which led to it seem to have concentrated the minds of the larger farmers on the iniquities of competition from small farmers and commoners. The Fishlake Bye-Law Book shows the farmers there introducing clover into the open fields in 1740 and having similar problems to Hatfield in finding a suitable cropping course in subsequent years. From mid-century there is evidence in Fishlake of an increased determination to keep interlopers from the commons. Regular drifts resulted in the fining of men from Thorne, Moorends and Cowick. About 1778 joint drifts with the Sykehouse Bye-Law men started. A detailed list of trespassers of 1784 shows how serious the problem was. Apart from 29 horses, 41 beasts and 160 sheep belonging to several men, John Saunders had 120 sheep and 8 beasts, William Cawkle had 4 horses and 20 sheep and William Dunghill had 2 horses and 2 beasts. In 1787

> *the Three parreishes* [Fishlake, Hatfield and Thorne] *goined and drove the whole Commons Belonging to the Maner of Hatfield and touche on the trespassers as follows for every Hors 5s. and every Beas 3s. and for ye sheep 6d.*

After this date the Fishlake Book peters out, as the Hatfield one had done thirty years earlier but the implication of the joint drifts is clear: that the larger farmers of the Manor wanted enclosure. Their desire for enclosure was not simply a result of their dissatisfaction with the abuses on the commons or of the difficulties of running the open fields through the village courts at a time of change; it was a result of what

Figure 15. Hatfield Grammar School. Built by John Hatfield I 'on a little lyn land (flax close)' in 1682/3. The school was founded early in the seventeenth century by Thomas Wormley. In the nineteenth century it was taken over by the Travis Charity as an elementary school. The extension on the right was built 1890. *The Author*

they had seen in the many parishes round about where parliamentary enclosure had already taken place.[28] Also, for much of the century a debate had been carried on in the country at large on the merits or otherwise of enclosure and by mid-century many of the supporters of it had begun to attack commoners as criminals and idlers who were far too independent and needed, for the national good, to be disciplined by being turned into farm labourers.[29] It seems unlikely that Hatfield and Fishlake farmers were unaffected by these views. It is, perhaps, significant that in the year of the first combined drift of the commons advertisements appeared in the new, Doncaster published *Yorkshire Journal* on the future of the commons. The first, headed 'Hatfield Inclosure', referred to the decision of a meeting in Thorne to apply to parliament for a bill to enclose and divide the commons. The second called a meeting at the *Bay Horse* in Hatfield to reject enclosure and to support a 'Deed of Association' to regulate rights of pasturage.[29] Nothing appears to have come of either proposal but in the later years of the century many of the larger farmers were buying up land to increase their influence over the future of the Manor. Attempts at enclosure had possibly been made before 1787 and there were three attempts to introduce a bill before it was finally passed in 1811. The delay was partly a result of the sheer size of the Manor and of difficulties with the Lord, the Marchioness of Hertford, but it was obviously recognised in Fishlake that the last days of the Bye-Law Court had come as there were only two entries in it between 1787 and the last entry in 1808. This was three years before the passing of the bill which ended the communal farming system in the Manor and the main reason for the existence of the Court.

Notes and References

1. Darby H C, *The Medieval Fenland*, 1940 (reprinted 1974), p 42.
2. Hoskins W. G, *Local History in England*, 1959, p 75.
3. Apart from Darby, see Thirsk J, *English Peasant Farming*, 1957 (reprinted 1981).
4. Brocklesby R. 'Hatfield Court Rolls', National Register of Archives, Northern Section 1958–59, *Bulletin* No 3 May 1960, pp 28–46.
5. Kerridge E, *Agrarian Problems in the Sixteenth Century and After*, 1969, p 19.
6. Leeds Archives, TN/HC/C5 Rentals.
7. Limbert M. *The Drainage of Thorne Waste in the Nineteenth Century*, Thorne and District Local History Association Occasional Papers No. 5, p 1.
8. British Museum (BM) Eg 3160, Mss 13674, 'Map of the Bounders of Haitfield Rectorie made by Nicholas Prole of Thorne', 1669.
9. By the time of John de Warenne's death in 1347 Ashfields Park and a small park called the Haye in Fishlake had been disparked and let to tenants. Hatfield Great Park was partly disparked but the majority, c.1100 acres survived until the drainage. I would like to thank Ms Lynne Heley late of Sheffield University for this information.
10. BM, MR 336, Map of 1633. The map of 1639 by Josias Arlebout was redrawn by Thomas Smith and published in Read, *History of the Isle of Axholme*, 1858.
11. Rackam O, *Trees and Woodland in the British Landscape*, 1976, p 153.
12. York City Archives, ACC 104 0/20. A survey of deer after the severe winter of 1615 claimed: red deer, 677 living, 534 dead and fallow deer, 1755 living, 1365 dead. An estimate in 1607 gave 1000 in total! I thank Mr David Hughes for this information.
13. CSPD, 88. Chas. I, 1628–9, p 515.
14. Brocklesby, *op cit*, p 43.
15. BM Eg 3389 (Leeds Papers Vol. LXVI) 'Survey of Hatfield taken in ye year 1634'.
16. Public Record Office, LR/2/193.Jl., 'Survey of Hatfield Manor'.
17. Ravensdale J R, *Liable to Floods Village Landscape on the edge of the Fens A.D. 450–1850*, 1974, p 151.
18. Caulfield C, 'A Reporter at Large: Thorne Moors'. *The New Yorker*, Feb 4, 1991, p 63.
19. Doncaster Archives, PR/FISH/ADD/1, Bye-Law Book, 1582–1674. This was in private hands until recently and in very poor condition. I would like to thank Mr Robert Downing, late of Hatfield, for lending me his transcription. The book has now been carefully restored, P17/6/A/1 Bye-Law Book, 1680–1808. PR/1/1/1 and 2, Hatfield Town Books, 1692–1755.
20. Hey D (ed), *The Oxford Companion to Local and Family History*, 1996, p 473. 'The vestry . . . was originally the room where parish meetings were held. Membership of the vestry comprised the minister, churchwardens, and leading parishioners . . .'
21. Barras N I, *Stainforth and its History*, 1984, p 6.
22. Probably refers to the junction between Turnbridge Dike and the remnant of the Don which was cut off by a sluice nearer to Thorne.
23. Borthwick Institute of Historical Research, University of York, Probate Inventory of Robert Moore, 19 Oct. 1691. I would like to thank Professor David Hey for the transcript of this inventory and many more.
24. Hundoak was a furlong within the West Field, it was not a town field.
25. Leeds Archives, TN/HC/B19, Frank Moore to Robert Hopkinson, 1 January 1741.
26. Young A. *Northern Tour*, 1770, pp 102–7. Brown R, et al, *A General View of the Agriculture of the West Riding*, 1799, App. p 37.
27. Leeds Archives, TN/HC/B19, 1740–41.
28. In the first surge of parliamentary enclosure, 1750–80, there were nine enclosures of commons and wastes in the immediate neighbourhood.
29. Neeson J M, Commoners: *Common Right, Enclosure and Social Change in England*, 1993 (reprinted 1995), pp 19–34.

7. THE HISTORY OF THE BRASS BAND MOVEMENT UP TO 1914: DONCASTER'S CONTRIBUTION

by Philip L Scowcroft

IT IS OFTEN SAID THAT brass banding is heavily weighted towards the North of England, Lancashire and Yorkshire especially (though other parts of the country would contest the generality of this assertion) and it comes as no surprise to learn that many of the early attempts to establish brass bands and band contests were in those counties. The longest lasting of these contests was the 'Open', started at Belle Vue, Manchester in 1853 and still flourishing, but there were others, for example at Burton Constable, near Hull, at Halifax and Sheffield and, in 1859 and 1860, Doncaster.

Doncaster had, since at least the 1790s, heard military bands, usually those of the local militia, yeomanry and volunteer regiments, particularly when these assembled in the town for annual training periods. Outdoor concerts were given during these periods, normally in South Parade, still one of the town's major thoroughfares, and these

Figure 1. The Thurlstone Band pictured in 1858; the band did not appear in the Doncaster contests of 1859–60 but is reasonably representative of those that did. Trombones, 'Cornopeans', Ophicleides and Saxhorns may be seen. *Brian Elliott/Barnsley Archives*

Figure 2. Bandstand at the Botanical Gardens, Sheffield.

became so popular that the Doncaster Philharmonic Society formed a Promenade Band in about 1851 specifically for open air concerts and appealed for the £60 necessary to provide instruments. This mixed woodwind and brass ensemble, twenty-one strong, was, however, short lived despite some 'promising' performances noted by local newspapers; but the coincidence of firstly, the availability and growing popularity of cornets and the instruments of the saxhorn family (Figure 1) and secondly, the move to Doncaster of the Great Northern Railway's Locomotive Works (then, and still, known locally as the 'Plant'), the town's first major industry, in 1852–53, produced one or two purely brass bands during the 1850s. The cornet a piston, called 'cornopean' in England at that period, reached this country in 1834 and quickly caught on, partly because of the brilliant playing of Monsieur Koenig, composer of the celebrated *Post Horn Galop* and much else, whom Doncaster heard twice, in 1844 and 1849, when he appeared there with Louis Jullien's 'unrivalled' band in orchestral promenade concerts. Saxhorns, introduced to this country in the 1840s, were probably first heard in the town on 22 April 1850 when the Distin family, contemporary travelling brass virtuosi, played on instruments which had been presented to them by the former French king, Louis Philippe. The Distins returned to Doncaster the following April.[1]

In November 1854, Thomas Dodgson, a local musician, was appointed Bandmaster of a new band for the Doncaster troop of the 1st West York Yeomanry which initially mustered five 'cornopeans', one D Flat saxhorn, one E Flat bass, one ophicleide, one valve trumpet, one brass trombone and a brass drum. This was not quite a 'typical' brass band as it included a trumpet and also an ophicleide, a keyed instrument popular in early Victorian times, but such 'non-standard' instrumentation was common at that early period.

We hear briefly of a Great Northern Loco Band, dressed in 'a very neat uniform', playing hymns around the town at Christmas, 1852;[2] this may have been an *ad hoc* ensemble but certainly by April 1856 the Great Northern Railway Mechanics' Institution had established a drum and fife band and a Plant Works Brass Band eighteen strong (two sopranos, six cornopeans, two tenor horns, one baritone, three trombones, two ophicleides, one bombardon – probably an E Flat bass – and percussion) which by the summer of 1858 was giving regular concerts out of doors. Its conductor was one George F Birkinshaw, a Barnsley man by birth, who had become known in Doncaster as Bandmaster (1853–56) of the 3rd West York Militia; he was the father of a celebrated Black Dyke cornettist of the same name. Birkinshaw quickly secured contest successes with his railway band: Third Prize at a competition in Lincoln on 6 June 1859 and First Prize (£15, a substantial sum then) at Peterborough on 5 September 1859.[3] In 1860 it visited the Botanical Gardens in Sheffield (Figure 2) and emerged with Second Prize.[4] Its concerts, attended by as many as 500 on fine days, featured operatic selections – from, for example, Flotow's *Martha*, Verdi's *I Masnadieri, Luisa Miller* and *Rigoletto* and Ricci's now-forgotten *Scaramuccia* – marches and dance music, much of the latter by Birkinshaw himself: *Festive Polka, Promenade Galop, Rouse Polka, Spring Flowers Galop* and *Pas Redouble.*[5]

This upsurge of interest in brass music, coupled with a strong feeling, prevalent by that time, that musical entertainment should be provided for the working classes, crystallised into a brass band contest held on 29 August 1859 in 'Mr King's grounds', adjoining the Horse Fair (now called Waterdale), near Doncaster town centre. Cheap railway excursions from neighbouring towns, patronised by at least 470 people, were laid on and prize money of £25 and a silver cup provided. The contest duly took place; unfortunately rain put a damper on things, though it cleared up in the evening for the fete and fireworks. Cleckheaton Band won, playing a medley from Verdi's *La Traviata* after Doncaster Railway Foundry Band (so described) – who eventually finished third – had led at the half-way stage. Between 4000

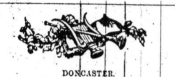

and 5000 people were present. Ten bands appeared together;[6] the judges were Henry Farmer (Nottingham), H Newham (Nottingham Cavalry), Thomas Dodgson and Enderby Jackson, a great figure in the early days of brass bands and whose *Yorkshire Waltz* was played on this occasion by the Gawthorpe Band.

A repeat, under the grandiose title of the Second South Yorkshire Brass Band Contest, was planned for the following year and was duly held in Nether Hall Park on 25 June 1860 (Figure 3).[7] The rewards offered were £12 plus a silver cup (First Prize), £10 (Second), £5 (Third) and £3 (Fourth); a grand fete with military displays and fireworks again followed the contest proper, as did also the playing of the *Hallelujah Chorus* and Mendelssohn's *Wedding March* by all the competing performers (340 players), which had necessitated a rehearsal that morning (11.30 am) in Doncaster's then new Market Hall. The contest, at 2 pm, had seventeen participating bands (Heckmondwike Albion; Oakley; Cleckheaton Victoria; Bramley; Bradford; Kingledew's, Leeds; Wike Independent; Dewsbury; Doncaster Volunteer Rifle Corps, which was the Doncaster Plant Works Band restyled;[8] Baildon; Dodworth; Black Dike [sic] Mills; Countesthorpe; Waterloo; Leeds Spanish Leather Works; Morley; and Holmfirth Temperance) – Dewsbury won, with Cleckheaton second. Doncaster secured the Fourth Prize, beating Black Dike, who were to be winners of the very first National Contest at the Crystal Palace the following month. The pieces played were 'own choice', mainly the operatic selections which were to remain so common as championship test pieces for at least half a century thereafter, though Waterloo offered the *Grand Prize*

DONCASTER.

THE Musical Public are respectfully informed that the SECOND SOUTH YORKSHIRE BRASS BAND CONTEST will take place (by the kind permission of Mr. Wm. Eyre,) in NETHER HALL PARK, on Monday, the 25th day of June, 1860, under the immediate Patronage of

The Worshipful the MAYOR OF DONCASTER,
C. J. FOX, Esq., Ex-Mayor,
The Right Honourable the Earl of SCARBROUGH,
JAMES BROWN, Esq., M.P.

The Prizes to be awarded on this occasion will amount in value to nearly FIFTY POUNDS! including Two superb SILVER CUPS! the Gift of the Inhabitants of Doncaster and the Doncaster Licensed Victuallers Association.

The Entry List contains the following highly celebrated Champion Bands of Yorkshire:—

Heckmondwike Albion Band.
Oakley Band.
Cleckheaton Victoria Band, winner of the First Prize at Doncaster, in 1859.
Bramley Band, winner of the First Prize at Sheffield and Hull, also Second Prize at York and Darlington, 1859, and Second Prize at Lincoln, 1860.
Bradford Band, first time of playing at any Contest.
Ingledew's Leeds Band.
Wike Independent Band.
Dewsbury Band, winner of the First Prize at Sheffield, and Second Prize at Hull, 1858.
Doncaster V. R. C. Band, winner of the First Prize at Peterbro', 1859.
Baildon Band, winner of £50, in a Match with the Dewsbury Band, 1859.
Dodworth Band.
Black Dike Mills Band, winner of the First Prize at York, and Second Prize at Hull, 1859.
Countesthorpe Band.
Waterloo Band.
Leeds Spanish Leather Works Band.
Morley Band, winner of the First Prize at Hull, 1857 and 1858; and Newcastle-upon-Tyne, 1859.
Holmfirth Temperance Band, winner of the First Prize at Aston Park, Birmingham, 1859.

At Half-past Eleven in the Morning there will be (by permission) a GRAND REHEARSAL in the MARKET HALL, of Handel's 'Hallelujah Chorus!' from the Oratorio "Messiah," and Mendelssohn's 'Wedding March!' by the whole of the Bands.

The Contest will commence at Two o'clock. Each Band will play Two Pieces of their own selection. After the Bands have played their first pieces, the whole will be united and form a MONSTER BRASS BAND of upwards of THREE HUNDRED and FORTY MUSICIANS! and will play Handel's "Hallelujah Chorus," and Mendelssohn's "Wedding March." At the close of the Contest there will be a

GRAND FETE CHAMPETRE!

ASSAULT AT ARMS!—Comprising Feats of Swordsmanship, Bayonet Exercise, by Professor GREGORY, of Savile House, Leicester Square, London, and Assistants; also the celebrated Indian Club Exercise, as performed before Her Majesty the Queen.

RIFLE PRACTICE! ARCHERY! AND DANCING!

The whole to conclude with a Brilliant DISPLAY of FIREWORKS, at dusk. Amongst other numerous and Original Devices introduced will be

THE ARMS OF THE BOROUGH OF DONCASTER!
Made and Fired by Mr. SEAMAN, of Hull.

Cheap Excursion Trains from Boston, Horncastle, Lincoln, Peterbro', Nottingham, Grantham, Newark, Retford, Bradford, Leeds, Wakefield, Pontefract, Sheffield, Masbro', Barnsley, Keadby Grange Bridge, Thorne, and all the intermediate Stations.

ADMISSION:—Tickets purchased on or before 23rd of June for the whole day's Entertainment SIXPENCE each. On the day of the Contest ONE SHILLING each.

Excursionists on producing their Railway Tickets will be admitted at Sixpence each.

A limited number of Tickets for the Grand Rehearsal in the Market-Hall, will be issued 6d. each.

Tickets may be had of all the Book and Music Sellers, and at the usual places. Agents have also been appointed in all the surrounding Villages.

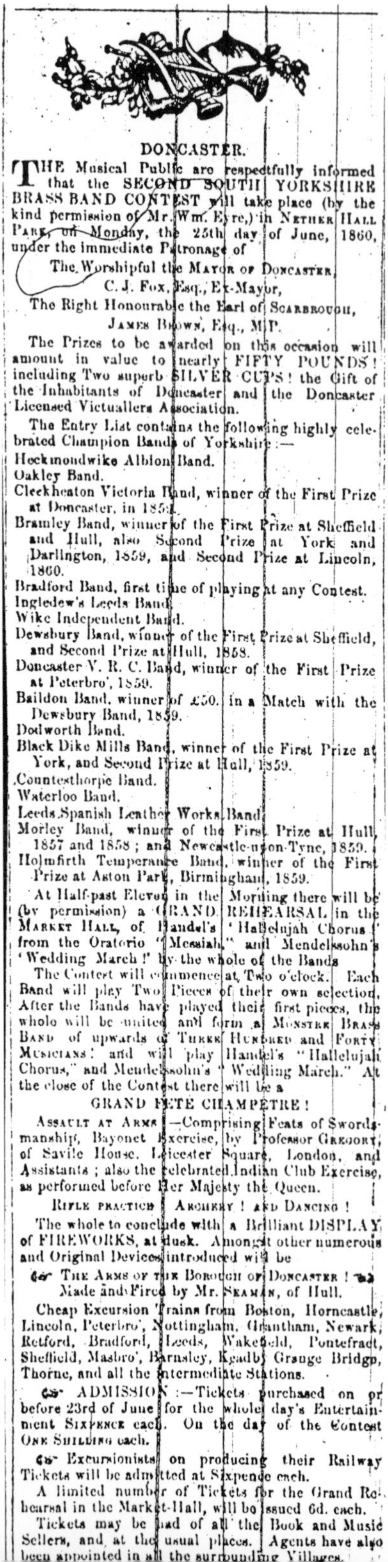

Figure 3. Advertisement informing the Doncaster public of the SECOND BRASS CONTEST scheduled for Nether Hall Park on 22 June 1860.

Quadrilles by Enderby Jackson, who was again present and indeed conducted the massed bands in the Handel and Mendelssohn. The contest was a great success, aided by the weather, which, after a rainy morning, kept fine, but there was no repeat the following year, or indeed at all, though on 17 18 and 19 September 1861 Birkinshaw organised a 'Promenade Concert' in Nether Hall Park with his own band, accompanied by fireworks, balloon ascents, comic songs and other features. Birkinshaw soon afterwards left South Yorkshire for the Bradford area and Doncaster entered a quieter phase as far as brass banding was concerned, though one not altogether without incident. It continued to enjoy the mainly alfresco efforts of its local military bands, the Volunteer and 1st West York Yeomanry (later Yorkshire Dragoons) Bands, which latter was conducted for many years either side of 1900 by Lieutenant Samuel Suckley, a competent band trainer and composer of marches and dances like the *Elsie* and *Sandringham* waltzes. Both were apparently purely brass formations, the Yeomanry usually being heard during their annual Doncaster training week. Regent Square, the *Salutation Inn* forecourt, Hall Cross Hill, a field at Thorne Road, St James' Bridge, The Holmes and Market Place were some of the outdoor 'pitches'.

Volunteer and Yeomanry bands combined in a Grand Military Concert at the Corn Exchange on 27 October 1887, the programme including Boieldieu's *Caliph of Baghdad* overture and selections from *The Bohemian Girl* (Balfe) and *Lucia di Lammermoor* (Donizetti). This was by no means the only time the Volunteer Band played in the Corn Exchange. The Volunteer Band's conductors after Birkinshaw included J Redfern, in the 1860s and early 1870s, and S Wilson, later in the century. With reorganisations nationally of the Volunteer effort in the period up to 1914 this band was later restyled 2nd York & Lancaster Regiment Band and, from 1908, the 5th KOYLIs. Its repertoire over the years interestingly reflects the times and contemporary composers. Waldteufel's waltz *Souvenir* figured in 1881; a concert in 1883 included the march *Tel-el-Kebir* (after a British victory in Egypt the year before) and the *Iolanthe Valse* arranged from Sullivan's operetta; a selection from *The Gondoliers* appeared in 1891. In 1894 it was 'acknowledged to be one of the best in the district'.

From time to time new brass ensembles were formed; during the 1890s Hexthorpe Brass Band (from 1892), Doncaster Borough (from 1893, under David Cameron's musical direction), Doncaster Temperance (from about 1898) and Oxford Place (from 1898), based on a town centre Methodist church and then conducted by W H Tuxworth, were all active. The Salvation Army had established a band in Doncaster in 1888, soon after the formation of the local Corps. At times five, even six, of Hexthorpe, Borough, Temperance, Oxford Place, Volunteer, the intriguingly titled Druid's Band (about which I know nothing) and Salvation Army appeared together, notably at the (outdoor) Friendly Societies' Demonstrations between 1898 and 1901 and at Infirmary Demonstrations held at various outdoor venues from the early 1890s onwards. Each band contributed separately. On 12 August 1900, for example, Hexthorpe played Wallace's overture *Lurline*, Borough a selection from Donizetti's opera *Marino Faliero* and Temperance *Memories of Balfe*; the offerings of the Salvation Army (*Break Forth into Joy*) and Oxford Place (a selection, *Steadfast and True*) were appropriately devotional (Figure 4). Besides the bands, choirs and, on one occasion, a concertina band, also figured in these Demonstrations. From the mid-nineteenth century onwards communities in the Doncaster region, like Thorne, Conisbrough, Stainforth and Tickhill formed bands and of these Conisbrough and Tickhill at least appeared at these Demonstrations.[9]

Brass band contests emerged again in Doncaster from 1898 onwards; on 30 June that year one was held near the Racecourse as part of the Doncaster Agricultural Show. This was in three sections: a quickstep (i.e. march) contest, won by Rotherham Temperance (Doncaster Temperance was the only other participant but its rendering was described as 'very rough'); a test piece

Figure 4. William Booth (1856–192? founder of the Salvation Army, was a gre exponent of brass band music, often usi bands at his meetings.
Shire Publications/Nottinghamshire Record Office

selection – Donizetti's *La Favorita* – won by Besses o' th' Barn with Black Dike second (Doncaster Temperance also competed here); and an 'own choice selection' contest.[10] Besses also won this, playing their then-famous selection from *Die Walkure* (Wagner, arranged by Alex Owen) with Black Dike again second, playing a Spohr selection.[11] Doncaster Temperance contested with a fair degree of regularity at this time, winning Third Prize in a contest at East Ardsley (May 1899), said by the local press to be the first prize secured by a Doncaster band since Birkinshaw's palmy days in 1860. They earned a Fifth Prize in the National Championships at the Crystal Palace in 1904, Fourth Prize in 1905 and Fifth Prize again in 1906.

Further Doncaster contests followed, organised, like that of 1898, by Doncaster Temperance, now called Doncaster Temperance Prize Band. On 14 April 1900, in a paddock adjoining the *Salutation Inn*, Dannemora Steel Works (Sheffield) won the 'selection' contest, Cleckheaton Victoria the 'march' contest. The following year (6 April) eleven bands competed – of them, only Dodworth (Barnsley) still exists today – each again playing a march and selection as test pieces. In the former (Ord Hume's *BB and CF*) Rotherham Borough were victorious, in the latter (Donizetti's *Belisario*) King's Cross (Leeds) Band.

Oxford Place, which organised Brass Band Festivals at the Church in the latter years of Edward VII's reign, and Hexthorpe (Figure 5) were still extant after 1907, by which time Borough had faded out of the picture and the Volunteer Band, as we have seen, was being absorbed into the newly-established Territorial Force. In 1909 Doncaster Corporation made money available – a new departure, this – to pay bands for regular outdoor summer performances in various places around the town.[12] An Excelsior Silver Band was formed in December 1909 (their Bandmaster, Fox by name, emigrated to New Zealand in 1911) and Britannia Silver Prize Band gave charity concerts during World War I; these and other ensembles may not have had very long continuous lives, though a Britannia Band was still in being in 1927. In any event by 1914 many of the recently sunk local collieries were establishing their own bands, several of whom, like Bentley Colliery (which was winning prizes and giving concerts by 1912), Carlton Main Frickley Colliery, Markham Main and

Figure 5. Bandstand in 'The Dell', Hexthorpe Flatts. *Brian Elliott Collection*

Brodsworth Colliery, were to achieve distinction in the fullness of time. But that is another chapter in Doncaster brass history.[13]

Notes and References

1. On their saxhorns (or 'newly invented euphonic horns' as they were described) they played the *Quartette* from *Lucia di Lammermoor*, a *Fantasia on the Daughter of the Regiment* (both Donizetti) and a *Cuckoo Polka*.
2. *Doncaster Chronicle*, 31 December 1852. It celebrated its anniversary with a supper in June 1853.
3. Performing selections from *Martha* (test piece) and *Luisa Miller* (own choice).
4. See E D Mackerness, *Somewhere Further North: A History of Music in Sheffield* (Sheffield: Northend), 1974, p 68. The Doncaster Band had to defend themselves physically against disappointed rivals afterwards.
5. Birkinshaw also composed marches and had previously written a Trio for cornets and arranged *Lift Thine Eyes* (from Mendelssohn's *Elijah*) as a cornet trio.
6. Cleckheaton, Doncaster Railway Foundry, Gawthorpe, Hemsworth, Meltham Mills, Mirfield, Ossett Temperance, Thorncliffe Victoria, Dodworth and Conisbrough (conducted by a Mr Thickett). As three others failed to turn up, Doncaster Victoria, Boulton and Brodsworth (village) bands played in a non-competitive capacity. Between them they played selections from operas by Weber, Ricci, Flotow, Bellini, Donizetti and, represented by five different operas, by Verdi.
7. Nether Hall, now local government offices, still stands but its adjacent park has long been built over.
8. The Doncaster Plant had its own Volunteer company, formed in 1859 following a war scare with the French and also contributed its Band to the local Volunteer effort. See the writer's 'The Doncaster Plant Works and the Mid-Nineteenth Century Volunteer Movement' in the *Journal of the Railway and Canal Historical Society*, v. 31, 1993, pp 22–24.
9. A Tickhill Victoria Brass Band gave its first concert in February 1866; it lasted for about twenty years, being replaced in 1887 by the Tickhill Jubilee Brass Band which endured until 1939, conducted by successive members of the Clarkson family. During the 1890s a separate Tickhill United Band existed for a time. For more detail see D Stockley, *Tickhill Jubilee Brass Band* (Author, 1995). On Thorne see my 'Thorne Music and Musicians', *Thorne Local History Society Publications*, Occasional Paper No 16, 1994.
10. Black 'Dike', as they were still styled, gave four concerts in Doncaster, three of them in the Corn Exchange, then the town's premier concert hall, during 1898. At the Corn Exchange in January they gave afternoon and evening concerts; at Broxholme Grounds in May over 3000 people came to hear them.
11. The adjudicator's detailed comments on the Spohr were printed verbatim in the *Doncaster Chronicle* and are of considerable interest. Newsletter No. 39 of the Spohr Society of Great Britain reprinted these comments in full.
12. The Doncaster Public Subscription Prize Band (twelve players) – possibly the Temperance Band under another style – received £48 for playing at Hexthorpe Flatts twice a week and twice a day on public holidays. Hexthorpe Brass Band (eight players) were allotted £25 for playing similarly on another local open space, Sandall Beat. These financial rewards seem reasonably generous, bearing in mind the financial values of the day.
13. The files of the *Doncaster Gazette* and *Doncaster Chronicle* (in Doncaster Central Library) furnished much of the material for this article.

8. DONCASTER PEOPLE OF TEN GENERATIONS AGO

by David Hey

BEFORE THE COMING OF THE RAILWAYS in the mid-nineteenth century, Doncaster was widely regarded as an elegant and prosperous market town. Joseph Hunter, the great historian of South Yorkshire, described it in 1828 as a wealthy and beautiful place,[1] and five years earlier, Edward Baines of Leeds, the compiler of the first commercial directory of the West Riding, wrote that it was 'one of the most clean, airy, and elegant towns in the British dominions.'[2] He thought that there were few places in the kingdom 'in which so great a portion of the inhabitants possess independent fortunes', and where the neighbourhood was 'remarkable for opulent families'.[3] Nor was it just Yorkshire people who wrote in this vein. Viscount Torrington, normally the most critical of men, wrote in 1792, 'Doncaster looks well in approach; and is well-built, well-paved, wide-streeted town . . . The Market Place, the Butchery, and all about it, is in good stile',[4] and Arthur Young wrote in 1770, 'Doncaster is a clean, well-built town; the streets broad and well paved'. (Figure 1)[5]

Much of the best surviving architecture is of the late-Georgian and Regency styles, but even in earlier times Doncaster impressed its visi-

Figure 1 The tower of St George's Church; a broad street and wide pavements are clearly evident in J Curtis's engraving of French Gate and High Street (from Friars' Bridge) c1802.

tors. Daniel Defoe described it in the 1720s as 'a noble, large, spacious town',[6] and in 1697 Celia Fiennes wrote, 'Doncaster is a pretty large town of Stone Buildings, the streets are good'.[7] Doncaster certainly looked the best town in South Yorkshire. It was also the most independent, for it alone had a mayor and corporation and was free from manorial control. The borough was co-extensive with the township of Doncaster, but the corporation also acted as manorial lords over the medieval soke or lordship, which included Hexthorpe and Balby, Loversall, Rossington and Potteric Carr, Wheatley and Long Sandall, and small detached portions to the north at Tilts and Langthwaite. The Mansion House (Figure 2), which was built to a design of James Paine in the late 1740s (and altered by William Lindley at the turn of the century), remains the most splendid civic building in South Yorkshire.

Yet little is known about the social and economic history of the town during this prosperous era. A number of worthy and substantial local histories were published during the nineteenth century, but since then many more documents have become available for study and new approaches to the subject have been developed. The probate inventories that form the basis of the present essay have not been used by previous local historians, and indeed, their condition suggests that both they and the wills to which they were attached had not been

Figure 2. James Paine, busy at Nostell Priory and Cusworth in the 1740s was chosen as the architect of the Mansion House. Paine's design included lower wings to balance the three-bay centre but these were never built. This engraving, taken from Miller's *History of Doncaster* (1804), shows the House just before the addition of William Lindley's attic storey.

opened since they were rolled into bundles and tied with scraps of parchment 250 or more years ago. The excitement of discovery adds much to their interest and value, for no other collection of documents gives such a vivid picture of the everyday surroundings and personal possessions of local people.

Until 1858 the church had responsibility for proving wills. From about the reign of Henry VIII to the middle of the eighteenth century it was normal practice to demand that 'a true and perfect inventory' of the personal estate of the deceased person should be drawn up before letters of administration were granted to the executors. This was done to reduce the possibilities of fraud. Unfortunately most of the inventories appraised within the diocese of York before 1689 have been destroyed, and the earliest example in this selection is dated 1694. Personal estate comprised such goods and chattels as furniture, utensils, farm stock, trade goods, debts, etc, but did not include the value of buildings, land, or other real estate. The inventories, there-fore, do not give a complete picture of an individual's possessions. Nevertheless, the personal estate is usually listed in fascinating detail, in a way that no other collection of documents can match.

The appraisers were two, three or four local men who need not have had any particular qualification for the task. Usually, they were friends and neighbours. In rural communities men occasionally earned repu-tations as efficient appraisers and they were frequently called upon and were paid a fee. In Doncaster, however, there were a number of able men who could perform the task and only a few of them signed their names with a mark. Even so, these inventories are full of contra-dictions and what seem to us to be absurdities of style. There was no standardisation of spelling, and the same word was sometimes spelt in different ways on the same line. Pewter, for instance, is spelt *peuter, peutter, pewther, pewder, puter* and *puther* in this selection, and cushions is spelt *kushens, cushings,* and *quishions.* Furthermore, there was an almost complete disregard for punctuation, capital letters were used haphazardly, and many of the words used are now obsolete. Where a word is obsolete dialect, spelt phonetically in difficult handwriting, there have been occasional problems of interpretation.

In some cases, an inventory was drawn on the day of death, but usually there was a delay of a few days or weeks, and occasionally of several months. Where such delays occurred, we cannot be certain that an inventory is complete, and, indeed, bequests in wills some-times refer to items of property that were not recorded by the appraisers. The goods to which a husband was entitled in right of his wife were also excluded, and this helps to explain why such things as beds and bed linen are not always listed. On the other hand, most inventories frequently list the last pot and pan and have been drawn up with great care. Very few poor people left either a will or an inventory, but men of moderate means as well as the rich are represented here. There are former mayors and aldermen, gentlemen and an attorney, a draper and a butcher, an apothecary, schoolmaster, widow, and a painter-and-undertaker. Without these inventories these people would have been mere names to us, but now we have a complete record of their household possessions and their stock-in-trade.

The appraisers normally begin their list with the Latin word *imprimis* (firstly), and then valued the *purse and apparel,* that is the loose money and personal clothes of the deceased. They then went from room to room and listed each item, except for the odds-and-ends that they described as *hustlement.* In Doncaster, the main living room was frequently described as the *house,* a usage that is still common in the North and which dates back to the time when houses were simple, one-room buildings that were open to the rafters. In some examples meals were cooked in the *house* rather than the kitchen, though in other cases the *house* was apparently a sitting room with a fire. Seven people used the equivalent southern or midland term, the *hall,* but in no case is the word used to describe a room in which meals were prepared. By this period, the term was also used in the present sense of entrance hall, and there are two cases here where it is used in this way. Furthermore, Godfrey Inman called his heated sitting room the *Hall House,* and William Kellam and John Addinell had a dining room.

In most cases the cooking was done in the kitchen, and only James Smyth, the blacksmith, had an unheated kitchen that was used merely for preparing food in the manner of many contemporary farmhouses. A few of the wealthier men had heated *back kitchens* in addition to their main kitchen. In this selection, there were also five brewhouses, six cellars, five butteries, three pantries and three kilnhouses (for baking, and for drying malt).

The centrepiece of either the kitchen or the house was the range, with its open coal fire. Attached to an iron bar ('gallow balk') in the chimney were ratcheted, wrought-iron pot-hooks, known as 'reckons' or 'reckon hooks', from which a large iron or bronze cooling pot was suspended over the fire. The coals were held by a grate, fender and 'yate' (or movable gate), on which could be placed a grid-iron or 'brandreth', or a 'winter', which was an iron frame or loose bar to fit on the bars of the grate in order to hold anything that was to be heated. The various pans included 'skilletts', which had three short legs and a long handle, a smaller version known as a 'posnet', and a 'kettle', which at that time was an open cooking pot or pan, not at all like the modern object. Meat was roasted on a spit, which was secured at each side by a 'rack' and by large 'fire-dogs' known variously as 'landirons', endirons', 'froggs', or 'cob-irons'. The spit was revolved mechanically by a 'jack' with an elaborate system of weights and pulleys. Underneath, to catch the meat juices, was a dripping pan. Around the hearth were also bellows, tongs, pokers ('fire-points'), fire-shovels, fire-irons, toasting forks and frying pans. An iron 'fire scummer' was used to take the ash out of the hearth, but a 'brass scummer' was used to ladle the scum from a cooking pot. Near the fire there was some-times a 'close hedge' or 'winter hedge' (a clothes horse) and occasionally screens to cut out the draughts. Food that was ready for serving was kept warm in a 'chafing dish'.

The equipment that was used in preparing food included kneading troughs, sieves ('tems'), pasty pans, rolling pins, funnels ('tunnels'), dredges, choppers, cleavers, mortars and pestles, skewers, cullenders, and tubs and pails, variously described as kits, kimlins, piggins and soes. Meat was salted in troughs or kits, and salt was kept in boxes ('salt-pyes') attached to the mantelpiece, or in salt-cellars known simply as salts. Food was eaten from wooden platters ('trenchers'), or more commonly from pewter plates and dishes, or from pottery described as 'Holland ware' or 'Delph ware'. Vessels such as flagons, tankards and 'porringers' (bowls for soup or porridge) were also normally of pewter, but occasionally of silver. Cutlery is rarely mentioned, though John Addinell had 'Six spoones . . . Eight Tea Spoons' in 1728. He also had a tea kettle, a tea table, a painted picture tea board, and a copper coffee pot.

Chairs were described in numerous ways. They were arched or armed, made of wood, cane or set-work, rush-bottomed, bass-bottomed, wanded or turned, and sometimes covered with leather, red leather, or Russian leather, which was oiled and very durable. The cost of early wooden furniture was far less than that of soft furnish-ings such as cushions and hangings, but by the late seventeenth century walnut veneers and other refinements were appearing in the homes of the rich. Tall 'buffet stools' were, however, still used, and high-backed 'langsettles' were still necessary to keep out draughts when sitting round the fire. Tables were frequently described as either oval, square or round, and draw, folding, French and Dutch tables all seem to have been gate-legged to enable them to fold. John Addinell also had a slate table, a tea table and a card table. The table linen included such items as a huckaback table cloth and twenty huckaback napkins, a damask sideboard cloth, two muslin sideboard cloths, and a diaper table cloth and eighteen diaper napkins.

In origin, the parlour was the downstairs bedroom, the private extension to the one-roomed 'house' open to the rafters. In Doncaster, four people in our sample were still using their parlours in this way, though of course by then the rooms were chambered over and there were other bedrooms upstairs. Three people had parlours which were used as sitting rooms rather than bed-rooms. There was very little variety in the type of bed, though 'trundle' or 'truckle' beds on casters were commonly used for children. The bedstead normally had a short curtain, or valance, around it, and coverings described as 'hillings'. Pillow-cases were known as 'pillow-beares'. The tradesmen and craftsmen normally had their shops and warehouses attached to their domestic property. Like the farmers, they worked at home. Six of the fourteen people in this selection had a shop, and several others had workrooms of one description or another. The trades reflected Doncaster's importance as a thoroughfare town and as a great regional market centre. At the time of Daniel Defoe's visit, the landlord of the post-house was the mayor of the town, and Doncaster was 'full of great inns'. The War Office enquiries into accommodation in 1686 reveal that Doncaster had 206 guest beds and stabling facilities for 453 horses. This compared with 119 beds and 219 stables at Sheffield, 64/109 at Barnsley, 63/72 at Rotherham, 57/69 at Bawtry and 17/32 at Thorne. The inventories include that of Thomas Mapplebeck, innkeeper, and that of Abraham Pillin, a carrier on the London route, who had 'sixteene, pack-horses and mares, with packsadles, pack-clothes, Cords, Wanteyes, Collers, garthes and furniture', worth £104 (See Chapter 1).

Doncaster's corn market was one of the most important in the north of England, and its wool market was justly famed throughout the North and Midlands. Sometimes, as many as 6,000 fleeces were sold here each Saturday during the summer, and buyers came from Derbyshire, Leicestershire, Lincolnshire, Norfolk, Nottinghamshire, Warwickshire and Yorkshire. The West Riding clothiers obtained much of their supplies this way. Doncaster was involved in the manufacture of textiles through the hard-knitting of tough, hard-wearing woollen stockings and of underwear. The inventories of Dorothy Wells and Nicholas Curtys contain references to this trade. The town also produced some woollen cloth and had a guild of weavers, walkers, shearmen, etc.

The corn market was held around the wheat cross, meat and fish were sold in the shambles, poultry were sold on Goose Hill, and permanent shops had been erected in or alongside the former churchyard of St Mary Magdalene at the heart of the market place (Figures 3 & 4). They were separated by narrow, little lanes, with names such as Shoe Lane, Meal Lane and Roper Row that described their various specialisations. The Butchers' Cross stood outside the market place at the junction of High Street and Baxter Gate until its removal in 1725, when it was said to have been 'a hindrance to coaches and carriages turning to the market place'. William Cooke was a prosperous butcher, with a slaughter house, three stalls and a shop, and livestock valued at over £505. Drapers such as William Walker were also gathered in and around the market place, but such was the congestion by about 1700 that some of the shoemakers left to set up their stalls at the west bar of the town in St Sepulchre Gate. The shoemakers had their own guild, and three of them are represented in this selection of inventories. They may have obtained their leather from the tanners in Fishergate, down by the river north of the market place.

Here are the inventories of the goods and chattels of fourteen Doncaster people who died between 1694 and 1728. They form only a small group, for at that time the population of Doncaster was around

Figure 3. Doncaster's market place and the layout of the main town streets can be seen on this basic plan, adapted from a c.1769 map.

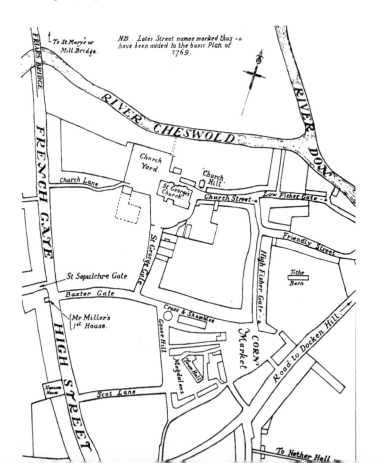

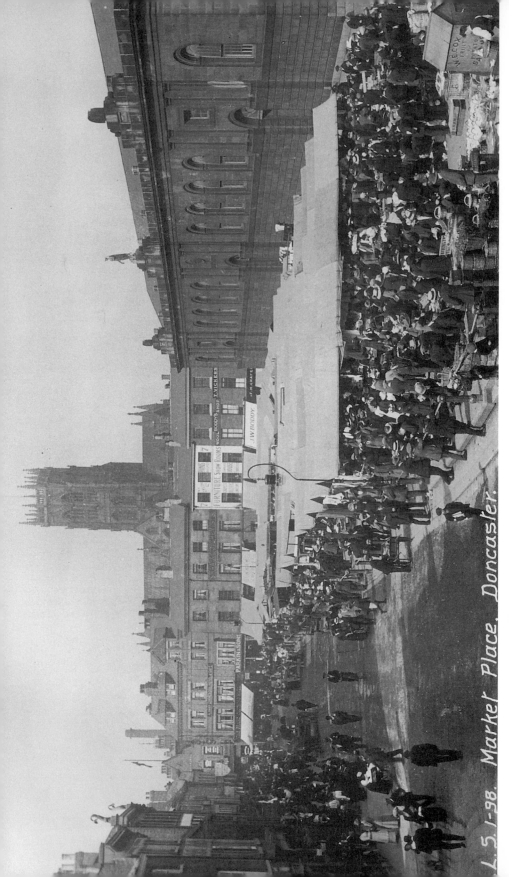

Figure 4. The busy Market Place in c1905 (from an Edwardian picture postcard).

5,000. Nevertheless, the inventories contain a good cross-section of the trades of the town, and they provide new information about people who would otherwise be shadowy figures, mere names in records.

The Inventories

1 Godfrey Inman, Grocer, 11 October 1694

Godfrey Inman had £120 worth of goods in his shop and warehouse,

but unfortunately they are not listed in detail. His son, William, inherited the business, together with two houses, two barns and a kilnhouse. His other son, Godfrey, was a chirurgeon, or surgeon, in Doncaster, and he received two closes in Wheatley under the terms of the will. The elder Godfrey's daughter, Ann, was to inherit £150 when she was 21 or when she married, whichever was the earlier. A Mr Godfrey Inman was taxed on six hearths in the Market Place in 1672 (Figure 5).

A true and perfect Invantorey of all the goods and chattels Rights & Credits of godray Inman Late of Doncaster Deceased Groser [Grocer] Taken this Eleventh Day of October 1694 By us John Burton Richd. Kellam Hump[hrey] ffrith & Robt. Skaife as follow[eth].

Imprimis The Said Deceased purs & Aparrell vallued att, £10.

In the Shopp: *all ye Groser haber Dasher and Lumber wares,* £70.

In the ware house: *all the Groser wares,* £50.

Figure 5. The Inman family are likely to have known Francis Smith (1719–82), whose trade card tells us that his shop was 'near the Shambles'. Smith was a leading Doncaster grocer, vintner and tobacconist, who also provided banking facilities. 'The Grocer', according to R Campbell's *London Tradesman*, 1747, 'deals in Tea, Sugar, Coffee, Chocolate, Raisins, Currants, Prunes, Figs, Almonds, Soap, Starch . . . Rums and Brandy, Oils, Pickles, and several other Articles fit for a Kitchen and the Tea-Table'.

In the Hall House: *3 Tables thirteen Chears 12 Kushens new and old two Carpits one Long Settle Vallued att with ye Range,* £3.10s.0d.

In the Kittchin: *22 Puter Dishes 19 Trencher plates 4 puter Candle Stickes one Bras Candle Stick, 2 Chees plates 2 Tables,* £4.5s.0d, *2 Close Stoole pans five chamber pots & one quart pott one fflagon one great Table 4 Tankerds,* 18s.0d, *3*

Bras pots 3 Bras pans one posnet 1 Bras morter & Iron pestell one Bras warmeing pan 2 Skellits 2 Bras Scummer 2 Bras Ladles one Bras ffish plate one Small Bras Candlestick, £3.10s.0d, one Jack one Rang Spits & other Iron Things, £3.

In ye Great Chamber over the Shopp*: one Silver Tankard & 8 Silver Spoones, £8, one Bed and the furnature Belonging there to, £4.10s.0d, 12 Settworke Chares fower other Chares one wanded Chare one Screene 2 Stooles one Range & Severall picters and two Tables, £5.*

In ye Sarvants Roome*: one Bed, 6s.0d.*

In the 2[n]d Chamber & one Little Chamber Adjoyning to it*: 3 Beds & ffurnature to them Belonging, £9, 2 Chests of Linen, £10.*

In the Chamber over ye Kittchin*: one Bed & ffurnature, £6, 6 Chears 8 Stooles two Tables & one Range £2.*

In the Garrett*: one Bed & ffurnature and other goods, £2.*

In ye Seller*: a parcell of Coles & 6 Barrells and one pare of Racks, £2.10s.0d.*

In ye Back Kittchin*: one pan & Bottom Grate & tubs, £3.*

In the Charcole House Chambers*: one Load Charcole, 10s.0d.* [fuel for drying malt]

In the Killne House Chambers*: one Load of hay 2 quarter mault two old Skreels & mett, £2.16s.0d.*

In the Barne*: Barley Thrashen & un Thrashen, £10.*

One Hay Stack of 4 Load, £2.10s.0d.

One Horse and pigg & ox, £6.

Tottall: £219.5s.0d.

2 Abraham Pillin[g], Carrier, 9 October 1695

Abraham Pillin or Pilling was possibly the most important carrier in Doncaster. The corporation records show that when the mayor went to London to see James II about the town's charters, it was Pillin who escorted him. A tradesman's token that has survived is marked 'Abraham Pilling, 1665, A.E.P.' on one side, and 'Carrier of Donkester. His Halfe Penny' on the reverse. He was taxed on four hearths in Frenchgate in 1672, and in his will he bequeathed 'all my Messuage or Tenement in Frech Gate where Dorothy Phillips dwelleth', together with a barn or laith in Far St Pulchergate, to his wife, Frances. He made other bequests to his married daughter, Mary Patrick and her son, John, to his younger daughters, Sarah and Mara, to his grandson and namesake, and to his son, William, who had been absent so long it was not known whether or not he was still alive. His inventory shows that he had a team of sixteen pack horses, a considerable amount of fodder, and a warehouse.

A True and perfect Inventory of all the Goods and Chattells of Abraham Pillin late of Doncaster in the County of Yorke Carryer deceaced viewed and appriazed by us whose names are here under written the ninth day of October AnnO Dom[ini] 1695.

Imprimis his purse and apparell, £10.

In the Kitchin: *a range a paire of froggs a gallowbalk and reckons, fire shovell, tongs and fender, 10s. 0d, A Jack with Line and pullyes, 10s. 0d, some brass and Iron things in the Corner-end, £1, ffour spitts three Iron Candelsticks two smoothing Irons with heaters, a pair of bellowes an Iron toasting forke, 10s. 0d. A brass pott, two posnetts, a brass Morter, and a pestill, four brass panns, two Iron potts, £1. 15s. 0d, pewter dishes, plates, flagons and all other things in the pewter case, £4, Two litle oak Cuberts, 4s. 0d, An Iron driping pan, and warming pann, 5s. 0d, A longsetle five Chares and Cushings, a Case of drawers, a seeing-glass, a litle table, water kitt, a salt pie, 13s. 4d, A pewter salver, two pewter Candeseticks, with a little white ware and other huslement, 3s. 0d.*

In the Buttery aJoyning to the kitchin: *a parcell of pewter and other husle-ment, £2.*

In the Hall: *A range, 3s. 0d, A draw table four buffet stooles, one forme, 15s. 0d, ffive seeled Chares, and five Cushings and a Childs Chare, 16s. 0d, ffive red Lether Chares, £1, A Clock With weights, and a brass Candlestick, £1. 6s. 0d, Two Cuberts, a Langsetle, a sett Cushing, with other hushelments, 10s. 0d.*

In the Parlour: *a range, 3s. 0d, Two feather Bedds a bedstead, a paire of Blankitts a paire of sheets, a Rugg, hangings, vallens and Curtaines, bolster and Pillowes, £5, An Ovell table, 14s. 0d, A Chist of drawers, £1, Seaven Lether Chares, £1. 4s. 0d, A Langsetle, bedstead, and a litle feather bed and other things belonging it, £1. 10s. 0d, Two silver tomlards, a silver Cupp, and six silver spoones, £12, A seeing Glass, window Curtaines and Iron rodd and other huslement, 3s. 0d.*

In the first Chamber: *one bedstead and hangings, £1. 10s. 0d, Two Chists, two stooles, with other huslements, 10s. 0d.*

In the Second Chamber: *a range, 3s. 0d, One feather Bedd Boulster and Pillowes, a bedstead Counterpaine, Rugg, a paire of Blankitts, a paire of sheets, hanging vallens and Curtaines, £6, Six Chares and Cushings, two stooles, a litle table a hanging shelfe, and other huslements, 16s. 0d.*

In the third Chamber: *One range, 1s. 0d, A bedstead, ffeather bedd, Bolster, Pillowes, a Rugg a paire of blankitts, a paire of sheets, hangings vallens and Curtaines, £5, Three Chares, three stooles, som Cushings a langsetle a litle table, two stands, and other huslement, £1.*

In the fourth Chamber: *two Chists, two Screens, som wood boxes, a paire of Pistols and houlsters and other husement, £1.*

In the Milkhouse: *one hogshead four barrells one soe two flaskitts, salting kitts, milk vessells and other hustement, £1. 2s. 6d.*

Linnen in the house not before menconed viz. Six paire of fine sheets, two paire of corse sheets, three dozen and a halfe of napkins, two table clothes, £5. 11s. 0d, Table linning constantly useing ith house, 10s. 0d.

In the Servants Chambers: *a parcell of Oates, £15, a parcell of Beanes, £3, a parcell of Malt, £4, two lodes of Rye, 14s. 0d, a lode of Wheat, 13s. 0d, Two Cowes, £6. 10s. 0d, A Pigg, 12s. 0d, sixteene pack horses & Mares, with packsadles, pack-clothes, Cords, Wanteyes, Collers, garthes and furniture belong them, £104, Severall parsels of hay, £16, a parcell of Coles & some old wood, £4, grass in the Closes, £1.*

In the Warehouse: a balk, scales, weights and other huslements, £1.6s.8d.
Booke debts whereof some may be desperate, £15.
[no total]
Thomas Crosby, John Briggs, Daniel Whitaker, Robert Butterwood .

3 Nicholas Curtys, Alderman and Apothecary, 31 October 1695

Nicholas Curtys described himself as apothecary in his will, but the appraisers of his inventory referred to him as alderman. He was mayor in 1686. He lived in French Gate in a tenement, 'part of which I purchased of Nicholas Walker, gentleman, and part of Edmund Howson, gentleman'. He may possibly have come from Dronfield, for he left forty shillings to the poor of that parish, as well as a similar sum to the poor of Doncaster. He made small bequests to his nephews and nieces, and £50 to his son, William, if this was claimed. The rest was given to 'Gathured, my loving wife'. It is disappointing that the inventory does not give details of the £30 worth of 'goods in the Shopp'. The barrel of tobacco in the cellar may well have been part of his stock-in-trade. Other items of interest include the knitware in the Passage Chamber and the malt and beans that were stored in two chambers in the High Street (Figure 6).

Figure 6. Inside an apothecary's shop (from a seventeenth century print by Faithorne).

The Inventory of the goods and chattells of Nicholas Curtys Allderman Apraised October 31, 1695.

Imprimis his purse and Aparrell, £7.

All the goods **in the Shopp** *with Chists & Shelves, £30.*

The Debt Booke, £5.

In the Hall: *wood goods and Clock, £2.10s.0d, Plaet Cubbard & Range, £10.*

In the Kitchin: *the Cubard & what is in it, £1, Allsoe one cubbard more, 2 Long-settles, 3 Chaires & 4 Stooles, 12s.0d, Puther in the Kitchin, £2, Brass Potts & Panns with other Iron things belonging to the Kitchin, £1.10s.0d.*

In the Little Roome next the Buttery: *one table, one Cubard, with severall peutter dishes, £1.10s.0d.*

In the Sellar: *Several Barrells & Runlets one Kimlen & one Barrell of Tobacco, £2.10s.0d.*

In the Butterey: *2 Stills and a Limbeck with other husslements, £1.10s.0d.*

In the Chamber over the Kitchin: *of Mault, £1.10s.0d.*

In the Chamber over the Shopp: *with all manner of ffurneture, £4, One Coaech Chaeire, 6 other Cheaires, 5 Stooles, one table, & one lookeing-glass with other odd Mattars, £1.10s.0d.*

In the Passage Chamber: *one Bed with furneture & one Chist with Knitt-ware, and some other od Matters.*

In the Chamber over the Hall: *one Bed with all Nessesarey ffurneture, 4 Chaeires, 6 Stooles, one table, and 2 Cubards, one Seeing-glass with other Husslements, £5.5s.0d.*

In the 2 Clossets belonging the Hall Chamber: *3 Trunks with Linnen, one Box, one Skreene, with other Husslements, £8.*

In the Garrett: *one Bed with ffurneture, one small parcell of Oaets, one parcell of Wheat, one parcell of Wooll, one Sadle with other Husslements, £6.*

In the Backsyde: *the Coaels, 3 Potts, 3 Panns, with other Husslements, £4.*

In the Stable: one small parcell of Coaels, with 2 fflaskets and other Husslements, 13s.4d.

In the Bruie-house: *severall bunches of Latts with other Husslements, 10s.0d.*

In the 2 Chambers in the High Streete: *Mault by estemation, £20, Beanes by estemation, £1.16.0d.*

Totall £132.16s.4d.

Edward Bassett, John Tymm.

4 James Smyth, Blacksmith, 21 April 1696

James Smyth's shop was 'next the Streete', but there is no clue as to which of Doncaster's streets this was. He died intestate, and the administration of his estate was granted to his widow, Ann, and to John Moxon, a Doncaster joiner. The inventory is particularly interesting because it lists the tools and equipment in the smithy.

A true and perfect Inventory of all the goods and Chattels of James Smyth of Doncaster in the County of York blacksmith deceased apprised on the one & twentieth day of Aprill Anno 1696 at Doncaster aforesaid by Christopher Shaw, Robert Harpham John Mogson and Thomas Squire as followeth.

Imprimis his purse and apparell, £3.

In the house: *one range and froggs, 1 fire shovel & tongs, 1 fender, 1 yate & reckon hooke, 10s.0d, 2 paire of fire shovells & tongs, 1 pestill, 2 spitts, 1 tosteing fork, 1 winter, 1 shreading knife, 2 Iron Candlesticks, 1 hand bill, 5s.6d, 1 jack with Rope and pulleys, 8s.0d, 1 warming pan, 1 Chafeing dish & a cover, 2 brass ladles, 1 brass scummer, 1 skellitt* (Figure 7) *1 brass Candlestick, & a paire of brass weigh scales, 6s.8d, 8 pewter dishes, 18 plates, 2 salts, 2 porringers, 1 tankard-pewter, 1 pewter chamber pott & a mustard pott, £1.11s.6d, 2 brass potts, 1 posnet, 1 brass morter, 11s.9d, 1 dresser with shelves, 5s.6d, 1 square table & 1 ovell table, 6s.0d, 7 archt Chaires, 7s.0d, 3 quishions, 1s.0d, 1 Cradle & a rugg, 3s.0d, 2 buffet stooles, & 2 little chaires, 2s.0d.*

In the buttery: *5 small pewter dishes, 1 porringer & 6 spoons, 3s.0d, 3 brass panns small, 1 brass ladle, 1 copper cann, 1 sauce pann, 4s.0d, 18 trenchers, 1 haire temms, & 1 lanthorne with other hushelment, 3s.6d.*

In the Chamber over the Shopp: *1 bedstead, matt, curtaine rodds & curtaines, £1, 1 fether bedd boulster, 2 pillows, 1 paire of blankets, 1 paire of sheets, and 1 rugg, 2s.2d, 1 truckle bed with beding, 7s.6d, 3 paire of fine sheets & 3 paire of cours sheets, £1.18s.0d, 3 dozen and a half of napkins, & table cloths, £1.16s.0d, 1 chest of drawers, 10s.0d, 1 ovall table, 8s.0d, 6 archt chaires, 9s.6d, 1 little range, 1 trunk & stand, 1 wanded chaire, 1 voider, 1 seeing glass, 1 chimney piece with other hushlement, £1.4s.6d.*

In the Chamber over the house: *a bedstead with beding, 14s.6d, 1 Close press, 1 little table, 1 cimlin with other hushlement, 6s.8d.*

Figure 7. A **skillet** or **skellet** was a saucepan made of brass, copper or iron with three feet and a long handle. Used for boiling liquids, stewing etc. A smaller version was called a **posnet**.

In the backside: a small percell of coales, 1 flaskett, 1 waterkitt & 1 tubb with som wood & other hushlement, 7s.0d, 1 stone trough, 4s.0d.
Kitching: 1 brewing pann topt with lead, grate & dore, £1.1s.6d, 1 litle tubb 4s.6d.
In the backshopp: 1 paire of bellows, & anvill, & stocks, £3.10s.0d.
In the Shoppe next the Streete: 1 pair of bellows & anvill, £4.10s.0d, 12 new rasps and files, 6s.0d, 1 paire of vice, 5s.6d, 13 stone of hors shoos at 3s.6d. per stone, £2.5s.6d, 3 fore hammers, 5 hand hammers, & 5 litle hammers & 2 butresses, 12s.0d, 8 paire of tongs, & 3 paire of pincers, & 23 punches, & sates, 10s.8d, 3 stakes [? torn] *tools,* 2 iron ladles, 3 blacks & 1 sleck trough, 7s.0d.
Sum totall £31.10s.3d.

5 William Wright, Schoolmaster, 29 May 1696

William Wright did not leave a will, so we do not know whereabouts in Doncaster he lived or where he kept his school. The inventory shows that, like most schoolmasters at that time, he had other sources of income from by-employments. He had a kilnhouse, and he also kept two cows and three pigs. His books were valued at fifteen shillings, but the titles are not given. The administration of his estate was granted to his widow, Elizabeth, and to John Wright, a Doncaster barber.

A True and perfect Inventory of the Goods and Chattles of William Wright of Doncaster Schoolemaster Deceased taken and Apprized (by us whose names are under written) the twenty ninth day of may one thousand six hundred ninety six.

Imp[rimi]*s. His purse and Apparrell,* £5.
In the house: One range 1 pair froggs fire shovell and tongs 1 fender A Gallow bauck and Reckons a pair racks 3 Spitts and other Iron Things in the Corner End, 15s.0d, One Jack with Cord & pullies, 10s.0d, One cubberd 12 Cushions & 1 press, 15s.0d, One warming pan a Skellitt a Chafing dish 3 Candlesticks 3 Salts and a mustard pot, 19s.6d, A dish cover 3 little stools 2 little tables and some huslem[en]t, 4s.4d, A parcell of bookes, 15s.0d.
In the Kitching: Six brass potts 3 little pans a skellit and a Sawce pan, £1.1s.6d, One Gallow bauck 2 pair pott hooks A dozen trenchers and some huslem[en]t, 5s.0d.
In the Parlour: A looking Glass, 2s.2d, Two Stand bedsteads with Curtains & vallance 2 feather beds with all furniture, £4, A trunle bedstead with bed and furniture a table & a Cubberd, £1.2s.6d, A little table a Chair 2 Cushions 2 buffit stools 2 Chests a Longsettle and some huslem[en]t, 6s.8d.
In the Buttery: Nine little pewter dishes 10 tankerds 5 flaggons a pewter Cup & a bottle a bason & 4 Chamber potts, £1.0s.9d, One Dresser a pewter Case 9 Holland plaits & a Jugg a Buffitt Stool 2 forms a few trenchers a few spoons & some huslem[en]t, 9s.4d.
In the Cellar: One Kimling a Copper Can with some Huslem[en]t, 4s.8d.

In the Parlour On the far side the Entry: Two tables 3 forms a Chest & a
range with a pair of froggs, 6s. 8d.
In the Chamber over the house: One Stand bedstead with beding and all furniture, £2. 6s. 8d, Six Leather Chaires a seiled Chair an ovall table 2 Covered Stools
a trunk a Chest a Desk & other odd things, £1. 10s. 9d.
In the Chamber over the Parlour: Two Stand bedsteads with beding and all
furniture, £3. 13s. 4d, Two little tables 2 oake chairs a turned Chair a Wanded Chair
a Chest with other odd things, 6s. 4d.
In the Kilnhouse: One Iron Grate a hair Cloth a flaskitt a water kitt a temsing
tub & temse with some huslem[en]t, 13s. 4d.
In the Chamber over the Buttery: Skree[n] a mett a parcell of Malt, £3.
In the Backside Chamber: A parcell of Charcoale, 1s. 6d.
In the Backside: Wood and coales, 6s. 8d, A buckitt & a rope & 2 watering
troughs, 1s. 8d, Three piggs & 2 troughs, 12s. 6d, a parcell of manner [manure],
4s. 0d.
In the Stables: 2 Cows, £5, Racks & maungers, 6s. 4d.
[total] £36. 13s. 2d.
Robert Martin, Thomas Croft, ffrancis Wright, Jno. Ambler.

6 Henry Hardcastle, shoemaker, 14 January (1696/7?)

Henry Hardcastle died intestate and his occupation is not recorded in
his inventory. However, the items near the end of the inventory show
that he was a shoemaker. In August 1697 letters of administration for
his estate were granted to his widow, Ellen, and to William and
Lawrence Wainman, two Doncaster shoemakers.

*Inventory of the goods and Chattles of Henry Hardcastle of Doncaster deceased
Apprized the 14th. day of January by us whose names are under writt.*

Figure 8. A salt pye was a wooden box
with a flat back and sloping lid kept near
the fire for storing salt.

*Imprimis his purse & Apparell, £1. 10. 0d, Money in
the house, £10, Money upon bond by Thomas Croft,
£20, By Samuel ffirth, £10, By Henry Kay, £10, By
Margaret Hamur desperat, £10.*
In the house: One range, a paire of ffroggs, & a
ffender, fire shovel, & tongs, gallowbauck & reckon
hookes, 15s. 0d, A jack & materialls & 3 spitts a rack,
13s. 4d, A warming pann, a posnitt, & 3 brass potts,
& 2 panns, £1. 5s. 0d, severall Iron thing in the
Corner, 5s. 0d, Three Tables, 1 fform, 1 buffett stoole,
16s. 0d, 6 rushia Chaires, £1. 16s. 0d, 2 seiled Chaires
2 stooles & a bass-bothamd Chaire & a salt-pye
(Figure 8) 4s. 6d, A screene a looking glass, a lantern
& a watter kitt some white ware, 10s. 6d, 2 fflicks of
beefe, & a flick of baccon, 15s. 0d, a tinn dripping &
half doz. of Case-knives, 3s. 0d.

In the Parlour: A bed & bedstead hangings & vallance, Rugg & blankitts & other furniture, £4, 6 Chaires, 12s. 0d, A hanging shelfe a wanded Chaire & other hushlement & 2 Bibles & other books, 5s. 0d, 5lb. of hemp, 2s. 8d, A large huggaback table-cloth half a doz. of napkins, a towell, a voider cloth & a huggaback towel, 14s. 0d, 2 paire of sheets 3 paire of pillowe bears, half a doz. of ordenary napkins, 4 paire of cours sheetes & 2 paire of cors pillow-bears, £2, A little table-cloth, 1s. 0d, Two silver spoones, a childe spoone, & a tumbler, £1. 10s. 0d.

In the buttery: Eleven pewter dishes, £1. 6s. 8d, half doz. of plates, 2 poringers, 2 candlesticks, 2 fflaggons 2 tankards, a chamber-pott, a salt, a mustard box, 15s. 0d, A Chaire a pudding pan, a doz. of trenshers, & 2 small runlitts with other hushlement, 7s. 0d.

In the Chamber over the house: A bedstead, Curtaines, & Vallance & rodds, a feather bed boulsters & pillowes, a paire of blanketts, a Rugg, & natt, & Corde, £3, A table, a livery Cubberd, a Chest, 2 trunks, 3 boxes a doz. of bottles, 2 voiders, £1, A parsell of peggs, 1s. 6d, A parsell of Wood-heels, & turffes & other hushelment, 5s. 0d.

In the Chamber over the Shop: A bed stead & half-bed & other furniture to it, £1, A trundle bedstead, 2s. 6d, A press, 4s. 0d, A skep with other hushlement, 5s. 0d, 7 hides, £5. 12s. 0d, 10 Calf skins, £1. 5s. 0d, Offeild Leather drest, & a paire of offeils, 16s. 0d, 3 Butts & other sole Leather, £1. 10s. 0d, 4 doz. of shooes, £4. 14s. 0d.

In the Shopp: Lasts, boote trees, sham treese & Clams & seats, £1. 13s. 4d.

In the backside: A parsell of Coales, 8s. 0d, A Soe & a flask, 5s. 0d, 3 Sheepe, 15s. 0d.

[no total]

William Whitaker, John Mawhood, Thomas Creakill, ffrancis Barker.

7 Thomas Mapplebeck, Innkeeper, 19 January 1697/8

In his will, Thomas Mapplebeck described himself as innkeeper. His son and heir, Thomas, was not yet of age, so 'my good friend', William Whitaker of Doncaster, alderman, was put in charge of his tuition, and 'my brothers', Nathaniel of Campsall, butcher, and Hastings of Fishlake, blacksmith, were appointed trustees. The Mapplebecks seem to have been a Campsall family, for bequests were made to the children of Robert Mapplebeck of Campsall, husbandman, and of Robert Wintringham of Campsall, butcher. It is unfortunate that the inventory does not list the rooms, but the number of beds (24) gives some indication of the size of the inn.

A true and perfect Inventory of the goods and chattells of thomas Maplebeck late of Doncaster deceased Apprized and sold the nineteenth day of January one thousand six hundred ninety seaven by us whose names are under written. mp[rimis] his purse and apparrel, £54. 9s. 0d.

Goods in and about the house: *One Longsettle one pair racks one little table* *one pair bellows another table a brass pott and a Copper Cann, £1.8s.0d, One little old range another range and a pair froggs two looking glasses three Iron Candlesticks two seiled Chaires and a **sad Coloured bed**, £6.9s.3d, One Candlestick a little brass pan two hand Candlesticks a large Iron Candlestick a winter three petty panns and two tankards, £6.12s.0d, **One bed** and Bedstead with furniture a Seiled Chair an old warming pan a skellitt a fire Shovell an Iron pott and pott hookes two brass pans a brass pott a brass posnitt four brass sticks a skellitt a sauce pan and a warming pan, £5.16s.0d. **One Green bed in the sun** with furniture an Iron dripping pan five old Cushions a bowle a milking piggin a pair of tongs a Candlestick a painted bason, £3.18s.4d, **One bed** with furniture in the four bed Chamber, £2.12s.6d, **One bed** bedstead and beding a spitt a winter a sett of sad Coloured hangings a Chamber pot a pair tongs and three pewter dishes, £5.16s.9fid, **one bed** with furniture two seiled Chaires eight plaites a bowle an ovall table and two covered stools and **another bed** with furniture, £7.11s.0d, One little range a Chamber pott a white bason two Glass bottles another chamber pott two Curtaines a brass Candlestick three Chaires two Cushions and **a bed** with furniture, £4.4s.8d, **One bed** with furniture a range a fender a pair of froggs a pair tongs a fire shovell a Gallow bauck 6 Chaires a table a livery Cubberd and **another bed** with furniture, £6.13s.0d, Three pewter dishes a bed with furniture a Green Covered stool a Lark [sic] spitt six sett work Chaires two pewter dishes two brass Candlesticks a Large salt a pewter dish and a half Doz. plates, £6.16s.10fld, Two pewter dishes six plaites a fflanders Chest a dish ring a **feather bed** with furniture a grate fire Shovell eight plaites more a Malt Skreen an old stand a Candlestick an old pair of snuffers and a **trunle bedstead**, £4.7s.10d, A mett a Smoothing Iron a Squ[i]rt two old tubs two meat piggins a Chest a brass fish plaite a dish Cover a tin broiler with a dripping pan **a bed** with furniture a grate a little Cubberd a deep dish a Longsettle **another bed** with furniture, £8.18s.3d, **A trunle bedstead** with hangings three pewter porringers three meat piggins an Iron Candlestick a brass Candlestick two old kitts a bowle **a bed** with furniture a Chest a little brass fire Shovell **another bed** with furniture and a Smoothing Iron, £5.9s.6d, An old pan a pair of Yern Windles a fish Skummer a toasting fork A parcell of mainer [manure] **an old feather bed** two tankards two Reckons a Chamber pott another tankard two dishes a little salt another Chamber pott & a reckon, £4.7s.10fld, A Chamber pott a flaskitt a stand another flaskitt a brass Candlestick a little hay a mash tubb with things belonging it a fire shovel a napkin beater a pott and pott hookes six Leather Chaires & a Large Covered Chair, £3.5s.4d, An **old bed** an old stool a looking glass a pasty pan a pair tongs a Large brass pott with a grate a Grid Iron five Chaires a table a rugg a Coverlitt a toasting fork a water dish a bottle a tunill a little Chaire a Spitt a duck & a drake, £2.10s.0d, Six plates a sauce pan two Chests a tunhill six sett work Chaires a seiled Chaire a spitt eight old Chaires a Cubberd another old Chaire an old Stool a maund a pease hooke a hair tems a Skellitt a gathering tubb & a guile tub, £5.4s.9d, A half hogshead two Iron teames a hogshead a Chest **a bed** and furniture a pair of tables an old fire shovell a mortar & pestill some old pewter **a bed** with Double Hangings & all furniture 6 Chaires 2 Chamber potts a little kimlin Some ffeathers a silver tankard six Chaires more, £21.19s.2d, Two gold rings a parcell of Malt a parcell of oates a parcell of hay, £83.6s.0d, A Steel Mill, £1.2s.0d,*

Two dressers two pewter Cases a table a Chaire a Jack with pullies weight Cord and Case a Crud Skummer a Chopping knife a long table 2 formes an oval table 2 longsettles a Cubberd a desk a Square table the Kings arms **a bedstead** *another Long table 2 formes a little table* **a bedstead** *another table a forme and benches six pictures a draw table an eight square table 2 little tables an old table a livery Cubberd a hanging against the wall another little table a forme a long settle an old Chaire a range* **a bed** *with furniture, £8.12s.6d,* **A ffeather bed** *two ruggs a tub a table a forme a dresser a salting tub a Chest a kneading trough an desk a Chalking board a little table with benches and knatting against the wall a hogshead of ale a Close stool & pan a Copper a trough lined with lead 2 dressers a shelf a frying Pan three tubbs forty four pound fl of pewter a parcell of hay four forks two shovells a wheel barrow a parcell of Coales a soe a buckitt rope & Chain a bell some shelfes the belroom two sows a press a range a Gallow bauck a pair of froggs a fender two reckons one hogshead of bear a silver tankard a salt a taster, £80.10s.8fld, A Close press a little table seven dishes a pye plaite a bason twenty nine pound & a half more in plaites three dishes more a warming pan a Skrue six pair sheets a Doz. of napkins a table Cloth two pillow bears two Chamber potts a brass ladle a Stander for a smoothing Iron a tray a driping pan a Copper can a limbeck Rich. Carrs Room a Cow* [sic] *& a Silver Tumbler, £13.18s.3/d, Twenty eight pair & a half of sheet two little table Clothes an old table Cloth seven table clothes more two Doz. & an half of Napkins five towells & 1 Pillow bear, £5.18s.0d, Eleven sheep and some swine, £3.12s.0d, A parcell of wood nine hogsheads a Land Skipp and some pictures a parcell of knitt ware £30.13s.5d.*
[no total]
John Tomlinson, Jno. Wright.

The appraisers also listed 33 debtors (26 of them 'desperate') who owed a total of £83.5s.4fid. 'for services at the inn', in sums ranging from a few shillings to a large desperate debt of £28.4s.2d. owed by 'Mr. Godfrey Copley'. Five loans (all but one 'desperate') or 'debts upon bond' accounted for a further £37.15s.0d, owing to the innkeeper. However, Mapplebeck also owed 31 people a total of £154.7s.3d, which included £1.1s.6d. for 'Excise', and bills, probably medical expenses incurred during his illness, of £60 and £10 to 'Dr Jno. Cooke' and 'Dr Jno. Mawhood'. Such information illustrates the widespread but often precarious nature of credit and money lending at the time.

8 Robert Parkin, Mason, 1 June 1698

Robert Parkin died intestate and the administration of his estate was granted to two Doncaster gentlemen. His standard of living was typical of a craftsman of those times. His inventory is interesting for recording the names of his tools and for showing that he earned extra income from two butchers' stalls in the market.

A true and perfect Inventory of all the goods and Chattells, rights and credits of Robert Parkin late of Doncaster in the county of Yorke Mason deceased taken and apprised the first day of June 1698.

Impr[im]*is His apparell, £1.*

In the house: *A range frogs & fender, 13s. 0d, One Jack pullies Spitt & a Reckon, 6s. 8d. fire shovel fire point & tongs, 5s. 0d, Two Winters two old toasting forks a frying pan two beef forks & a slicer, 5s. 0d, A warming pan a Skellet ladle & three bad Candlesticks, 5s. 0d, A Cubberd two seel Chairs two turned Chairs & two old Cushions, 8s. 0d, One Counter a little table & an old tub, 3s. 6d, two temses nine trenches an old trundle bedstead an old langsetle bed and some other hustlements, 3s. 0d, Two Iron potts a brass & a pair of pot hookes, 4s. 0d.*

In the Parlour Chamber: *One bedstead Curtains & Vallence, 15s. 0d, a feather bed a bolster two pillowes two blanketts & a rugg, £2. 5s. 0d, An old feather bed two bolsters a pair of old blanketts two Coverletts an old rugg & a pair of hangings, £1. 10s. 0d, One little table Chest & forme two Stools an old Chair an old flock & Chaffe bed & some other huslement, 7s. 0d.*

In the Parlour: *Three tables & a forme, 8s. 0d, Six old red covered chairs, 6s. 0d, two old bass bottomed Chairs & a wanded Chair, 3s. 0d, a Chest, 4s. 0d, two sadles, 6s. 0d, two brasses a coper can a stone Mugg & a plate, 2s. 0d, four stone and five pound of pewter, £2. 3s. 0d. three plaister flailes & trough two trowells a plevett a paving pick two slate hammers three triangles a plum rule & a runspindle, 5s. 0d, a grinding stone & two short laders, 3s. 6d.*

A Sow, 10s. 0d, old hay, 13s. 4d.

five course sheets three pillow beares a table Cloth & Six Napkins, 15s. 0d, a Cradle rugg, 1s. 6d. a Lease from the Corporacon for two butchers stalls, £18.

£32. 10s. 6d

[appraisers names not given]

9 Mr William Cooke, 19 July 1698 (Figure 9)

William Cooke was a butcher, and one prosperous enough to have earned the title 'Mr'. He had a slaughter house, three stalls and a shop in or near the market place, and at the time of his death he had 81 beasts, 33 cows, a calf, over 200 sheep, five horses and a few pigs, most of which were presumably awaiting slaughter. The scale of his business gives some idea of the importance of Doncaster livestock market at that time. He died intestate, and the administration of his estate was granted to his widow, Mary, and to Dorothy Wells, whose inventory appears elsewhere. Two of his upstairs rooms are described as being next the street, and next to the church.

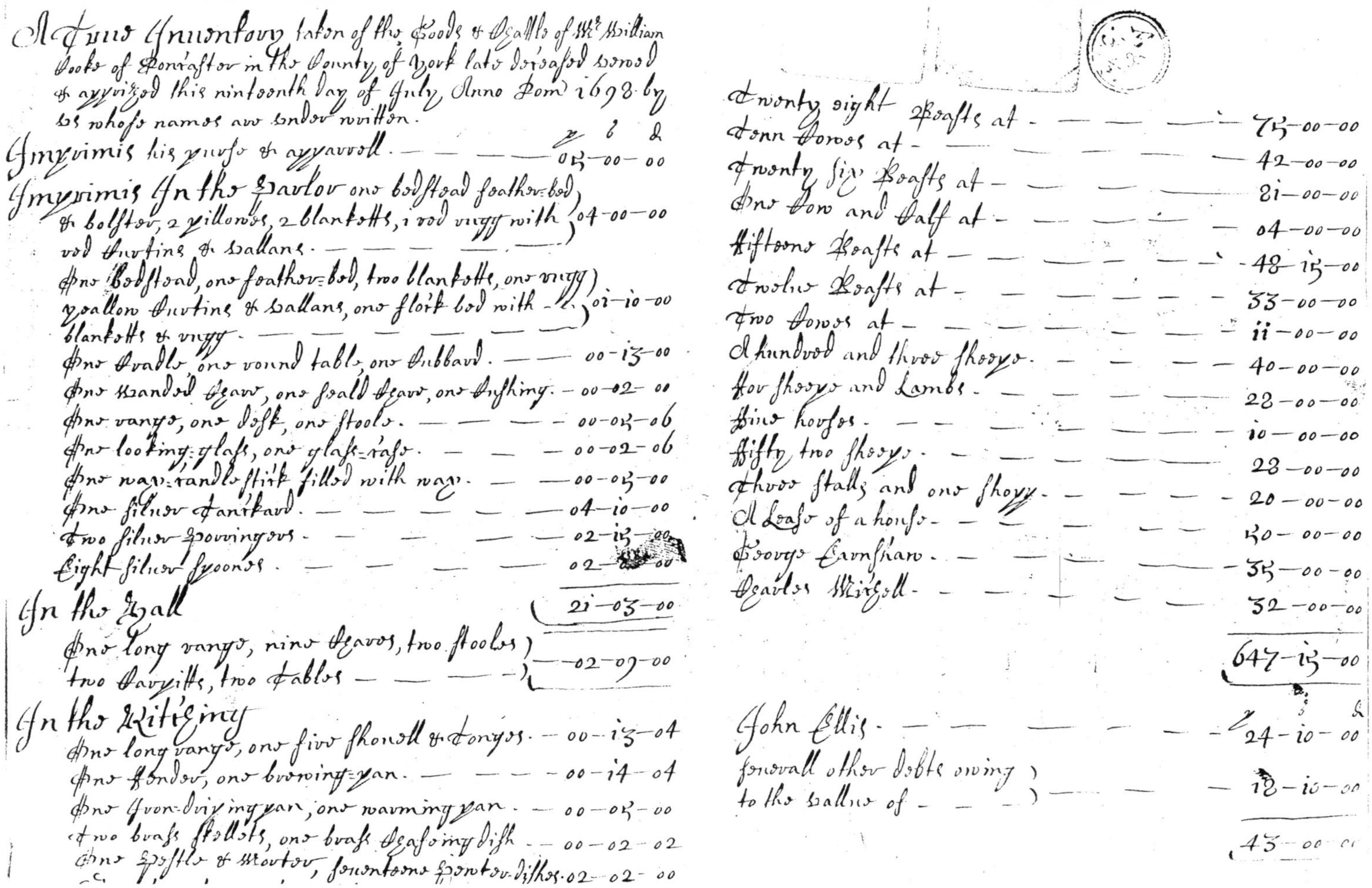

An Inventory taken of the Goods & Chattels of Mr William
Cooke of Borough... in the County of York late deceased
& appraised this nineteenth day of July Anno Dom 1698 by
us whose names are underwritten.   £ s d

Imprimis his purse & apparell ——————————————— 05—00—00

Imprimis In the Parlor one bedstead featherbed
& bolster, 2 pillows, 2 blanketts, 1 rod vett with   } 04—00—00
rod curtins & vallans ——————————————

One bedstead, one featherbed, two blanketts, one rugg)
yallow curtins & vallans, one floit bed with   } 01—10—00
blanketts & rugg —————————————

One cradle, one round table, one cubbard ——————— 00—13—00

One standed chest, one deall chest, one dressing — 00—02—00

One ... one deske, one stoole ——————————— 00—03—06

One looking glass, one glass case ——————————— 00—02—06

One ... flitt filled with ... ——————————— 00—03—00

One pewter standard ————————————————— 04—10—00

two silver drinking vers ——————————————— 02—15—00

Eight silver spoons ——————————————————— 02—00—00
                                                                    ————————
                                                                    21—03—00

In the Hall
One long ranges, nine chaires, two stooles)
two ... forms, two tables   } 02—07—00

In the Kitchin
One long ranges, one fire shovell & tongs — 00—15—04
One fender, one bowting pan — 00—14—04
One frying pan, one warming pan — 00—03—00
two brass kettles, one brass dropping dish — 00—02—02
One brass ... & ... forks ... 02—02—00

Twenty eight beasts at ———————————————— 75—00—00
ten stores at —————————————————————— 42—00—00
twenty six beasts at ———————————————— 81—00—00
one sow and half at ———————————————— 04—00—00
fifteen beasts at ——————————————————— 48—15—00
twelve beasts at ——————————————————— 53—00—00
two sows at ————————————————————— ii—00—00
standerd and three sheepe ——————————— 40—00—00
for sheepe and lambs ——————————————— 28—00—00
nine horse ————————————————————— 10—00—00
fifty two sheepe ————————————————— 23—00—00
three stalls and one sow ——————————— 20—00—00
A ... of a house ————————————————— 50—00—00
... farmer ———————————————————— 35—00—00
... dishes ————————————————————— 52—00—00
                                                                   ————————
                                                                   647—15—00

John Ellis ——————————————————————— 24—10—00
severall other debts owing)
to the valew of   } 18—10—00
                                                                   43—00—00

Figure 9. A copy of the original probate inventory of Mr William Cooke. Borthwick Institute of Historical Research, University of York

A True Inventory taken of the Goods & Chattle of Mr. William Cooke of Doncaster in the County of York late deceased vewed & apprized this nineteenth day of July Anno Dom. 1698 by us whose names are under written.

Imprimis his purse & apparrell, £5.

*Imprimis **In the Parlor**: one bedstead feather bed and bolster, 2 pillowes, 2 blanketts, 1 red rugg with red curtins & Vallans, £4, One bedstead, one feather bed, two blanketts, one rugg yeallow Curtins & Vallans, one flock bed with blanketts, & rugg, £1.10s.0d, One Cradle one round table, one Cubbard, 13s.0d, One Wanded Chare, one seald Chaire, one Cushing, 2s.0d, One range, one desk, one stoole, 5s.6d, One looking glass, one glass case, 2s.6d, One wax candlestick filled with wax, 5s.0d, One silver Tanckard, £4.10s.0d, Two silver Porringers, £2.15s.0d, Eight silver spoones, £2. **In the Hall**: One long range, nine Chares, two stooles, two Carpitts, two Tables, £2.9s.0d.*

***In the Kitching**: one long range, fire shovell & tonges, 13s.4d, One ffender, one brewing pan, 14s.4d, One Iron driping pan, one warming pan, 5s.0d, Two brass skellets, one brass Chafeing dish, 2s.2d, One Pestle & Morter, seventeene pewter dishes, £2.2s.0d, Six & twenty pewter plates, 14s.0d, Two pewter Candlesticks, two solvers 2 fflagons, 6s.6d, Two Chamber potts, one tinn Cullinder, 2s.0d, Two Tables, one dresser, seven Chares, 6s.6d, Two brass Potts, two brass Pans, 12s.0d, One Posnett, one Jack, 5s.6d.*

***In the Street Chamber**: One ffeather bed, one boulster two Pillowes, one paire of blanketts, one yealow rugg, brown curtains & vallans, £2.10s.0d, Six sett work Chares with covers, £2, One square table, one rang, one stoole, one Chest, one Trunk, 8s.6d.*

***In the Chamber next the Church**: One ffeather bed, one bolster, one coverlead, Curtins & Vallans, £1.5s.0d.*

***In the Slater house**: One block, two bills, two ropes, £2.0s.6d.*

One Sow with 10 piggs, one houlding, £1.10s.0d.

Coales and all other huslement, £2.10s.0d.

Sir paire of sheetes with other linning, £2.

Twenty Cowes, £105, Twenty eight Beasts, £75, Tenn Cowes, £42, Twenty Six Beasts £81, One Cow and calf, £4, ffifteene Beasts, £48.15s.0d, Twelve Beasts, £33, Two Cowes, £11, A hundred and three Sheepe, £40, ffor Sheepe and Lambs, £28, ffive horses, £10, ffifty two Sheepe, £28, Three Stalls and one Shopp, £20, A Lease of a house, £50.

George Earmshaw, £35, Charles Mitchell, £32.

£647.15s.0d

John Ellis, £24.10s.0d.

Severall other debts owing to the vallue of, £18.10s.0d.

Rents owing to Sir George Cooke, £60.

Peter Hudson jn, Thomas Crosby, Sammuell Ayre, Anthony Burcks.

10 William Kellam, Gentleman, 28 October 1700

William Kelham was described as Attorney-at-Law in the parish register when he was buried on the 10 May 1700. He died intestate, and the administration of his estate was granted to his widow, Ann, and to Richard Firth, a Doncaster gentleman. The Kelhams were a prominent local family, and the final items in the inventory give some indication of the extent of William's property. Attorneys had become increasingly prominent in English towns during the second half of the seventeenth century. They were professional people of gentlemen status.

An Inventory of ye Goods and chattells of William Kellam gen[tleman] *dec*[ease]*d Apprized by Us whose names are underwritten ye Eight and twentieth day of October Ann D*[o]*m*[ini] *1700.*

Impr[imi]*s His Purse and Apparrell, £5.*

In ye **house**: *One Range End Irons ffender Grate Yate ffire Shovell and Tongs, 10s. 0d, A Jack ffour Spitts and two Ruinns, 10s. 0d, A driping Pann two Smoothing Irons two Warming Panns two Pair of tongs two ffire Shovells with Severall other brasse and Iron things, 13s. 4d, Two Pasty Panns and a Dish Cover a Pudding Pann, A Lanthorne And a Candle Case, 2s. 2d, A Hanging Cupboard and A Tems, 1s. 6d, Three little Tables, 4s. 0d, Eight Chares & a Steele, 10s. 0d, A Dripping Pann & a ffender a Toasting Iron & a brasse Pann, 7s. 0d, A Dresser and pewter Case, 6s. 8d, Nineteen Pewter Dishes two Ruinns ffive Candlesticks a Psalt a Pepper box and mustard Pott a pewter bottle, £2. 13s. 4d, Twenty Plates, 6s. 8d, A Pewter Tancard, 1s. 0d, A Seeing Glasse, 6d.*

In ye **Kitchen**: [illegible for one line, and] *Six chares and three Stooles, 12s. 0d, A Pair of Racks one other pair of racks a Spitt, 13s. 4d, A Brasse Panne & Pott one other brasse Pott a Bill with some Hushlement, 18s. 0d, Thirteen Plates ffour Pewter Dishes two Copper canns a fflaggon two tinne Dripping panns a Psalt a Pewter Possit Pott & ffive porringers, 10s. 0d, A Range and End Irons A Gallow Bauke ffire Shovell & Tongs, 7s. 0d, A Lead and Grate, 19s. 6d, A Brasse Pott & an Iron panne two little brasse Pannes with Toasting fforke, 13s. 6d, A Dresser and an Old Lanthorne One Candlestick and other Hushlements, 2s. 6d.*

In ye **Brewhouse**: *ffour Tubbs three fflasks two water Kitts a Range a Tub cover and other Hushlements, 15s. 0d.*

In ye **Pantry**: *Two Meall Tubbs a Psalting Tubb Dresser and Shelves with other Hushlements, 5s. 0d.*

In ye **Office**: *Two Chares and a Deske & Green Table and a Parsell of bookes, 12s. 6d.*

In ye little **Dineing Roome**: *A little Table two bouks and three Pictures, 4s. 0d.*

In ye **Street Parler**: *A Clock, £2. 10s. 0d, Two Tables and twelve Russia Lether Chares, £3. 10s. 0d, Six little Pictures, 6s. 0d, Two Window Curtaines & a Carpett, 1s. 6d.*

In ye **Little parler**: *A Range, 2s. 0d, Two Tables and a Carpett, 8s. 0d, Seven Sett worke chares, £1. 1s. 0d, Two Wood Chares, 1s. 6d, Eleven Pictures & a Seeing Glasse, 11s. 0d.*

In ye **Seller**: *Twelve Barrells a Dresser Board two Dozen of bottles and a Hanging Shelfe, £1. 1s. 0d.*

In ye best Chamber: *Bed bedstead and bedding, £5, A Chest of Drawers 2 Tables two Stands a seeing Glasse & Eleven Chaires, £5.5s.0d, Seven little Pictures and two large Pictures, 12s.0d, Six Small Pictures and ffour Window Curtaines, 3s.6d, Grate ffire shovell and Tongs, 12s.0d, A parcell of Images on the Chimney Piece, 5s.0d, Two little Silver Tancards Ten Silver Spoones 3 Castors ffour Silver Psalts and two Silver Cupps, £16.10s.0d.*

In ye little Chamber: *Bed bedstead and bedding, £3, A Table & Stands and Seeing Glasse, 5s.0d, ffive Chares two trunks & a ffir box, 16s.0d, A Hanging shelfe a Table Cloth and Carpett, 3s.0d, Twelve Chaire Quilts, 6s.0d.*

In ye Clossett: *One Deske three Trunks and Nine Boxes, 15s.0d, A Parcell of Holland Ware, 5s.0d, A Parcell of Glasses, 1s.0d, A Parcell of Bookes, 2s.6d.*

In ye Matted Chamber: *Bed bedstead and Bedding, £4, Window Curtaines, 1s.0d, A Pallatt Bed & Beding, £1, A Close Prasse, 5s.0d, A Close Stoole & one other little Stoole, 2s.6d, Eleven Knives & Eleven fforkes, 10s.0d. A Huckaback Table cloth and twenty Huckaback Napkins, 16s.0d, A Damaske sideboard Cloth, 3s.0d, A Diaper Table Cloth & Eighteent Diaper Napkins, £2.5s.0d, A parcell of Linnen in a Trunk, £3, A little Table and a Seeing Glasse, 2s.6d.*

In ye Clerk Chamber: *Bed bedstead & bedding, £1, A Langsattle & other Hushlements, 3s.4d.*

In ye Servants Roome: *Bed bedstead & bedding, £1, A Longsattle & other Hushlements, 3s.4d.*

In ye Meale Chamber: *A Kimbleing & Kneading Trough two Shelves a Watering Pann a Chopping Block a Desk, 5s.6d, A Tems & a Bird Cage, 1s.6d, A Still and a Limbeck, £1.10s.0d.*

In ye Nursery: *Two Beds bedsteads & Beding, £3, A Chest a Rugg & ffour Pillows, £1, Two little Chests and a Deske, 5s.0d, A Painted Screen, 12s.0d, A Pair of Virginalls and Dulsamore, 15s.0d, ffour Pictures, 1s.0d.*

In ye Stable: *A Saddle and a Corne Chest and two Bridles, 4s.6d.*

In ye Backside: *A parcell of Coales and Some Turves, £1.10s.0d, A Cow, £2.10s.0d, Corne upon ye Land being one Acre and a Halfe, £1.10s.0d.*

The House Backside & Garden, £40, The Meese Stead in ffarr St. Pulchergate [St Sephulchre Gate] in Doncaster, £1, Two little Closes in Hexthorpe Lane, £4.10s.0d, The house and land att Auckley, £5, A house in Doncaster John Smeaton lives upon, A Shop in ye Markett Place belonging to the Same house with two Stalls in the Shoemarkett, £20.

The Debt Booke, £150.

Totall of all ye pages: £310.18s.0d.

ffran. Watson, Philip Bessett, John Scott, John Smith.

11 Dorothy Wells, Widow, 29 December 1700

During this period many people in Doncaster earned part of their living from knitting stockings and underwear. Dorothy Wells's inventory is most informative in this respect, and in her will she instructed her executors, 'Not to sell or dispose of any of my Households Goods

But devide and share my Knitt ware betwixt themselves'. She owned houses in Marsh Gate, St Pulcher Gate, and near to the Butcher Cross, but does not say which one she lived in. Mr William Kellam, the attorney (inventory 10), was given twenty shillings to buy a ring, in recognition of his work in drawing up the will. She made several bequests to her married daughters and their children, and set aside £20 for her funeral expenses.

A true and perfect Inventory of all the goods & Chattells of Dorothy Wells of Doncaster widd[ow] *deceased Apprized the twenty ninth day of Desember Anno Dommini 1700 by us whose names are hereunto subscribed.*
Imprimis her Purse and Apparell, £50.
In the house: *all the severall goods standing & being there, £4.*
In the Kitchin: *all the severall goods standing & being there, £1.10s.0d.*
In the Brewhouse: *all the severall goods standing & being there, £6.*
In the Buttery: *all the severall goods standing & being there, £4.*
In the little Parlor: *all the severall goods standing & being there, £1.10s.0d.*
In the Streets Parlor: *all the severall goods standing & being there, £7.10s.0d.*
In the Streete Chamber: *all the severall goods standing & being there, £5.2s.0d,*
All the several Linnings being in the Street Chamber, £8.5s.0d.
In the Chamber over the house: *all the several* [goods] *standing & being there, £1.10s.0d, 8 Knitt peticoates, 15 paire of Knitt drawers, 17 Knitt wastcoates, £13.5s.0d.*
In the Garratt: *a certaine percell of Wool & a quantity of oyle, £2.3s.0d.*
In the back Chamber: *a certaine Trunk with other hushlement, £1.1s.0d, More 9 doz. of Cappes & Socks & 23 paire of hose, £5.17s.9d, More 2 Petticoates 3 Wastcoates & 8 Cappes, £2.*
In the Sellers: *2 Rundletts, one Safe with other hushlement, 6s.8d.*
Two Ranges & one Dresser **in the Roome wherein one Mrs. Hall dwelleth,** *£1.10s.0d.*
A certaine parcell of Coales **in the backside,** *13s.4d.*
A certaine parcell of Hay **in the haychamber,** *10s.0d.*
Halfe of a Cowe which was betweene the said Dorothy Wells & one John Tymm, £1.10s.0d.
Due to the said Dorothy upon Bonds from severall persons, £263.1s.0d.
£385.11s.3d.
Confirmed by us:
Robert Butterwood, Thomas Creakell, peter Hudson ju., Apprizers.

12 William Walker, Alderman, 20 January 1717/18

William Walker was a draper, whose merchandise is listed in great detail in this inventory. The trade was one of the wealthiest in the town, and he was mayor on two occasions, in 1689 and 1702. In his will, which was made on 12 November 1704, over thirteen years previously, he left 'all my Messuages Cottages Barnes Closes lands tenements & hereditaments', together with his personal estate, to his son, William. Until William was 21 or was married, Mr Robert Seaton and John Mawhood were to act as guardians and the elder William's sister, Katherine, was to manage his affairs. If the younger William died, the estate was to pass to William, the son of Mr John Walker, the alderman's brother, and Katherine was to be provided with £1,000 or £500 if she had married.

An Inventory of the Goods Chattles & personall Estate of William Walker late of Doncaster in the County of York Alderman Deceased taken & Apprized by John Whitelaw William King & Richard Blomley the Twentieth Day of January Anno Dom. 1717.

Impri[mi]*s His Purse and Apparell, £10.*
In the Kitchen: *A Range A ffender A Galley Balke tongs and ffire shovell, £3.10s.0d, 2 Drippin Panns, 10s.0d, 8 Spitts, 15s.0d, A Jack Cord and Lead Weights, £1.2s.0d, 2 warming Panns 2 Chafeing Dishes One Brass Scummer, 11s.6d, A ffire Shovell & tongs A Grid Iron 2 Shreding Knifes & other thing in the Corner, 6s.8d, A ffrying Pann, 1s.4d, 3 Brass Morters and Pestell, 12s.6d, 2 Smoothing Irons & heaters, 4s.0d, A Clevor 2 Pasty Panns, 3s.6d, 19 Dishes & Salvers w[eig]ht 67 lb. at 8d., £2.4s.8d, 20 Old Plates, 11s.8d, 1 Dozen of New Plates, 14s.0d, 3 ruins, 3s.0d, 3 Brass Candlesticks, 3s.0d, A Pewter Bottle & Muster Box, 6d, A Close Stoole Pann, 4s.0d, A Copper Coffee Pott & Puding Pann, 3s.10d, 4 Knife 4 fforks & Lanthorn, 2s.0d, 5 Chairs, 3s.4d, A Ovell Table, 4s.6d, Long Settle, 2s.6d, A Cupboord, 4s.0d, 2 Dressers & pewter Case, 8s.0d, Petty Pans & other Hustlem[en]ts, 2s.0d.*
In the Hall: *A Range ffroggs and Stands, £1, 1 Long Table, 12s.6d, A Large Ovill Table, 12s.0d, One Ditto Walnut Tree, 8s.0d, 1 Ditto, 6s.0d, 6 Leather Chairs, £1.1s.0d, 1 Square Table & Drawer, 5s.6d, 2 Arm Chairs, 5s.0d, A Long Settle, 4s.0d, A Childs Chair, 1s.6d, A Pair of Tables, 10s.0d, 2 Green Carpetts, 6s.0d, 2 Large Picters, £1, 2 Pair of Buck Horns, 1s.6d, A Looking Glass, 2s.0d, 2 Brushes, 1s.0d.*
In the Parlor: *A Range, 2s.6d, A Ovill Table, 4s.0d, 1 Dozen of Leather Chairs, £3, A foulding Table, 7s.6d, 2 Large Picters 4 Smaller, £2, Curton Vallans & Rodds, 6s.0d.*
In the Pantry: *18 Dishes A Pasty Plate w[eig]ht 62 lb. at 8d, £2.1s.4d, One Pewter fflaggon, 2s.6d, 5 Measures, 7s.6d, Glass Case and 12 Glases, 8s.0d, half Dozen lb Candles, 2s.6d, A Napkin press and Beator, 3s.0d. A Pair of Boots, 5s.0d, A Wax Candle Stick, 3s.0d.*
In the Chamber over the Hall: *4 Stools, 2s.6d, A Bedstead and Curtaine rodds, 11s.0d, A Press, 3s.0d, 1 Box, 1s.0d.*
In the Chamber over the Parlor: *A Bed Bedstead and Boulster, £4, 2 Large*

Cane Chares, 18s. 0d, 1 Dozen of Cane Chares, £4. 4s. 0d, A Chest of Drawers, £3, A Desk and fframe, 5s. 0d, Window Curtons Vallans & rodds, 6s. 0d, A Square Table, 5s. 0d, A Lookeing Glass and dressing Boxes, 6s. 0d, A Close Stoole Box, 4s. 0d, A Range, 2s. 6d.

In the Chamber over the Pantry: 6 Cane Chares, 15s. 0d, A Bed Bedstead & Boulster, £3, 2 More Cane Chares, 14s. 0d, A Table, 3s. 0d, Window Curtons and Rodd, 2s. 0d.

In the Chamber over the Entry: 2 ffeather Beds 4 Blankitts 1 rugg 2 Boulsters & Bedstead, £4, 2 Cane Chares, 5s. 0d, 2 Trunks, 5s. 0d, A Square Table, 2s. 6d, A Side Table, 2s. 6d, 4 Boxes, 2s. 0d, Window Curtons and Rodd, 2s. 0d.

In the Chamber over the Shop: A Bed and Bedstead, £2, 3 Boulsters 8 pillows, £1. 8s. 0d, 1 Chest, 2s. 0d, 2 Ruggs 1 Pillow 1 Oak Chest, 15s. 0d, 2 stooles 2 Chairs, 2s. 6d, 1 Close Stoole Box 2s. 0d, 3 Empty Boxes, 1s. 0d.

In the Garrett: hustlem[en]t, 5s. 0d.

In the Kitchin Chamber: A Bed and Bedstead, £1. 15s. 0d, One Other Bedstead & Hustlem[en]t, 4s. 0d, A Table, 1s. 0d.

In the Warehouse: 4 cwt. Iron Weights A Pair of Scales a balk and other Lead Weights, £2. 5s. 0d, A buckett and Chaine, 3s. 0d, A Boarded fflore & Petition, £1.

Goods in the Shopp Vallued by Nicholas Walker and John Aldam: One Piece Light Brown Cloth 18 yards a 6/6, £6. 1s. 10d, 1 Do. Sad Coloured Cloth Broad at 6/-, £5. 12s. 6d, One Do. Light Gray, 16 Yds at 7/6, 1 p[iece] Light Drab broad 4 yards at 7/-, £1. 11s. 6d, 7 Yds fine Black at 11/-, £3. 11s. 6d, 3 Yds fine Wo. Black Cloth at 11/-, £1. 13s. 0d, A Remd. 1/Yd Do. 8s. 6d, 1 Do. $1^1/_8$ yd at 5/-, 14s. 1d, 2fi Yds Drab Cloth at 4/6d, 11s. 3d, 1fl yds. Green Broad 1fl Yd at 4/-, 15s. 0d, 1 Yd. Sad Col[oure]d at 4/-, 14s. 0d, 3 Remds. 1flYd a p[iece] 3flYd. at 4/-, 15s. 0d, 1 Do. Copper Coloured 1fi Yd at 4/-, 6s. 0d, 4fl yds Black Course at 5/-, £1. 3s. 9d, 2fl yds Course Devenser at 4/-, 11s. 0d, One Sad Coloured Druggett 11 yds at 22d, £1. 0s. 2d, 1 Do. Gray 7 Yds at 22d, 12s. 10d, 1 Copper Col[oure]d Saggathy 19fi Yd at 20d, £1. 12s. 6d, 1 Brown Due Roy 13fi yds at 18d, £1. 0s. 3d, 1 Brown Serge 7/ yds at 18d, 10s. 10d, 1 Do. Brown 13/Yds at 18d, 19s. 10d, A Parcell of Remds, 20fl at 16d, £1. 7s. 8d, A parecell Shalloons, 28 at 12d, £1. 8s. 0d, A p[iece] of Cold fustan 8s. 6d, A p[iece] Do. Brown, 15s. 0d, 1 Do. White, 18s. 0d, 1 Do. fine, 18s. 0d, 17 yds White at 9d, 12s. 9d, 15 yds fine White Pillow at 14d, 17s. 6d, One Coars Do., 17 Yds at 18d, 11s. 4d, A P[iece] Canvas, 19 Yds at 10d, 15s. 10d, 9 Yds Shalloon Blew at 14d, 10s. 6d, A P[iece] Coars Gray Kersey 16 yds at 22d, £1. 9s. 4d, 1 P[iece] Do. Gray, 17 yds at 22d, £1. 11s. 2d, 1 p[iece] Brown Kersey, 3fi yds at 2/4, 7s. 7d, a P[iece] Brown Coars Do., 23 Yds at 2/4, £2. 13s. 8d, a Re[nan]t Blew Devonser, 7s. 0d, 9 Yds Broad Blew Cloth at 6/-, £2. 14s. 0d, a Parcell Blew Remnants, 6s. 0d, 10fi yds ffrize Base at 8d, 7s. 0d, a p[iece] ffine Broad fflannill, 17 yds at 14fi, 18s. 10d, a p[iece] fine Twild fflannill, 20fi yds at 20d, £1. 17s. 7d, 16 yds Black Base at 4d, 5s. 4d, 21fi yds of fine Narro[w] fflannill at 11d, 19s. 9d, 19 Yds Base at 3d, 4s. 9d, 41 Yds Narro[w] fflannill at 11d, £1. 17s. 7d, 53 Yds Narro[w] fflannill at 9d, £1. 19s. 9d, 65 Doz[en] of Coat Buttons at 4d, £1. 1s. 8d, 130 Doz[en] Breasts at 2d, £1. 1s. 8d, 2 Doz[en] Stay tape at 8d, 1s. 4d, 3/ of Mohair at 5/-, 16s. 3d, 14 Oz. Thred at 1d, 1s. 9d, 2 Oz. Silk at 15d, 2s. 6d, The press's and Compters in the shopp, £6. 18s. 0d.

In the Barnfold: *A Waggon 2 Carts, £14, Manure in the folds, 14s. 0d, Do.* **in the Dove Coat** [Dovecote] *6 qr. 5 Metts at 17s, £1.8s.0d., An horse, £4.10s.0d, 3 Load of Wheat at 9s, £1.7s.0d, 11 Load & a Mett Pease at 5s, £2.16s.8d.*

In Plate: 170 Ounces at 5s, £42.10s.0d, A Silver Watch, £3, A dymond Ring, £6, Old Pieces of Silver Coyn, 10s. 0d, 4 Gold Rings, £2.10s.0d.

Linnen: A Remnant of huckaback, 8s. 0d, 2 Pair Old Pillow Drawers, 3s. 0d, Six Pair Sheets Do. Old, £1.5s.0d, A Table Cloth & 13 Napkins, 11s. 0d, A Table Cloth & 2 Dozen of coars Huckaback Napkins, 18s. 0d, An Old Sheet and 4 Towells, 4s. 0d, A Damask Table Cloth & 12 Napkins, £1, 2 china Dishes & other China, 14s. 0d, 56 Yards of White Dimothy for A Bed, £2.10s. 0d, Some Old Books, 10s. 0d.

In the Milkhouse: *30 Dozen of Empty Bottles, £2, 2 Shelves, 3s. 0d, A Winter Hedge, 2s. 6d, A Salting kitt, 2s. 6d, A Kimling, 4s. 0d, An old Pump, 2s. 6d, a h[ogs]head, 2s. 6d, Hustlem[en]t, 3s. 0d.*

In the Colehouse: *A Pair of Large Racks, 18s. 0d, A Pair of Smaller Racks, 3s. 0d, One tubb & table fframe, 1s. 0d.*

In the Brewhouse: *A Lead and Grate, £2, 2 Tubbs, £1.10s.0d, 2 More tubbs 1 Empty Barrell, 4s. 6d, a Soe 2 flasks 2 Kitts One Tunnell a Ladeing Piging & a Boule, 11s. 0d, A Range Galley Balk & Reckins, 12s. 6d, A kettle, 10s. 0d, A Brass Pott, 6s. 0d, A Posnett, 4s. 0d, An Iron Pott and Iron Pann, 8s. 0d, A Stew Pan & A Sauce Pann, 5s. 0d, A Watering Pan, 2s. 0d, Hustlem[en]t, 4s. 0d.*

In the Brewhouse Chamber: *18 Boards at 20d, per Board, £1.10s.0d, a Steel Mill & a Hopper, £1, A Wyer Screen, 10s. 0d, A Deal Board, 1s. 0d, 2 Sides for a Lather, 1s. 6d, 4 Elme Boards 4s. 4d, Short Boards, 5s. 6d, A Mett of Rye Meal, 2s. 8d, ffeathers 3s. 0d, A Tiffany, 1s. 6d, Hustlem[en]t, 5s. 0d.*

In the Colehouse Chamber: *3 Load of Rye, £1.4s.0d, 3 Load of Wheat, £1.7s.0d, 2 Peck of Peas, 2s. 0d, 1 Empty Mett, 3s. 0d, 1 Underbeck, 3s. 6d.*

In the Stable: *A Saddle, 3s. 6d, A Pullen Call, 2s. 6d, Hustlem[en]t, 3s. 6d, A Spade, 2s. 6d, 3 tubbs & wood* **in the Hay house**, *10s. 0d, Coles, £3, Bricks, £1, Mannour, 15s. 0d, A Stone trough, 5s. 0d.*

In the Cellar: *6 Empty halfe h[og]sheads, £1.10s.0d, Brandy, £3, 10 Bottles of Brandy, £1, 11 Bottle of Syder, 5s. 6d, 3 Empty halfe Ankers, 3s. 0d.*

Wool **in the Chamber** *Sold to Mr. Dickson of Wakefield, £52.13s. 0d. One Elme Tree, £1.10s. 0d, One Tree in the Barne, £1, A pair of Wain Rayes, £1. An Oak Tree* **in the Sand Pitts**, *15s. 0d, More Wood there, 2s. 6d.*

An account of the Debts Due to the Testator of which part is paid & the other part desperate:

Mr. John Hawton, £1, Alderm[an] Rayney, £11.10s. 9fid, Mr. Renold of Bramwith, £2.15s. 6d, Mr. John Yarnold, £3.5s. 6d, Mr. Edward Hartley, 9s. 11d, Sister Burton, £2.5s. 0d, Capt. Hen. Arthur, £3.16s. 10fid, Thomas Lane Sadler, £7.3s. 5d, Mr. Johnathan Twithie, £3.4s. 8d, Coz. Wright Castleton Derbys, £4.15s. 6d, Sister ffroggott, £8.2s. 10d, Mr. John Satterfield, £1.2s. 6d, John Carr of Doncaster, 18s. 9fid, Merridith Richards, 2s. 10fid, Mr. Barnardiston of ffiningley, £1.0s. 7d, Leve. Wright of Wheatley, 8s. 0d, Mr. Hen. Bassett, £6.3s. 6d, Mr. William Wade, £4.4s. 9fid. Catherine Warde Widdow, 3s. 0d, William ffernley, 14s. 0d, Mr. Thomas Lee, 2s. 0d, Joshua Oxley, £2.4s. 4fid, Mr. Robert Seaton, 7s. 0d, Rowland Wood, £1.13s. 4d, Mr.

John Shaw, £2.3s.2fid, Mr. John Hall, 4s.9d, Bryan Cooke Esqr, 15s.5d, Mr. Hen. Broadhead, 10s.10d, Mr. Roger Perkins, 10s.2d, John Hirst of Rossington, 3s. 1fid, Mrs. Anne Ellerton, £1.13s.4d, Mr. Robert Moody, £1.4s.3d, Wm. Crawshaw Loversall, £1.6s.3d, Mr. John Key, £8.10s.0d, Richard Bingley Goldthorp, £3.13s.3d, Ald[erman] ffrance, 13s.7d, Mr. John Pugh, £2, Mr. Leadbeater, 14s.9d, Mr. Charles Arthur, £3, Richard Bonnington, 8s.8d, Mr. John Arthur Senr, £3.15s.6d, Mr. John Torksey, £1.18s.2d, Mr. Daniell Lees, £2.9s.10d, Mr. Jacklin of Wheatley, 5s.1d, Mr. Sunderland of Wadworth, £1.6s.11d, Samuell Smith Tayler, 5s.2d, Edward Smith Tayler, £1.13s.9d, Mr. John Howard Shay Hill near Manchester, £8.10s.0d, ffrancis Elwick, 15s.1d, Mr. William Mawhood, £7.8s.2d, Mr. Thomas Croft Junr, £15.4s.7d, Mr. John Twist, £2.14s.4d, Mr. Mollinax, 5s.0d, John Bower, 19s.0fid, Mr. Wm. King, £5.9s.3d, Mr. George Bradshaw, £7.5s.9d, John Harpum, £2.12s.9fid, Mr. Wm. Thwaites, £2.8s.9d, Mr. Payler Jackson, £2.15s.2d, Robert Ward, 14s.0d, Mr. Roger Wild, £5.13s.0d, Mr. Nathaniell Badge, £5.17s.2d, Walter Addie, £26.9s11fid, Mr. Tofield, £15.4s.5d, Mr. Thomas Arthur, £2.13s.0d, Mrs. Hall, £4.17s.9d, Mary Sharp, £4.5s.8d, Wm. ffayram, 19s.0d, Mr. Brooke of Adwick 11s.1d. = £107.7s.6fid.
Totall: £553.6s.3fid.

The list of debts includes a high proportion of people with the title, 'Mr.', which implies gentleman status. There is also some indication of the places of residence of the debtors. The debts are all small and are presumably book debts. Where the chances of recovery were small, it was normal practice to describe them as 'desperate'. The shop contains a wide range of fine and coarse cloths, flannel, etc. 'Kerseys' were coarse cloths, made originally in the Suffolk village of that name, but by this time manufactured in the West Riding. 'Serge' was a durable twilled worsted cloth, 'shalloons' were light twilled woollen fabrics, used especially for linings, 'fustian' was a thick twilled cotton cloth made in south Lancashire, 'drugget' was a coarse woven fabric used for floor coverings, 'sagathy' was a woollen stuff, 'Due Roy' was a coarse woollen fabric made in the west of England, and 'Devonsers' were presumably made in Devon.

13 Mr John Addinell, 11 March 1727/8

John Addinell had been Mayor of Doncaster in 1704, Eleven years later, the corporation accounts record 'Mr. Addinell's bill of £10.10s.0d. for painting the Town arms & for making & painting the banner' (i.e. for the mayoral procession). The inventory has several interesting references to his painting business and records the items in his work room and his colour room. He was also an undertaker, and the accessories of this business are listed towards the end of the inventory. John Addinell appears to have been a keen musician, with 'Four Instrum[en]ts of wind Musick', 'a Singing Book', and another work entitled, 'Introduction of Musick'. Inventories do not normally record the titles of books, but here we are given a rare glimpse of a gentleman's library. He died intestate, and the administration of his estate was granted to his widow, Ann, together with William Brooks of Doncaster, mercer, and George Holme of Rampton (Notts.), yeoman. He was living in French Gate in 1672, when he was taxed on four hearths.

An Inventory or appraizment of the Goods & Chattells of Mr. John Addinell deceased taken & appraized the Eleventh day of March 1727/8 by us whose names are hereafter subscribed.

Imp[rimi]s his purse & apparrell, £5.
One Range a Grate ffire shovell & Tongs & ffender Yate Grate & Rackens & Bow, £1.15s.0d, One Winter one pair of Briggs Toastin ffork, 1s.6d, One Jack & Materialls Drippin Pan & 3 Spitts & Rack, £1, One pair of Troans a Beef ffork & Sprittle, 6s.0d, One Mortar & Pestill, 6s.0d, Warming pan, 2s.0d, Eight brass Candlesticks & a pair of Snuffers, 8s.0d, One pair of brass Scales & Weights, 2s.0d, One Copper Coffee pot & Can, 4s.0d, Six thin Canisters six petty pans other matters, 8d, One Lead Tobacco Box a Tinn Cullinder, 2s.0d, Thirteen Pewter 72 lb at 7d, £2.2s.0d, Twenty pewter plates Two Salvers one Dish Ringe one mustard pott & salt, £1, One Clock & Case, £2, Twenty dozen of Cammell haire pencills in desk, 4s.0d, Eleven Camel Hair Tools, 6 Brushes, 3s.0d, Six painters thin knives, 4s.0d, A Sliding Rule and a Yard Rule, 2s.0d, Four Instrum[en]ts of wind Musick, 10s.0d, 2 Setts of drawing tools, and a Rule, 8s.0d, three yards of Buckram, 3s.0d, A Parcell of Colours in ye Desk, 10s.0d, One Wainscott writing desk, or Bewroe, £1.10s.0d, One looking Glass, 2s.0d, Two hundred of Gold in a Cupboard, 13s.0d, One Cupboard, 2s.0d, One Dresser & pewter Case, 6s.0d, Six wood Chairs, one Oval, one Sq. Table, 17s.0d, One arm'd Chair & a Screen, 3s.6d, In a small Box 13 knive, 17 fforks, 4s.0d, One dozen ordinary Ditto, 1s.0d.
In the Brewhouse: *One Range, one pair of Briggs, 8s.0d, One ffrying pan & a parshall Iron, 2s.0d, One Iron pan and pot-hooks, a Saw, 3s.6d, One brass pot sett, and grate and Doar, 10s.6d, One Brass pot, 18lb, 7s.6d, One brass pot, 14lb, 5s.6d, One Lead & Grate, £1.5s.0d, 2 Brewing Tubbs, Skreen, and Tunnil, £1, 2 cast mettle pans, a Saw & pann, a Ladle, 5s.0d, A Tinn dripping pan, Broiler a Egg Slice, 1s.0d, A Tea Kettle, Brass pudding pan, 4s.0d, Two Temeses and a serge, 2s.0d, Two Lanthorns and a parcell of potts, 1s.6d, Eight Pewter Dishes 19lb, 11s.0d.*
In the Vault: *Five half Hogsheads and a Barrel Gantry, £1, Seven dozen of Bottles at 16d, 9d, 4d, a parcell Shelves, 1s.0d.*
In the little Room: *Six Rush Bottom Chairs, 8s.0d, In Bewsett a parcell Delf China and Glasses, 15s.0d, Two presenters and a Gun, 18s.0d, Seven Prints & a painted picture Tea Board, 10s.0d.*
In the Hall and Passage: *One Close Hedge, 2s.6d, Six Leather Chairs and*

Langsedle, 10s. 0d, One Slate Table & a Wheather Glass, 10s. 0d, Four Pictures, two Prints, 10s. 0d.

In the Street Dining Room: *Twelve Cane Chares at 3s. 6d, £2. 2s. 0d, Six Pictures, 18s. 0d, One Range & a Chimney Board, 5s. 0d, One Tea table & Card table & Oval table, 12s. 0d, Two Tankards Six Spoones two Salts Eight Tea Spoons & pair Tongs, £11. 13s. 1½d.*

In the Stuff bed Chamber: *one bedstead & hangings ffeather bed 3 Blanketts & a Quilt & 2 Pillows & a Boulster, £2, One Chest Drawers & Table, £1, ffour Chaires, 3s. 0d, ffour Printes & a Seeing Glass fframe, 1s. 0d, A pair of Window Curtaines a Rod, 2s. 0d, A Trunk & a Desk, 1s. 6d.*

In the Red Bed Chamber: *One Range ffire Shovell Tongs & ffender, £1, One bedstead & hangings feather Bed & Bolster Two pillows 13 blanketts & a Covering, £3. 10s. 0d, One Wallmittred Scrutore, £2, One Oak Close Stool & pan, 5s. 0d, ffour Chaires & a table, 5s. 0d, A Seeing Glass & Window Curtaines, 6s. 6d.*

Dark Closset: *A Bedstead & 2 Basketts, 2s. 0d.*

In the Best Chamber: *One bedstead & Hangings ffeather Bed Bolster 2 Pillows 3 Blanketts & a Quilt & window Curtaines, £6, A Chest of Drawers & comod Table, £2, Seaven Pictures, 16s. 6d, A Larg Glass & Corner Cupboard, £1. 5s. 0d, One Range ffire Shovell Tongs & ffender, £1, ffour arm'd Chairs One lasy Chaire, £2.*

Chamber over Little Room: *One Bedstead Hangings ffeather Bed Bolster 2 Blanketts & a rugg, £1. 5s. 0d, A large old Chest & table, 5s. 0d.*

In Maids Room: *A Bedstead & ffeather bed Rugg & Blankett, 15s. 0d.*

In Culler Roome: *Blue Black 14lb, 18s. 8d, Vardigrease 6lb, 18s. 0d, Dutch Pink lb, 1s. 0d, ffrench Oaker 14lb, 4s. 8d, White Copperes 2lb, 1s. 8d, fforty Brushes, 18s. 0d, A Parcell of Pencill Sticks, 1s. 0d, Amber 20lb, 6s. 8d, India Red flake White Blue Verditer, 10s. 0d, 60 small Barrills Lam Black, 8s. 6d, ffour suites Coffin ffurniture, £1. 4s. 8d, A Small one for a child, 2s. 6d, One piece of a bagg of Hopps, 8s. 0d, Eighteen yards of canvis, 6s. 0d.*

In the Work Roome: *Oyle & Culler & work in Materialls and an Ingeon, £3. 10s. 0d, a Steel Mill, 10s. 0d.*

In Stables: *2 Whips 2 Sadles & other Materialls, £1, a provender Chest Comb & brush & Spade & Shovell & Cowle Rake, 10s. 0d, A parcell of muck, 2s. 6d, Two Stees & other huslem[en]t, 5s. 0d, A Cow, £3, A mare, £5, An old Grey Horse, £1, A Bottle Cratch 18 Bottles 2 washin Tubbs, 12s. 6d.*

In Laithe in laith Gates: *a Mourning Coach a Horse a Chair & Harness belonging, £13.*

A parcell of Stoops & Railes in Orchard & the Reversion of a lease of a Layth at Bardicke in St. Pulker Gate, £1.

The Bookes: *The English Latine Dictionary, 3s. 0d, Bailey Dictionary, 2s. 0d. Nelsons Justice, 4s. 0d, ffestivalls & ffeasts, 2s. 0d, 3 Gibsons ffarriers, 5s. 0d, A Guide to Devotion & Sa[ca]ram[en]t, 10d, 1 Bible, Two Bibles & a prayer Booke, 5s. 0d, Exercise of Holy Liveing, 4d, The Gazeteer, 1s. 6d, Introduction of Musick, 6d, A Booke of Syfers, 4d, Coles Dictionary, 8d, Miscellanys Poems, 1s. 0d, Instructions, 3d, a Singing Book, 3d, a Latine Homilie, 4d, Whole Duty of man, 4d, Liberty of Conscience, 2d, ffemales Excellency, 2d, [Chris]tian Grounds of Religion, 2d,*

Kit[c]hin Phistick, 2d, 2 Herrald Bookes & one old One Donquivedo & study brass, 8s. 0d.

The pall, £20.10s.0d, ffifteen Cloakes, £12.12s.0d, Nineteen Scoines, 19s.0d, a parcell White Lead, £4, 7 Yds Green Cloth, 18s.0d, A parcell of Linnen, £2.10s.0d, 2 Smoothing Irons, 8s.0d. A parcell of old mourning, 5s.0d.

The Totall sume is £153.4s.7fid.

As Appraized by us: Roben Moody, Mark Skelton, Leo. Wilberfoss, Anthony Pool, George Kitching.

Addinell had several interesting items connected with his painting business. 'Cammell haire pencills' are thin, but strong paint brushes, of the sort used by script writers. 'Buckram' was a coarse linen cloth, stiffened with paste, and used as canvas. 'Two hundred of gold' may have been either paint or gold leaf. The 'Ingeon' [engine] in the work room was probably used for grinding colours. 'Vardigrease' was a green pigment, Copperes' was vitriol, 'ffrench Oaker' was ochre, and 'Blue Verditer' was blue-green pigment.

The pall, cloaks and scoines were all part of the mourning equipment provided by an undertaker.

Among the religious books, 'Nelsons Justice' was a popular work written by Robert Nelson in the late seventeenth century.

14 Richard Blomyley, shoemaker, 27 December 1728

In his will, Richard Blomyley described himself as a shoemaker (Figure 10), with 'messuages, houses, lands and tenements in Doncaster'. Shoes and leather are recorded in his shop at the end of his inventory. After making small bequests to his relations (including £20 only to William Blomyley junior, 'he haveing much disobliged me'), he left his estate to Richard Blomyley of Woburn in Bedfordshire, the younger son of his uncle, Robert. He also provided his sister, Mary, with £10 per annum, 'and alsoe the bed bedding & furniture of the Room where she lyes'. The vicar of Doncaster was given £5 to distribute as charity. Another clause reads, 'I order & appoint that my funeral be decent & all my Relations be Invited & have a pair of gloves given them and that there shall be Ten Bearers who shall have scarves'.

An Inventory of all the household Goods of Mr. Ricd. Blomyley Deceased taken ye 27th of December 1728.

Imp[rimis] Purse & Apparell, £5.

In ye Kitchen: *1 Range & fire Shovell & briggs and other things belonging,*

12s. 0d, 13 pewther Dishes and 1 salver, £1.1s. 0d, 24 pewther plates, 9s. 0d, 1 pewther Case, 2s. 6d, 12 Long Cubert, 5s. 0d, 1 Iron Drping pan 1 Rosting iron 1 Chafing Dish, 2s. 0d, 2 Copper potts & two Sauce pans, 10s. 0d, 6 Leather Chairs & 2 Tables, 12s. 0d, 1 Warming pan, 1s. 0d, 3 Spitts & 1 pudding pan & 1 Iron Cleaver, 4s. 0d, 1 brass Morter & 1 surquthing Iron & 4 Candlesticks, 6s. 0d, 1 Seeing Looking Glass, 3s. 0d.

Goods in ye back Kitchen: *One Wood Kitt & other huslement, 7s. 6d.*

Goods in ye pantry: *1 Dresser, 1s. 6d, 4 pewter Dishes, 4s. 0d, 1 pewther flaggon & other huslements, 1s. 6d.*

Goods in ye Hall: *1 Range & fire shovell & tongs, 2s. 6d, 2 tables & six Chaires, £1.1s. 0d, 1 pair of Chist of Drawers and Delf, 15s. 0d, 1 Large Glass, £1. 1s. 0d, Window Curtains & Cushins, 10s. 0d, pictures, 15s. 0d.*

Goods in the Chamber: *1 Bed & Bedding, £5, 5 Coverd Chairs and 3 Stooles, £1, Two Window hangings, 4s. 6d, 1 Large Glass and pictures, 15s. 0d, 1 silver tanckard, £7, 1 Silver Chairs & 2 Tables, 12s. 0d, 1 Warming pan, 1s. 0d, 3 Spitts*

Figure 10. Inside a shoemaker's shop, from a painting, *The Shoemaker* by G Terborch, 1660s. The shoemaker is making a woman's shoe, using an awl to make a hole in the leather for the thread. Notice his foot on a heel block and an assortment of hand tools on a make-shift table to his right. *Northampton Museum*

& 1 pudding pan & 1 Iron Cleaver, 4s. 0d, 1 brass Morter & 1 surquthing Iron &
4 Candlesticks, 6s. 0d, 1 Seeing Looking Glass, 3s. 0d.

Goods in ye back Kitchen: One Wood Kitt & other huslement, 7s. 6d.

Goods in ye pantry: 1 Dresser, 1s. 6d, 4 pewter Dishes, 4s. 0d, 1 pewther flaggon
& other huslements, 1s. 6d.

Goods in ye Hall: 1 Range & fire shovell & tongs, 2s. 6d, 2 tables & six Chaires,
£1. 1s. 0d, 1 pair of Chist of Drawers & Delf, 15s. 0d, 1 Large Glass, £1. 1s. 0d,
Window Curtains & Cushins, 10s. 0d, pictures, 15s. 0d.

Goods in the Chamber: 1 Bed & Bedding, £5, 5 Coverd Chairs and 3 Stooles,
£1, Two Window hangings, 4s. 6d, 1 Large Glass and pictures, 15s. 0d, 1 silver
tanckard, £7, 1 Silver Jill & 4 spoons, £3.

Goods in ye little Chamber: 1 Bed & Bedding & other huslement, £1. 10s. 0d.

Goods in a Nother Kitchen: 1 Range & 1 Jack & Gallow balk & other things,
£2, 2 Dressers, 5s. 0d, 1 Copper and brewing Vessells, £3.

Coales **in the backside**, 10s. 0d.

Goods in the Celler: 6 barrills 1 Gantry, 10s. 0d.

Goods in ye Shopp: Upper Leather, 18s. 6d, Soal Leather, 11s. 0d, 7 pair of Mens
shoes, 11s. 0d, Lasts, 10s. 0d, 19 pair of Women & Girles Shoes, £1. 1s. 0d, 13 pair of
boys and Girles Shoes, 13s. 0d, Cork, 8s. 0d.

£44. 5s. 0d.

Appraised by us: John Davis, Geo. Hibbard.

Notes and References

1. Hunter Rev. J. *South Yorkshire*, Vol 1, London, 1828, p. 1.
2. Baines E. *History, Directory & Gazeteer, of the County of York*, Vol. 1, Leeds, 1822, p. 167.
3. *ibid.*, p. 169.
4. Andrews, C B, ed., *The Torrington Diaries Containing Tours Through England and Wales 1781 and 1794*, vol. III, London, 1934–38, p. 28.
5. Young, A. *Tour Through the North of England*, vol. 1, London, 1771, p. 110.
6. Defoe, D. *A Tour Through the Whole Island of Great Britain*, London, Everyman edition, 1962, vol. II, p. 181.
7. Morris, C. ed., *The Illustrated Journeys of Celia Fiennes, c1682–c1712*, London, 1984, p. 89.

Acknowledgements

This is an edited version of a study produced by the writer and his University of Sheffield and Workers' Educational Association local history class, held in Doncaster and published by the University of Sheffield Department of Extramural Studies in 1975. The wills and inventories are housed at the Borthwick Institute of Historical Research, University of York, and the transcripts appear by permission of the Controller of Her Majesty's Stationery Office.

9 A FIELD GUIDE TO DOVECOTES OF THE DONCASTER AREA

by Brian Elliott

Figures in brackets refer to illustrations

THE YORKSHIRE DOVECOTE SOCIETY'S exhibition held at Cusworth Hall Museum two years ago (and promoted by the British Trust for Conservation Volunteers) was both a celebration of dovecotes as buildings of architectural and historic interest and an exercise in raising awareness of the importance of conservation. Cusworth was an appropriate setting for this purpose since an interesting dovecote located in the village was demolished in the 1960s, a situation unfortunately repeated many times at nearby locations. Since an account of Rotherham area dovecotes was subsequently completed and published by the writer in 1996 the present contribution, covering the more extensive Doncaster MBC area, serves as its companion, and the illustrations in particular may be of interpretative value for neighbouring areas.

Eleven Doncaster area dovecote sites, either extant or lost, were identified at the Cusworth exhibition, located at Auckley, Barnburgh,

Dovecoate sites mentioned in the text.

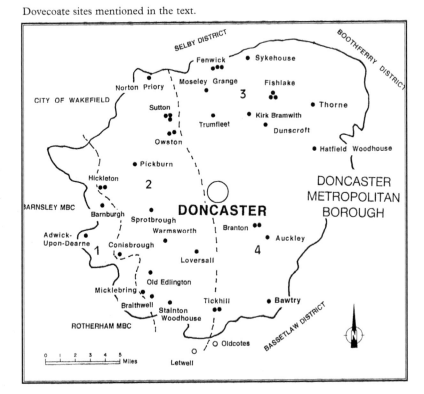

Campsall, Conisbrough Castle, Fishlake (three sites), Hampole, High Melton, Thorne and Tickhill. The predominantly agricultural character and size of the Doncaster MBC area initially suggested that there would be many other sites. One of the anticipated difficulties of research versus recording and writing is when to call a halt to fieldwork in the face of further discoveries. This study, therefore, is very much a preliminary survey, based mainly on fieldwork, is certainly unfinished, and therefore offers scope for more research. Nevertheless some 39 sites have been identified. Although the vast majority are on private property, the response of owners to my often unexpected visit has been extremely helpful, not only for allowing access but also for providing ladders and health and safety advice!

Dovecotes were once an extremely common landscape feature, from medieval times found in the grounds of monasteries, manor houses, country houses, rectories, and, by the eighteenth century, on many farms. Unfortunately, with declining usage and abandonment numbers of dovecotes have been drastically reduced in recent years, many remaining examples are in a poor state of repair and others converted, with varying aesthetic success to other uses. However, the listing of dovecotes as either individual buildings of merit or with other farm buildings for 'group value', has assisted the survival of some of the better known examples. The Planning Department of Doncaster Metropolitan Borough has a good record in this respect with some twenty listed examples identified. Yet the increasing demand for 'character' properties has placed pressure on local authorities to grant planning permission for conversion. Usually this means the destruction of unique dovecote interiors, though an award winning example at Sykehouse, demonstrates that this not need be the case. Unfortunately, worthy examples do escape scrutiny. Many of the dovecotes built from the late seventeenth century are, at least for the layman, difficult to identify since they were often an integral part of other farm buildings. Later additions to formerly free-standing examples also obscures recognition. An extreme example of this occurred when the writer visited a site in the Rotherham area, its owners being totally unaware of their substantial eighteenth century ex-farm dovecote. Dovecotes, therefore, continue to be somewhat neglected examples of vernacular architecture despite having many architectural and historical virtues.

In the Doncaster area we shall see that dovecotes range in age from medieval to Victorian and have a wide diversity of styles, from architectural showpieces to utilitarian pigeon houses. Despite some regional characteristics, for example in the use of building materials, no two examples are exactly the same, even in the same village or across the same street.

'no Kingdom of the Worlde hath so many Dove-houses'

(Fynes Maryson, c 1680)

From medieval times until the eighteenth century doves or pigeons were a valuable source of fresh meat and eggs but there were strict legal restrictions on dovecote ownership. For centuries, the keeping of pigeons, like that of fish and rabbits, was a right limited to monastic houses, parish clergy and manorial estates. The nuisance value of marauding pigeons rather than equality of opportunity was bitterly resented by poor villagers who of course could not afford to build dovecotes, and had to put up with their crops being habitually raided for the benefit of the parson's or squire's table. No doubt an occasional bird or two found the family pot despite the prospect of severe punishment. 'Professional' poaching, direct from dovecotes, became a serious problem in some areas, with owners 'fortifying' their pigeon-houses by means of iron spikes or 'tangs'. A single pair of birds, according to John Milton's friend Samuel Hartib who had estimated that there were 26,000 dovecotes in seventeenth century England, could consume four bushels of grain a year. Even a small dovecote could accommodate about 250 nestboxes, so pigeon keeping, even allowing for statistical vagaries, was a widespread form of alternative meat production. By the eighteenth century no farm was said to be complete without its dovecote. Documentary references also support the huge scale of pigeon keeping, though there were obviously regional variations in distribution, reflecting both the extent of arable farming and manorial monopoly. In 1552, for example, an Essex dovecote provided 1080 birds for the table between Easter and Michaelmas, the heaviest 'drawing' of 'three score pair' taken in August. A high status Elizabethan pigeon house at Lewis Priory in Sussex accommodated 3,228 birds. The massive brick-lined dovecote that can still be seen at the Home Farm of Temple Newsam, near Leeds was of a similar capacity. On average, 1,200 young pigeons were culled each year from Cambridgeshire dovecotes, according to William Gooch in 1811, and, more locally, as late as 1830 naturalist Charles Waterton kept more than a thousand pigeons in a round dove-cote at Walton Hall, near Wakefield, using the dung to manure his barley crop.

Legal restrictions on dovecote rights were changed in the Act of 1761/62 whereby any freeholder was allowed to build a pigeon house on his own land and tenants were allowed to erect dovecotes with permission of the landowner. But legislation coincided with improved farming and a decline in the demand for pigeon meat so there were relatively few traditional dovecotes built. However, owners and tenants, as we shall see, found space for pigeons by combining dove-cotes with granaries, stables, pigsties and poultry houses, the second or third storey towering over adjacent buildings. An occasional new dovecote combined function with decoration on eighteenth century estates, such as the splendid showpiece example at Letwell, near Worksop, whilst others, such as at Oldcotes, also just outside Doncaster MBC, were built as part of the model farm movement of the nineteenth century. The simplest and cheapest way of housing a small number of birds was in garrets of barns and granaries; and in the roof space of houses, with access for the birds via either holes in the gable wall or a purpose-built window, usually with an alighting ledge.

Distribution and Materials

Dovecote sites identified by the writer in the Doncaster MBC area can be seen by reference to the location map. The Borough has been divided into four areas so as to reflect common geological and topo-graphical features. Area 1, on the coal measure sandstones, at the extreme western edge of the borough, contains two very contrasting sites at Adwick-upon-Dearne and Barnburgh, the latter of regional importance. The Adwick dovecote is the only surviving sandstone-built dovecote, very similar to examples in the Barnsley and north Rotherham areas. Seventeen sites are marked on the four to five mile wide magnesian limestone escarpment, shown as area '2'. Made of local stone, in rubble and ashlar, though occasionally part brick (but often with brick interiors), this area has the earliest and most inter-esting examples. Thirteen sites have been identified in the low-lying area '3' to the north and east of Doncaster, especially in and around Fishlake. Here the mostly farm dovecotes are almost entirely brick-built and, as we shall see, of a similar size and design. A small group of seven cotes survive in area '4', three of them in Tickhill.

Area 1

Later outbuildings are attached to the once free-standing dovecote situated at the junction of Manor Lane and Harlington Road, Adwick-

Figure 1. The Adwick dovecote was once free-standing. Notice the blocked mullioned window opening in the gable. Adsetts Cottage can be seen in the background.

upon-Dearne and about twelve metres north-west of Adsetts Cottage, disguising its former importance as a small but free-standing manorial cote (**1–2**), probably dating (note blocked and partly obscured two-light mullion window in east gable) from the early eighteenth century. Constructed of the local dressed sandstone arranged in deep courses, with ashlar gable copings and pronounced kneelers, it also has a distinctive string course which wraps around the upper part of the first floor, at the cottage side passing under a square window and over a low doorway. String courses were often pronounced in order to stop vermin ascending the walls and entering the chamber. This upper entrance, with massive stone surround would have to be reached by ladder, allowing secure entry into the cote, which was a common arrangement. The lower doorway, also with massive stone surround, opened into a stable or store. Part of a small slit vent can be seen to the right of the door. The bird chamber contains brick-lined

Figure 2. Characteristic features at the front (east) side of the Adwick dovecote include square (ex-mullioned?) window opening, 'rat' course, low ground floor doorway and first floor access doorway into the cote.

nesting holes. Reliable oral evidence suggests that at least three other cotes existed in the locality within living memory, at nearby Poplar Farm and two at Harlington – one on the site now occupied by the

Figure 3. The Tudor octagonal dovecote can be seen at the edge of the overgrown grounds of the demolished Barnburgh Hall, overlooking open countryside, St Peter's Church to the left.

Figure 4. Barnburgh Hall, though much altered in the eighteenth and nineteenth centuries, was a building of considerable importance, this vignette taken from Hunter's *South Yorkshire*, Vol 1 (1828).

aptly-named *Dovecote Bungalow* and another adjacent to the *Harlington Inn*. Dovecote Farm, was also named after one of the Harlington cotes.

The magnificent dovecote at Barnburgh, despite its prominent position overlooking open pasture (**3**), is almost totally lost a good deal of the year amid encroaching woodland; but on a bright day in winter or spring its elegant proportions are clearly visible when approaching the village from High Melton. The dovecote was located in the grounds of Barnburgh Hall (**4**), off Hall Street, a building which, though much altered, was of considerable architectural and

Figure 5. Anne Cresacre, based on a 1528 drawing by Holbein. *Mike Burgess*

Figure 6. Access into the Barnburgh dovecote was via a typically low door facing the hall. This reduced the chances of the birds escaping. The keeper stepped down on entering, the floor level allowing for accumulation of manure. Notice the small two-light mullioned window, double rat ledge and attractive hipped roof with cupola or glover at the apex.

Figure 7. Detail of the delightful octagonal glover or lantern that allowed access for the birds.

historic importance, yet demolished by the National Coal Board in 1970. Documentary and recent archaeological evidence suggests that the hall site had a continuity of occupancy from at least the thirteenth century, principally as the medieval seat of the wealthy Cresacre family. In 1528 Anne Cresacre (5) married John More, whose ill-fated father, Thomas More, was shortly to be appointed by Henry VIII as Lord Chancellor of England. The great Tudor dovecote was probably erected soon after the marriage when the Hall appears to have undergone a rebuilding.

The Barnburgh dovecote (6–8) is the oldest and finest of only two surviving octagonal examples in the Doncaster area. It has a delightful cupola or glover (covered opening) at the

Figure 8. Fine masonry work can be seen in the interior of the Barnburgh dovecote. The wooden potence with its cross braces for resting the ladder on was intact. *Doncaster MBC Planning Department*

apex of the hipped stone-tiled roof, for access of the birds. The thick walls are composed of thinly-coursed rubble limestone quarried from the nearby escarpment with ashlar used for the large quoins, string courses and copings. Small windows are located midway on alternative faces, three with mullions whilst the typically low doorway, located on the north side, has chamfered jambs and an arched lintel. Inside the cavernous interior graceful ashlar piers can be seen attached to each angle, dividing neat rows of carefullyconstructed stone nestboxes with continuous alighting ledges below each tier which were also useful as footholds for the intrepid keeper. The fine conical stone-vaulted roof confirms both the skill of the Tudor masons and the high status of a structure which had an astonishing accommodation capacity of at least two thousand pigeons. Access to the 1600 nest holes for the collection of eggs and squabs (young birds) was via an ingenious device called a potence which consisted of a revolving central post extending to the full height of the walls, with projecting cross braces for attaching the ladder. This allowed the keeper to reach the holes without frequently having to climb down and reposition as would be the case if using conventional ladders. Circular and octagonal dovecotes were ideal for the use of potences.

Area 2

The pleasant landscape and scenery of the magnesian limestone belt includes several interesting dovecote types. At Conisbrough Castle, the top of one of the massive buttresses of the thirteenth century keep appears to have been adapted for possible use as a dovecote, which would make it one of the earliest examples in Britain (**9–12**). However, although possible dovecote usage is referred to in the English Heritage guide to the castle, and by Alan Whitworth of the Yorkshire Dovecote Society, on site interpretation favours a strategic purpose for the 'entrance holes'. Yet it was quite common for wealthy owners of medieval castles to keep separate pigeonhouses and occasionally incorporate small cotes within towers and the upper storeys of domestic buildings, so the Conisbrough example should not be discounted.

The fine dovecote at Hickleton (**13–14**) is one of the few structures remaining from the grounds of the Elizabethan mansion that was originally built by judge Francis Rodes, apparently for his son, Peter who appears not to have lived to enjoy the gift, the manor then purchased by attorney Sir John Jackson whose family occupied the property for four generations. Hickleton was sold to Michael Wentworth of Woolley

Figure 9. Conisbrough Castle: Five pigeon holes can be clearly seen near the top of the buttress to the right of the entrance doorway.

Figure 10. Detailed view of six surviving entrance holes leading into the hollow upper part of the buttress.

Figure 11. A close view of the barrel-roofed castle dovecote which is nine feet wide at the opening, narrowing to five feet. The height at the entrance is seven feet six inches, and, at the inner end, five feet seven inches. *Dimensions courtesy of A Whitworth*

Figure 12. The angled nestholes are clearly visible in this photograph of the castle dovecote interior, each measuring about six by five inches.

Figure 14. Interior view of the nestboxes of the Hickleton dovecote, made of brick with stone alighting ledges, each with a typical 'L'-shaped interior giving privacy for the birds.

Figure 13. The late seventeenth century Hickleton dovecote has a graceful hipped roof, with finial, and low central access door with massive lintel and surround. The clock is a c1970s addition. It once served the old hall.

(c1654–1696) whose widow, Dorothy (daughter of Sir Godfrey Copley of Sprotborough) lived at the hall, as did her daughter, Lady Pilkington. The estate descended to Godfrey Wentworth in 1729 who built the present Hickleton Hall to the south of the old hall which, to use Hunter's phrase 'he suffered to decay'. The dovecote, now in the garden of *Old Orchard House*, was probably built towards the end of the Jackson occupancy or shortly after the Wentworth purchase as it appears to be a late seventeenth century building. The Hickleton dovecote is a square structure of two storeys, composed of rubble limestone with large ashlar quoins. The hipped roof, with a ball finial at the apex is a modern copy of the original, minus the glover. The clock, a recent addition, circa 1970, hides a small window. Another, single light window is on the right side of the building. Above the low stone doorway can be seen the remains of the rat ledge. The interior contains almost 500 brick nest holes with a continuous alighting ledge made of two-inch thick limestone slabs. Although not as prestigious or as large as Barnburgh, the Hickleton cote nevertheless was in keeping with the needs and status of its gentry owners and serves as a useful local example of the development of dovecote design; and, like Barnburgh, has outlived the original house it once served.

Another notable dovecote, also a survivor, can be seen at Loversall (**15–17**), occupying a corner of the walled garden once occupied by the old hall and probably dating from the late seventeenth century when the Wolstenholmes still held the manor. Here we can see a fine rectangular structure that is a credit to the present owner, F A Tomlinson, who has carried out a sympathetic restoration of the listed

Figure 15. The Loversall dovecote is sited in a corner of the former walled garden of the old hall.

Figure 16. A fig tree now guards the entrance to the seventeenth century Loversall dovecote, one of the best preserved early examples in the Doncaster MBC area.

building, including stripping away horrendous rendering from the exterior walls, installing new interior roof materials and commissioning a replacement octagonal lantern, the perished 'original', part lead glazed and wrought iron cupola, having a '1769' date inscribed. As at Hickleton, the walls are of limestone rubble but here more distinctively banded but with irregular quoins and the 'rat ledge' is well pronounced, running continuously and at the same level, about two foot below the eaves. The roof is sharply pitched with shaped ashlar kneelers, one retaining its ball finial. The typically low central doorway, facing east, has a bonded ashlar surround, and to its left is a square six-paned window, repeated at the gable. Security was a most

Figure 17. Detail of the restored octagonal glover of Loversall dovecote. It has an attractive leaden roof and weather vane.

important consideration for dovecote design of this period, so such kitchen garden sites had considerable advantages where the owner and his servants could keep an eye on the nearby cote which was also such a convenient larder. The lower third or so of the cote was probably designed as a stable or store, whilst above (accessed via ladder through a square trapdoor, another common arrangement) and mostly in situ are, firstly, rows of stone nest holes and then in the gables, brick versions. The stone boxes have angular pieces projecting as alighting ledges whilst continuous rows of brick are used for this purpose in the upper area. There are about 900 nest boxes, therefore offering accommodation for well over a thousand birds. Several most interesting cotes survive on the limestone in the southern part of the borough. Probably contemporary with Hickleton and Loversall, though much altered and more at risk is the large free standing rectangular dovecote at Manor Farm, Micklebring Lane, Braithwell (**18**). Measuring about 10 x 6 yards, the two-storey and two bay construction is of rubble with alternatively placed quoins and shaped kneelers. The pantile roof has stone slate at the eaves. Running around the middle and upper walls is the remains of a distinctive string course or rat ledge. The ground floor appears to have been converted to stabling in the nineteenth century with subsequent storage and general farm use, brick being used to block

and repair two window openings. Birds probably entered through the square openings to each gable. Inside, to both floors, and in stone are about 600 well-constructed nestboxes (**19**) but without alighting ledges.

The rectangular seventeenth century cote at Old Edlington (**20**) is also composed of rubble magnesian limestone and has a pantile roof with stone slate eaves but there are no quoins. Its most distinctive

Figure 18. The large rectangular dovecote at Manor Farm, Braithwell has clearly been adapted for later farm usage but the basic design remains intact.

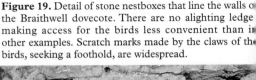
Figure 19. Detail of stone nestboxes that line the walls of the Braithwell dovecote. There are no alighting ledges making access for the birds less convenient than in other examples. Scratch marks made by the claws of the birds, seeking a foothold, are widespread.

features are the crow-stepped gables which are somewhat unusual for the area. The rat course is clearly visible running around the middle of the building and there is a low ground floor access door to the north side. As at Braithwell, bird access was via a square opening to each gable. Though blocked, the alighting ledge remains. Now situated in the garden of *Limestones,* a modern bungalow, the cote's location, a few yards east of the Norman hill-top church and the site of the demolished Edlington Hall, underlines its former importance during the Wharton and Molesworth ownership of the manor.

The main body of an octagonal dovecote at Stainton Woodhouse (**21**) probably dates from the eighteenth century, but, and somewhat unusually, an additional storey has been added, in brick, to accommodate a water tank. The magnesian limestone here is almost white in colour, the courses thinner towards the raised storey, but contrasting with the circa late-Victorian brick which supports a shallow hipped and pantile roof. The compartmented ground floor, (designed for pigs and poultry), has three door openings and three windows, one of the former having above it an entrance doorway (with sandstone surround) to the cote which via an external ladder, allows access to the pigeons (**22**). Characteristic windows openings with alighting ledges provide access for the birds. The interior is a most remarkable sight. There are about 1300 'U'-shaped nest boxes in excellent condition, constructed of clay tiles and lath and plaster, each section raised about eighteen inches by three wooden stilts supporting a single course of stone slabs, the nestholes ascending in fifteen tiers per side (**23**). Their construction involved making a grid of equal size square holes, using tiles as partitions and laths for 'floors' and 'roofs', the plaster then skilfully added to form near symmetrical openings.

The quality of workmanship, materials and shape of the nestboxes makes this dovecote of regional interest. The small linear settlement of Sutton, situated at the eastern edge of the magnesian limestone belt serves as an interesting case study of dovecote types. At Old Hall Farm (**24**), next to the *Anne Arms* a row of five arched pigeon holes (now blocked), leading to an interior loft, can be seen on the middle lower part of the east gable, a surviving example of what was a fairly common arrangement. Across the road, at Top Farm (**25–26**),

Figure 20. The interesting dovecote at Old Edlington has, unusually for the area, crow-stepped gables. The rat ledge and blocked window opening – with alighting ledge – can also be seen.

Figure 21. The octagonal stone and brick dovecote at Stainton Woodhouse remains an impressive landscape feature. The main access for the birds was via the (illustrated) window openings to the first floor, each having alighting ledges.

Figure 22. Detail showing the ground floor doorway and, directly above, the access doorway (with sandstone stone surround), being the entrance into the cote, via external ladders.

Figure 23. Interior view of the Stainton Woodhouse dovecote showing the symmetrical arrangement of tiers of nestholes with 'U'-shaped entrances. Notice the accumulation of manure, the nestboxes purposefully raised above floor level.

another simple version of pigeon accommodation is clearly apparent between the eaves and ventilation slits of an eighteenth century former barn. Here thirteen equally spaced nest holes each have protruding alighting ledges, still used by pigeons today. These may be individual nest boxes set within the walls ratherhan, as at Old Hall Farm, access holes to a loft. A short distance along the right side of Sutton Road, in the direction of Askern, a former free standing dovecote can be seen at Sutton Farmhouse (27). Probably early eighteenth century, it is composed of magnesian limestone rubble (plaster/cement rendering still evident) with ashlar used at the roof gable for shaped kneelers and copings. The roof is pantiled. The ground floor was designed for use as a stable, with the entrance door to the left and lit by a small centrally-placed unglazed square window. Typically, the entrance door for the birds was via a first floor doorway, reached by exterior ladders (or inside from the stable 'trap door'), above it a square

Figure 24. Nestholes can still be seen in the gable of Old Hall Farm at Sutton, next to the *Anne Arms.*

access window for the birds. Inside the cote about 500 nestboxes line the walls, constructed of brick, stone and plaster with protruding

angled pieces of stone inserted under each hole as alighting ledges (28). A few yards away, across the street at Vine Farm, within living memory, stood a similar free standing dovecote. Basic farm dovecotes such as these appear to have been quite

Figures 25–26 Pigeon/nest holes, each with alighting ledges under the eaves of the barn at Top Farm, Sutton.

common and those that survive, such as this Sutton example, do so as a consequence of the owners' and planning authority's rightful recognition of their importance as vernacular buildings.

The writer was involved in recording the stone and brick dovecote at what is now Warmsworth Court (**29**) during its conversion to a dwelling in 1985. Another, more recently converted example, named as *Dove Cote Cottage* is located in the pleasant village of Owston (**30**). The rubble limestone, two storey building retains a single storey wing

at right angles, formerly used as pigsties. The interior nestboxes have gone but the exterior features include a restored 'Y'-tracery window (with alighting ledge) to the roadside gable (**31**) and nestnoles in the north gable of the pig-stye. This cote was delisted in 1990 having previously been included for group value since it formed part of the Home Farm complex of the estate. However, a mile away, another listed cote is extant east of *Chapel House*,

Figure 27. The dovecote at Sutton Farm is composed of rubble magnesian limestone with a pantiled roof. Notice the first floor entrance door and third floor square window opening for the birds.

Figure 28. Interior of the Sutton Farm dovecote showing nestboxes of brick and stone with individual alighting ledges made of irregular pieces of inserted stone.

Figure 29. The stone and brick dovecote at what is now Warmsworth Court, during conversion to a dwelling. Brick nestholes can be seen through the first floor access door. There is a blocked bird entrance in a central position under the eaves.

Rushymore Road, Haywood. The sites marked at Pickburn and Sprotborough (**32**) have been included as typical examples of farm pigeon lofts. Returning to Hickleton, a small pigeon loft was incorporated below the pediment of the arched gateway at Hickleton Hall (**33**), more for architectural fancy than usefulness.

Area 3

Later, brick-built farm dovecotes predominate on the flatlands in the extreme north and east of the borough. The writer's visit to Riddings Farm, at Fenwick, was to view a single listed late eighteenth century combination cote but on the approach to the farm, on Lawn Lane, two other examples, were identified. The circa 1780 Riddings Farm dovecote (**34**), attached to an outbuilding, is of red brick with three courses of stone slates to its pantiled roof which, typically, project a storey above other farmstead buildings. The third storey has a blocked window to its front but

Figure 30. The recently converted dovecote at Owston still retains interesting exterior features.

Figure 31. Detail of the brick-lined round headed window with 'Y' tracery in the gable of the Owston dovecote. The window also retains its alighting ledge.

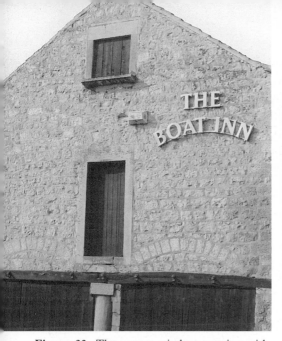

Figure 33. A few pigeons housed for ornamental purposes is evident via seven entrance holes over the pedimented late eighteenth century arched entrance to Hickleton Hall.

Figure 32. The square window opening with alighting ledge is a sure indication of a pigeon loft/dovecote over what appears to have been an arched cartshed at what is now *The Boat Inn* at Sprotbrough. The first floor boarded doorway probably allowed access into the cote or granary. Another loft/cote is extant in the old foldyard of the Copley farmstead, with access via external stairs.

an original, with almost decayed timber pigeon holes, is still intact at the farmstead side. A few yards away, to the right of the farm entrance, and probably associated with the ruinous Liley Hall is a most interesting small free standing dovecote, also of brick and pantile, but of a later build (**35**). Measuring just 4 x 5 yards, and two storeys, the upper chamber contains about 250 brick nestboxes. The ruinous remains of a substantial brick eighteenth century dovecote can be seen at Manor Farm, about a quarter of a mile westwards (**36**). The loss of the entire roof, first floor wall and part of the end gable reveals a cavernous interior of a dual purpose (stabling usage) rectan-

Figure 34. The dovecote at Riddings Farm projects, typically, over adjacent buildings.

Figure 35. The contrasting Riddings Farm and Lily Hall dovecote at Fenwick are in very close proximity to each other.

Figure 36. The ruinous condition of the Manor Farm dovecote at Fenwick provides us with an unusual view of the cavernous interior, full of nestboxes. Notice the first floor access door from the granary. The ground floor probably served as stabling.

gular cote that may have contained somewhere in the region of 900–1,000 brick nestboxes in the first storey. The main entrance appears to have been through a doorway linking the north gable to a barn and granary.

The brick dovecote at Moseley Grange Farm (**37**), is an integral part of outbuildings with a sandstone datestone proudly proclaiming its erection in 1878 'on the site of ancient farm buildings'. This example, a late product of the model farm movement, is a high status affair, as can be seen by the decorative brickwork at first floor and eave level, graceful semi-circular bird entrances and finial at the apex of the hipped roof. Inside, the nest holes, numbering 334, are of tile with entrance holes in the style of Venetian windows! The eaves retain iron spikes or 'tangs' to deter poachers, and the cote may indeed have been built for sporting purposes.

Figure 37. The brick dovecote at Moseley Grange Farm is an extremely late but high status example, dating from 1878, a product of the model farm movement.

Figure 38. The award-winning restored and converted dovecote and outbuilding at West End, Sykehouse illustrates a sympathetic usage of a listed building. This would originally have been the rear of the cote.

Figure 39. The front of the Sykehouse dovecote. The attached building to the right may have served as a granary/stables (notice the decorative ventilation holes in the brickwork). The first floor boarded access door is, as we have seen, a typical feature but the arched and tiled bird access holes are more unusual.

Figure 40. The interior of the converted Sykehouse dovecote still retains its brick nest-boxes with continuous lines of end-on brick alighting ledges. All too often such interiors are lost during conversion work.

Sadly, the interiors of even listed dovecotes are usually destroyed during conversion work but this has not been the case at West End, on West Lane, Sykehouse (**38–39**). Indeed, the design work of Clayton-Rodgers in partnership with Doncaster MBC's Planning Department has resulted in an award winning conservation project. The eighteenth century dovecote and attached outbuilding is of red brick, with two stone slate eave courses to the

Figure 41. *Orchard Lea's* brick dovecote has a large lunette window for bird access, a feature also present in several neighbouring examples.

Figure 42. The brick dovecote at Parks Farm, Dunscroft, near Stainforth Station, has some interesting architectural and design features.

Figure 43. Lunette window (detail) and steps leading to the dovecote entrance at Parks Farm.

restored pantile roof which also has the usual ashlar stone copings and shaped kneelers. The brickwork here extends to some decoration via a continuous frieze under the eaves. As we have seen in other examples, the central door at first floor level allowed the keeper/owner access to the birds via an external ladder. Unusually, one bird entrance is via four pairs of arched, tiled openings inserted in a small rectangular window under the eaves and above the boarded entrance door. The other entrance probably via a larger square window opening in the gable. The faces of the interior brick nestboxes (**40**) have been preserved and protected by coatings of transparent 'varnish', providing a most interesting feature for the residential part of the building, the lower floor used for business purposes. The owners, Mr and Mrs Bryan-Peach, have, therefore, restored the cote to excellent conservation standards as well as finding a commercial/residential use for the building. Of the three dovecotes in the Fishlake area the brick example at Park House Farm, probably early nineteenth century in date, with 250 nestboxes, is the best preserved. A small brick cote is extant on the west side of Trundle Lane. Off the east side of the same road is *Orchard Lea*, formerly Poplar Farm (**41**). Here can be found a typical late eighteenth/early nineteenth century brick dovecote containing about 600 nestboxes. The front has a first floor access doorway and an unusually large semi-circular or lunette window under the eaves. Pipestral bats have been in residence. Further eastwards, a similar, though large dovecote can be seen at Bankside Farm, Thorne. A small lunette window can be seen under the eaves of the interesting nineteenth century dovecote at Parks Farm, Dunscroft (**42–43**). The eye is also drawn to arched brick lintels over a small centrally-placed square window to the first floor (with blocked windows on either side?), repeated over twin ground floor windows and, part blind lunette, over the stable door. On the other facade the first floor access door is of a similar design, as is a small arched window lintel. Here access to the cote is via two flights of brick steps, also serving an attached outbuilding. Under the eaves of the pantiled roof are two decorative brick courses. Though purpose-fully designed for use in combination with a stable, granary and outbuildings, the now deceptive architectural features of this 'ordi-nary' cote would have been deemed it to be of some local status. Nearby, at South Bramwith Green (**44**), the dovecote is far less apparent until remains of the double row of bird openings are recog-

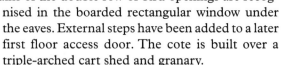

nised in the boarded rectangular window under the eaves. External steps have been added to a later first floor access door. The cote is built over a triple-arched cart shed and granary.

Several dovecotes are known to have been present in the Hatfield area and at Stonehill Farm, Hatfield Woodhouse a brick example, over an arcaded two bay cartshed is extant, though not as yet visited by the writer. The interior is apparently brick-paved and has brick nesting holes. As at Fishlake and Dunscroft there are lunette

Figure 44. The dovecote at Kirk Bramwith Green is sited above what appears to have been a triple arched cartshed. The boarded window under the eaves has two rows of bird openings still just intact.

Figure 45. The Branton brick dovecote, seen here to the right of the farmhouse, has unusual three-light gothic entrance windows and an attractive hipped roof.

Figure 46. The large brick dovecote in the former courtyard of the *Swan Hotel* at Bawtry.

windows, though blocked. The brick Trumfleet dovecote also remains to be investigated.

Area 4

The two-storey nineteenth century dovecote at a farm off Chapel Lane, Branton is of a square design, of brick, with a hipped stone roof 45). There is access, via exterior stairs into the cote via a first floor doorway which has a sandstone surround but the most unusual feature, sited under the eaves, is a three-light gothic window, in sandstone with remains of tracery in place in the end lights, making a rather grand bird entrance. Nearby at Brockholes Farm there is a brick dovecote incorporated into the loft of an outbuilding but the Auckley example awaits investigation.

Dovecotes were often incorporated amongst stabling at urban and country inns. A good example is extant in the market town of Bawtry where a large early nineteenth century cote was a prominent part of the courtyard buidings of the demolished *Swan Hotel* (**46**). Here, the brick cote towers over its adjoining buildings, its ground floor designed for use as a stable. There is a large lunette window over a stone alighting ledge to the third storey (the casement window has been inserted later). Above is a decorative course forming a dentilled band and in the gable a blind circular window or oculus. At Tickhill the apex of

Figure 47. The interesting stone and brick free-standing dovecote at *The Carpenters' Arms*, Tickhill.

Figure 48. The converted dovecote, Wilsic Road, Tickhill contrasts with modern housing nearby.

the wooden gable of former stabling and outbuildings of the *The Millstone* public house has several pigeon holes inserted over a prominent timber alighting ledge. Below is a blocked first floor loading or access door. Across the road (Westgate), next to the *Carpenters' Arms*, and much more obvious, is a splendid eighteenth century dovecote (**47**). Constructed of dressed magnesian limestone with a red brick upper floor, this example, despite inevitable alterations and additions, retains some dignity. There is a blocked lunette window in the west gable, blocked square windows to the front and a blocked ground floor doorway at the east gable end and modern replacement roof. Near the apex of the east gable is a square opening with four stone louvres inserted for convenient access of the pigeons. As at Bawtry, the ground floor was probably used as stabling. Finally, a tall dovecote of a similar style can be seen nearby on the Wilsic Road (**48**), but converted for domestic use. Here the pantile roof has been retained but the lower (stone?) storey has been rendered. The 'louvred' bird entrance is clearly visible in the west gable but blocked at the east end.

Acknowledgements

The writer would like to express his thanks to:
Mr T W Beastall, Mr & Mrs J Booth, Walter Brook, J & C Bowman, Mr Boyden, Mr & Mrs A Bryan-Peach, Mrs E Bungard (Sue Ryder Homes), Mike Burgess, Dan Byford, Mr & Mrs Clark, Mr C Cooper, Fred Creacey, Roger Curtis, Mr. D Green and Doncaster MBC Planning Department, English Heritage, Joe Fox, Steve Hempson (Robinson Hornsby), Brian Leesing, David Lodge, Richard Roberts, Alice Rodgers, the Earl of Scarbrough, Mr F A Tomlinson, Alan Whitworth & The Yorkshire Dovecote Society.

Bibliography

The following select bibliography may be of interest to anyone who wishes to pursue the subject in further detail:

Buxbaum, T. *Scottish Dovecotes*, Shire Publications Ltd, Aylesbury, 1987.
Brunskill, R W, *Traditional Farm Buildings of Britain*, Victor Gollanz Ltd, London, 1987 edition.
Cooke A O, *A Book of Dovecotes*, T N Foulis, London, 1920.
Elliott, Brian, 'Some Dovecote sites in the Rotherham Area' in *Aspects of Rotherham 2*, edited by Melvyn Jones, Wharncliffe Publishing Ltd, Barnsley, 1996.
Hansell, P & J, *Dovecotes*, Shire Publications Ltd, Aylesbury, 1988.
Hansell, P & J, *Doves and Dovecotes*, Millstream Books, Bath, 1988.
Jennings, G, 'Factory Farming, Medieval Style', in *Country Origins*, Autumn 1966 edition.
Lake, Jeremy, *Historic Farm Buildings*, Blandford & National Trust, 1989.
Peterkin G A G, *Scottish Dovecotes*, William Culross & Son, Perthshire, c1980.
Smullen, I, 'Home of the Dove', in *The Lady*, 30 July–5 August, 1966 ed.
Whitworth A, 'Yorkshire Dovecotes and Pigeon Lofts: A Preliminary Survey', in *Yorkshire Archaeological Journal*, Vol 65, Leeds, 1993.

For a more detailed listing see Whitworth A, *A Comprehensive Bibliography of Dovecotes*, Yorkshire Dovecote Society, Whitby, 1995. For membership details (of the Yorkshire Dovecote Society) contact Alan Whitworth, 10 The Carrs, Sleights, Whitby, YO1 1RR.

10. DONCASTER'S THEATRES: AN OUTLINE HISTORY

by Kate Taylor

SINCE DONCASTER'S GRAND THEATRE of 1899 was, more or less, the direct successor of its original theatre of 1776 it seems appropriate to outline the history of both in a single essay. But other theatres, notably the Circus or Empire Palace of 1885 and the Palace of 1911, have some immediate relevance and their history will be touched on here.

Doncaster's first theatre was unusual in that, whilst it was not uncommon for theatres to be built in the eighteenth century on land leased from a corporation, it was rare for the civic body actually to commission the building itself and to retain so firm a control over it.[1]

When groups of travelling players first performed in Doncaster it is impossible to say. Hatfield refers to two companies visiting the town in 1574, to other visits in 1610, 1616, 1636 and 1644 (when the players were arrested for performing the provocative *King or no King*) and to a riot in June 1684 when a drummer who had come into the town to announce the arrival of players was seized and imprisoned by Sir John Reresby's Grenadiers, and no doubt Doncaster was visited on less memorable occasions.[2] By the 1760s James Whitley's company of players was providing entertainment for the society which gathered at Doncaster for the September race week and Hatfield notes that in 1765 members of the Corporation rebuked the Mayor, who gained financially from the letting, for allowing them the use of the Town Hall. However, the following year performances were authorised there at race time provided that the company stayed no longer than two further weeks. Over the next few years their annual occupation proved both immensely popular and something of a nuisance to their hosts and on 4 October 1774 the Corporation determined to invite William Lindley (c1739–1818), who had been an assistant to the architect John Carr in York but was then advertising his services independently, to draw up plans for a playhouse.[3] These were accepted and the first stone was laid on 28 April 1775. The ground floor of the building housed shops. On the upper floor was a theatre typical of its period with a rectangular auditorium with boxes ranged on three sides, a central pit and a gallery above the boxes (Figure 1). Lindley received in all, when the building was completed, £1577 1s.0d. Meanwhile, Tate Wilkinson (1739–1803), the actor-manager operating the York circuit of theatres, had, partly through the interest of General (then Major) St Leger whom he had known since 1758, secured the chance to take his company to Doncaster for the race week in September 1775 when again performances were in the Town Hall.[4] The following August the Corporation agreed to lease the new Playhouse, above the shops in the Market Place, or Magdalens as the area was then called, to Wilkinson for £70 a year, the sum to be reduced to £35 if there was no race week.[5] Wilkinson was allowed £15.15s for furnishing the green

Figure 1. This splendid (c1930) model of Doncaster's first theatre can be seen on display at Cusworth Hall Museum. *Brian Elliott*

room. He was to give the Mayor of Doncaster a double ticket each year permitting two people to attend performances free. The new theatre, built Wilkinson notes 'under the direction of the friendly Alderman Rickard', opened on Monday 23 September 1776, the year the St Leger itself was founded.[6] 'And a very pretty and elegant theatre it then was,' Wilkinson recollected. For his first night Wilkinson chose *The Rivals* and *The Citizen*.[7] Thus Doncaster theatre became part of the York circuit with which it was to remain connected, leased to successive actor-managers, until 1832. In 1776 the circuit included the theatres at Hull, Leeds, Wakefield (where the new theatre had opened just three weeks earlier) and York itself. Wilkinson's company played additionally in Pontefract in 1779[8] and the actor-manager obtained the lease of the newly-built theatre there in 1789.[9] York and Hull were always the principal theatres in the circuit; at the former both the assizes and the races brought extensive patronage whilst the latter was profitable when vessels were laid up in the port during the winter months. The other theatres were opened more briefly, Doncaster for no more than four or five weeks at the most, usually commencing on the Tuesday of Race Week after a performance at Wakefield the previous evening and playing on only four nights out of six in the subsequent weeks. We may take the year 1791–2 as not untypical; the company's timetable then was:

> *Doncaster 27 Sept. 1791 to 29 Oct.*
> *Hull 1 Nov. to 3 Feb. 1792.*
> *York 7 Feb. to 16 May.*
> *Leeds 18 May to 30 July.*
> *Pontefract 1 Aug. to 18 Aug.*
> *York 20 Aug. to 27 Aug.*
> *Leeds 29 Aug. to 4 Sept.*
> *Wakefield 5 Sept. to 26 Sept.*
> *Doncaster 27 Sept. 1792 to 29 Oct.*[10]

The dramatic fare was similar to that of other provincial circuits. The programme changed each evening and included two substantial items with a variety of interludes comprising song and dance. It was commonplace to provide both tragedy and comedy, or tragedy and farce in a single evening's entertainment. Comic opera and pantomime (rather different from the modern notion of the genre and not then linked to the Christmas season) were also popular. Plays included those by Shakespeare and Restoration dramatists but the bulk of the fare was largely of ephemeral works by contemporary writers.

Wilkinson was ultimately well pleased with the Doncaster visits. Looking back in 1795 to the 1779 season there he said,

> *I recollect no particulars more than that the brilliancy of the company (in term of the assembled society) was then **very** conspicuous, and has been increasing every year as to fashionable attendance; and at the time I am scratching these lines I believe I may aver, for an assemblage of persons of distinction, as ladies and gentlemen, it now stands the foremost in Great Britain, and bids likely so to be on a lasting establishment.*[11]

Whenever he could Wilkinson brought the leading actors and actresses of the day to perform with his stock company at his various venues. Doncaster, however, rarely saw these stars, principally, as Wilkinson explains, because the London theatres were open, after any summer recess, by the time of Doncaster race week and secondly because of his outlay at Doncaster which he estimated at £200 a week was already so great as normally to preclude paying the additional fees demanded by stars. However, in 1799 Wilkinson brought Sarah Siddons (1755–1831) to Doncaster where she appeared for the first time on 24 September as Lady Randolph in Douglas. Two nights later, her second appearance, she played the part for which she was most renowned, Belvidera in Venice Preserved (Figure 2).[12] (Towards the end of her career Mrs Siddons played at Doncaster again, with her husband, for three nights in 1811 under John Wilkinson's management.[13])

Both Wilkinson and his successors sought the patronage of prominent local figures to bespeak a play and lend their name to the bills of the day. Patrons at Doncaster were comparatively rare. However there was always one night of the season when the bill was 'by desire of the worshipful the Mayor' and from 1780 onwards it was customary for the stewards of the races to give their names to the programme on the Friday of race week. In 1780 Viscount Galway gave his patronage to the first night of the season (25 September) and he and Lady Galway bespoke the players on 17 October 1796. (Married previously to the son of the Archbishop of York, she was very probably the Mrs Drummond whose name heads the bill of 21 October 1786.) Lady Cooke offered her patronage annually between 1785 and 1796 and no less a person than the Duke of Norfolk provided patronage twice (22 October 1789 and 20 October 1792). There were a number of bespeaks by the military: Colonel Balfour and the officers of the 23

Figure 2. *(Right)* Playbill for Sarah Siddons' second night at Doncaster. *By kind permission of the Dean and Chapter of York*

Mrs. SIDDONS's
SECOND NIGHT.

THEATRE, DONCASTER.

On Thursday Evening, September 26th, 1799, will be revived the Tragedy of

Venice Preserved,
OR, A PLOT DISCOVERED.

Duke,	Mr. MICHELL.
Priuli,	Mr. DUNCAN.
Bedamar,	Mr. DUNN.
Jaffier,	Mr. TOMS.
Pierre,	Mr. CUMMINS.
Renault,	Mr. MATHEWS.
Spinosa,	Mr. WOOD.
Elliot,	Mr. MARA.
Durand,	Mr. JARMAN.
Officer,	Mr HOPE.
Belvidera,	Mrs. SIDDONS.

To which will be added a MUSICAL ENTERTAINMENT, (in Two Acts,) called

No Song No Supper.

Robin,	Mr. MELVIN.
Frederick,	Mr. WOOD.
Crop,	Mr. DENMAN.
Endless,	Mr. MATHEWS.
William,	Mr. MICHELL.
Margaretta,	Mrs. J. WILKINSON.
Louisa,	Mrs. SOUTHGATE.
Dorothy,	Miss DUNCAN.
Nelly,	Mrs. CUMMINS.

To begin at SEVEN o'Clock.

BOXES as at York Assizes and Race Week, 4s.
PIT 2s. 6d.—GALLERY 1s. 6d.
Second Price, at the End of third Act,
BOXES 2s.—PIT 1s. 6d.—GALLERY 1s.

Tickets to be had of Mr. SHEARDOWN, Gazette-Office; and of Mr. SWALWELL, at Mr. Townrow's, Hall-Gate, and at the THEATRE, where Places for the Boxes may be taken from Eleven till One.—No Places to be had without Tickets.—No Servants admitted without Pay.—No Places kept after the first Act.

ON FRIDAY,
A PLAY and FARCE by *Desire* of the *Stewards* of the *Races.*
☞ Mrs. SIDDONS's *Third Night* on SATURDAY, when she will appear in
a Principal Character.

Welch (sic) Fusiliers (22 October 1784 and 15 October 1785), the officers of the 31st Regiment of Foot (30 October 1797) and Colonel Sir George Cooke and the officers of the 5th West Yorkshire Regiment of Militia (26 October 1798). The Doncaster Yeomanry Cavalry had an annual bespeak from 1794. During Tate Wilkinson's management there were also, bespeaks by Reverend Mr Cartwright, Mrs Childers, Mrs Copley, Mrs Farrington, H Overton and Mrs Ramsden.[14]

It was common at this period for local masonic lodges to bespeak plays and Tate Wilkinson, like other actor-managers, was himself a Freemason. However, at Doncaster, St George's Lodge gave explicit patronage to Wilkinson only once, on 8 October 1782. The latter part of the evening's entertainment was appropriate to the event with a pantomime, *Harlequin Free Mason*, and a 'magnificent procession' of the 'Grand Masters from the Creation to the present century'!

Whereas Wilkinson remained the lessee of Doncaster theatre for almost thirty years, until his death in 1803, others who followed him in control of the circuit remained both less successfully and more briefly. His immediate successor and son, John, became bankrupt in 1814, although under the complicated arrangements for the subsequent leasing of the theatres in the circuit he enjoyed the profits from a benefit performance at Doncaster (and elsewhere) until 1832. He was followed by Robert Fitzgerald, who died suddenly in 1818, Fitzgerald's widow for the remainder of her husband's lease, Robert Mansel, Samuel Faulkner and Thomas James Downe (jointly until Faulkner's suicide), Charles Cummins and, in 1830, William John Hammond (1797–1848), an actor with a breadth of experience behind him, a high reputation and perhaps excessive ambition.

Substantial alterations were made to the theatre in 1814 at a total cost of some £800: a semi-circular extension to the east, at the rear of the stage, provided a new green room and ladies' dressing rooms whilst the main entrance, now with a portico, reached by two flights of steps, was moved from the north to the west end. The annual rent was increased at the same time to £110.[15]

In 1821 the Corporation determined to let the theatre simply on an annual basis 'to persons who shall take the York and Hull theatres'.[16]

In 1831 the theatre was fitted with gas.[17]

By this time stage scenery, and especially that aiming at realism, had become a significant feature. One of the most spectacular productions of this year's season was a pageant of the coronation of William IV and Queen Adelaide with scenery, it was claimed, created from drawings taken 'on the spot'.[18]

Throughout this period, although with the loss of Pontefract, the itinerary of the York company remained much as it had been in Wilkinson's day with the Doncaster theatre opening only for the short September–October season.

Doncaster remained part of the York theatre circuit until 1832 but in 1833 W J Hammond, who had run the circuit for only three years, relinquished the other theatres and negotiated an independent lease for Doncaster at the same time leasing the Sheffield theatre, initially for thirteen weeks from 28 October 1833 for £150; in 1837 he took the Sheffield theatre for three years at £300 a year exclusive of gas, rates and taxes.[19]

For the 1833 season Hammond undertook a 'thorough renovation' providing a new stage, new machinery, two additional boxes and a new act drop.[20]

Hitherto known just as 'Theatre, Doncaster', the theatre was named the Theatre Royal in 1835 when Princess (later Queen) Victoria and her mother, the Duchess of Kent, stayed at Wentworth House for a part of the race week and Hammond advertised the performance on 18 September as under their immediate patronage. It seems unlikely that they actually attended, however, as the *Gazette* reported their departure that afternoon for Belvoir Castle.[21]

In 1836 Hammond leased the New Strand Theatre in London, in partnership with his brother-in-law, Douglas Jerrold but overreached himself in 1839 when he leased the Theatre Royal, Drury Lane, London and became rapidly bankrupt with debts of £8,000.[22] After imprisonment he surfaced again as lessee of the Liverpool Theatre Royal in 1843 but, unsuccessful again, he died in 1848 in America where he had gone in hope of repairing his fortunes.[23]

Hammond's tenure at Doncaster terminated after a three-week season in 1839. Provincial theatre was struggling in the middle decades of the nineteenth century. Circuits were breaking up and actor-managers, still maintaining their stock companies, were chancing their luck more widely, enabled to do so the more easily as the railway network developed. Difficulties were due in part to stern opposition from evangelical clergy, a dearth of new playwrights, competition from a new breed of touring companies bringing operas, and from virtuoso soloists who toured independently like the singer, Henry Russell or violinist Paganini who had drawn audiences from Hammond in Doncaster when, on 18 October 1833, he took part in a 'Grand Concert' at the new Concert Room near the Mansion House.[24] Then there were travelling diaramas (some of which were shown in Doncaster Theatre) which could be set up in any available hall. Later dining hours kept the upper-class patrons in particular away, and, it has been said, the *1830 Beer Act* prompted the lower elements of a theatre-going public to spend on drink at the expense of drama. The effects of the starring system too took its toll on actor-managers with audiences drawn only when the stock-company was enhanced by stars and the stars themselves demanding ever higher fees.

In the 1840s the theatre was leased on an annual basis to Thomas Lawless Ternan (c1799–1846), manager of the Theatre Royal, Newcastle-upon-Tyne from 1840–45, for a single year to William Robertson (c1799–1872) and, from August 1846 for seven years – though the lease was transferred after three – to Mercer Hampson Simpson.[25] Ternan had come from Rochester to take the lease of the Newcastle theatre in 1839 but remained there, in financial straits, little over two years. Robertson was a member of a prolific theatrical family associated with the Leicestershire and Lincoln circuit of theatres, which he had taken over from his uncle's widow in the 1830s; the circuit failed in 1847.[26] Simpson had become lessee of the Theatre Royal, Birmingham in 1840 where he was succeeded by his son in 1864.[27] He was also lessee at this time of the Theatre Royal in Liverpool.[28]

Before the 1840s the theatre was still open very rarely outside the September race season but other events in the social calendar then began to affect it. Robertson was the first to open the theatre, in May 1846, for Cavalry Week, an event which brought troops to Doncaster to train on the raceground, prompted the Mayor to give a grand dinner, included a service in the parish church and brought the patronage of Lord Milton, as Colonel Commandant of the First West Yorkshire Cavalry, and the officers to the theatre.

Although the practice of genteel patronage was dying out, the various lessees still enjoyed bespeaks by the stewards of the races, occasionally by St George's Lodge of Freemasons, and sometimes by local gentlefolk, including Mrs John Ramsdon, Mrs C Sotherton and Mrs L W Childers (in 1830), Mr and Mrs Lumley Savile (in 1834) and Sir Joseph and Lady Charlotte Copley (1851). Hammond also had the patronage in 1834 of the Gentlemen of the Woolpack Commercial News Room.[29] In 1844 E J Irwin, owner of the winner that year of the St Leger, *Foig-a-Ballagh*, gave his name to the performance on 19 September.[30] Officers of the voluntary military bodies continued to patronise performances throughout the century.

A more settled period came in 1849 when Edward Phillips Addison, then a member of Simpson's company, who had served as stage-manager at Doncaster,[31] took over the last years of Simpson's lease in

1849, remaining to undertake two seven years leases from 1853 to 1867, during which time he was described variously as 'of the Royal Princess Theatre, London'[32] and 'of the Royal Olympic Theatre, London'.[33]

Addison first responded to the initiation of a spring race meeting by opening the theatre in March 1850 for eleven nights, bringing members of the company from the Theatre Royal, Birmingham, together with Edwin Blanchard and his performing dogs. For his opening night, on 11 March, the double bill, with the typical contrasts of the period, comprised Shakespeare's tragedy, *Othello*, and *Cattle Stealers of the Mountain, or Rover and his Dog*.

In the later years of Addison's lease he sub-let the theatre from time to time, even for such important events as the cavalry week, but it opened still only very infrequently outside this or the race weeks and seems to have become, by the end of the tenancy, 'dirty and dilapidated'.[34]

Hatfield observed in 1870 that 'within the recollections of many' the theatre had 'fallen from its high position'. This he attributed to the failure of good plays, the lack of good actors and the 'extension of religious prejudices which has helped to crowd the lecture rooms and empty the playhouse'.[35]

From time to time money was, it seems, spent on the theatre and its fittings. Mercer Simpson, who leased it at £100 a year, was allowed £100 for refitting it with scenery and machinery and a further £50 for decorations.[36] In 1855 the building was re-roofed by the Corporation with 'best Westmoreland slate'.[37] In 1860 Addison, again paying £100 a year, was to spend £50 on new or additional scenery and decorations.[38]

Much more substantial alterations were undertaken in 1867 on behalf of the new lessee, John Coleman (c1832–1904) at a cost to the Corporation of £496. Coleman, who paid £130 a year for his lease, had a long, albeit very chequered, association with the stage, making the most of the fluid situation in provincial theatre. Having already been principal tragedian with the stock company at Bath and Bristol, he became the lessee when he was only twenty-one of the Sheffield theatre. In 1863 he bought the old Leeds theatre, in Hunslet, from Tate Wilkinson's family, leased the theatres at York and Hull and set about not so much renewing the old York circuit as creating a more extensive 'Great Northern' circuit which at one time included Lincoln, Liverpool. Glasgow and the Isle of Man as well as Doncaster and gave employment to three stock companies.[39] In 1879 Coleman became, briefly, lessee of the Queen's Theatre, London and in 1889 opened the New Olympic Theatre there.

For Coleman the proscenium at Doncaster was remodelled and painted in white and gold, and new private boxes with curved fronts were installed at each side of the stage. New provision was constructed for the orchestra separate from the pit and requiring the stage to be cut back. The pit floor was relaid to a different rake and new pit seats of deal supported by iron standards, covered with American cloth and stuffed with Alva Marina were provided. The floor of the boxes was repaired and covered with cocoa nut matting, the centre boxes had new sills, covered with velvet and with padded backs. Stairways and water closets were repaired. The theatre was decorated with a French paper which had entwined blue ribands on an orange ground. A new drop scene was painted by James Gates of the Theatre Royal, Covent Garden. Completely new gas piping and fittings were installed including 'an entirely new apparatus for checking and lighting the whole of the house'. Additional light came from a 'sunlight', lit by gas, where the centre of the ceiling had been cut away and where a ventilation shaft was provided. A standard lamp was erected in front of the theatre with the inscription 'Theatre Royal. Boxes'.[40]

The work was done within a six-week period. At the end of his autumn race week season, when the receipts had been 'much larger than for many years', Coleman referred to the theatre's having looked more like 'a dilapidated horse box than a place of entertainment' before the restoration.

The practice of providing a change of fare each evening had now largely gone and although Coleman still provided a double bill it was the same on each night of the week. It was clear that he intended to open the theatre only occasionally with his own company but he spoke of the likelihood of bringing other ones.[41]

Despite the investment on his behalf Coleman relinquished his lease within three years. Even in 1870 Doncaster had little in the way of commercial entertainment but what there was – for example a visit from a group of Christy minstrels or an evening of variety entertainment and song starring the dwarf tenor Henry Collard, customarily took place in the Guild Hall rather than the theatre which was, by then, of course, almost a hundred years old and rapidly becoming outmoded. On 3 June the Council-in-committee met to decide what to do with it but determined to keep control and seek to let the theatre for a period of three years.[42]

An inventory of effects at the theatre, belonging to the Mayor and Aldermen of Doncaster, drawn up at this time is interesting especially in revealing the extent of stock scenery. Besides chairs, tables, music stands, notice boards, cocoa nut matting and holland curtains to cover the fronts of the boxes when the theatre was closed, it refers to fifty sundry sets, ground and rock pieces of scenery in various sizes, three cottage scenes and one village set, together with the act drop and a landscape drop.[43]

The advertisement for the theatre to be let by tender drew at least four applicants including Addison, who offered £100 a year, John Senior of Doncaster who was prepared to pay £120, and Mortimor Murdoch of Bradford whose letter of application, offering £130 a year, reflects something of the state of provincial theatre at the time: he was prepared to open the theatre for nine weeks a year as well as producing a pantomime and added 'knowing how much theatrical property is depreciated by promiscuous sub-letting, such cases with me will be exceptional'.[44] Murdoch himself brought a 'company of London artistes' to the Doncaster theatre for a three-week run in June–July 1870 with a repertoire of plays including the perennially popular *Ticket of Leave Man* and *The Lady of Lyons*.

But it was the £130 tender of Captain Disney Roebuck, then touring the country, with his United Services Dramatic Company, that was accepted, perhaps because of his flattering observations: 'I was much pleased with the town of Doncaster and should, if I took the theatre, principally reside there.'

Roebuck had served at some point in the 23 Regiment of the Royal Welsh Fusiliers and in 1868 had been the manager at its opening of the Queen's Hall, Liverpool.[45] Like his predecessors, he opened the theatre only intermittently, sometimes presenting his own stock company and sometimes bringing in one of the rapidly-growing band of touring companies with ready-made shows. Roebuck himself, despite his promises, seems to have been rarely there. In 1874 his company was playing in the Cape of Good Hope.[46] Gradually, however, during Roebuck's tenure, the theatre was opened more frequently and at the end of his ten year lesseeship in 1880, it had become a venue simply for visiting companies on an ad hoc basis. The days of the stock-company led by its actor-manager, and with extensive and changing repertoire, were over. Companies were now got up to tour with a single production, usually a recent 'hit' from the London stage and staying for just a week (sometimes for only two or three days) in any one venue. In the last few years of his lesseeship and the last nine of his life Roebuck was manager of the Theatre Royal, Capetown, where he died in March 1885.[47]

With Thomas Brooke, who leased it from September 1880 and opened it on 13 September, for race week, the theatre had for the first time a proprietor who was not a member of the acting profession. Brooke was a Doncaster bookseller and stationer with a business in the High Street. The theatre was still in use only intermittently, for perhaps fewer than thirty weeks of the year hosting comic opera, brought by the D'Oyly Carte Company among others, as well as an eclectic range of touring plays. Very occasionally a patron would lend his name to a performance still, as when the Duke of Hamilton, whose horse, Ossian, had won the 1883 St Leger, supported Marie Majilton's production of *Round the Clock* on 14 September 1883.

The nineteenth century had seen an increasing use of other Doncaster halls, notably the Guild Hall and, from May 1873, the Corn Exchange, for entertainments. There were also visits from travelling circuses (featuring principally equestrian dramas and clowns), bringing their own arenas. In 1885 Doncaster gained its second purpose-built place of entertainment with the opening on 2 February of a more permanent Circus, adjoining the new Fire Station and with its principal entrance in the recently laid out Station Road. This was an ingeniously planned building, both designed and financed by the Doncaster architect, Frederick William Masters, which could double as a circus, with a central arena, and a theatre when the 'dress-circle' was adapted as a stage. Measuring 112 feet by 84 feet, it had in addition to the circle, a pit, promenade and gallery. There was ancillary stabling for the equine performers.[48] The first season was provided by James Clements Boswell and included horseback dramas such as *Cinderella* and *Dick Turpin's Ride to York* as well as more straightforward demonstrations of horsemanship. Boswell's occupation terminated with a benefit for the Infirmary on 28 March but the Circus was opened for a further season on 6 April by W B Harmston.

Perhaps dismayed by competition from the Circus, Thomas Brooke relinquished his lease in February 1886 and it was transferred to Samuel Henry Somerville who initially, and later at least intermittently, employed Henry S Dacre as his manager. Dacre exemplified a new breed of management. He had himself created touring companies for the purpose of presenting a single production at a succession of venues and had visited Doncaster in January 1883 with the comic opera *Olivette*. At the same time he had four other companies on tour with the farce *Pink Dominoes*, two comedies, *Truth* and *Betsy*, and the burlesque *The Corsican Brothers*. But he was also prepared to take on the running of theatres and the booking of visiting shows.

After a three-week closure to allow for alterations and elaborate redecoration, the theatre re-opened on Easter Monday, 26 April promising a 'new era in things theatrical in Doncaster' and now decorated in 'Japanese' style. The description of what must have become a remarkably garish auditorium is worth quoting:

> *The ceiling represents in the centre the sun surrounded by a cloudy sky, the several stars in order, encompassed with panels of rich tints, enriched with ornaments of olives and berries, tied with ribbons – the whole colony of which, enriched with two side friezes of storks in various positions, and grasses and bulrushes, lends a tone of elegance and repose . . . The top (gallery) tier is a series of urns, lilies and storks on an embossed gold ground and the box or circle tier is surmounted with rich crimson quilted satin and gold panels and fancy Japanese ornaments. The proscenium is laid out in a gold and turquoise blue frame . . . The dress circle has been entirely reseated and upholstered and the back, enriched by quaint Japanese figures and quilted satin panels in gold frames, has a most quaint and cheering view.*

The report also claimed that the upper boxes had also been reseated and 'now enable visitors to see the whole house without rising from their seats'![49]

It was now advertised as the 'handsomest bijou theatre in the provinces' and very shortly afterwards its name was changed to the New Theatre Royal.[50] By now it was open throughout the year except for a short recess in summer, with a change of company each week and a widely-varied diet.

Dacre mounted his own 'grand' Christmas pantomime in 1886, probably the first in-house Christmas production at the theatre, which he subsequently took on tour, and which was advertised as sparing the public 'the necessity of going to Leeds or Sheffield'.

Competition from the Circus ceased for some years when it was taken over in February 1887 by the Salvation Army and used for their services.[51]

Under the Somervilles (Mrs Somerville was the lessee in 1888[52]) the theatre may well have degenerated both physically and in tone: an Estates Committee minute of October 1892 refers to unauthorised alterations, determines that illicit openings in the wall must be made good and observes that 'in the opinion of the committee it is objectionable to open a bar in the theatre'.[53] In March 1894 Mrs Somerville applied for a renewal of the lease but the committee decided to re-let the theatre by tender. A little flurry of activity followed. Initially offered the lease, John William Chapman, described as an advertising and commission agent and then of Christ Church Road, Doncaster, withdrew his original tender and the theatre was offered instead to Richard Edgar, who had brought a touring company with *Nance* the previous December and who had bid £120 a year for five years, with a prospect of renewal for a further two years 'if the Corporation do not require the theatre at the end of that period' at £140 p.a.[54] Other plans for the Market Place were evidently being considered.

The entrepreneurial Chapman, who was also for some time a Doncaster councillor, ran a variety of agencies in Doncaster for example as a collection point for the Grantham and Doncaster and District Steam Laundry Company, and for Sutton and Co., general carriers. He was the booking agent for passengers for steamships and advertised that, as a bill poster, he had forty sites available.[55] He had also succeeded Thomas Brooke in providing a facility for booking seats for the theatre.

The arrival of Chapman as lessee and manager of the old theatre, which he renamed the Royal Opera House (these were the days of companies like the Carl Rosa and the Moody-Manners), was the herald of radical change.

By 1895 the tenant of the Circus was Henry Luigi Boswell and the manager-cum-ringmaster was Henry Metcalfe.[54] However in March of that year it was renamed the People's Empire Palace. The Doncaster Gazette reported that the lessees, the Amusement Catering Company, aimed to provide high class variety, that a new stage had been fitted and the ring would be filled with stalls seating, and that Will Hebden, lessee of the People's Empire in Wakefield, would serve as the business manager.

Quite when Chapman became involved in the management of the Empire Palace is unclear. The building had something of an identity crisis in 1895, advertising as the Grand Circus Hall in April, the People's Empire Palace from May onwards, with E W Vaughan doubling as manager and musical director, and again as the Grand Circus Hall in December. But as early as April a newspaper report congratulates Chapman on his programme there.

Chapman was able to renew the lease of the old theatre in 1896 but by this time he had certainly leased the Station Road Circus (apparently from Mr Masters) with an option to buy it, running it as the Empire Palace in tandem with the old theatre but for variety entertainment.[57] Moving pictures were shown in Doncaster for the first time on 30 November 1896 as part of the variety bill there.

The 1776 theatre had had its day. The Doncaster Gazette spoke of it as an 'eyesore . . . an ugly and dirty building . . . [the] source of very little profit for its owners, the Corporation . . . [and] source of great discomfort to hundreds of people when the stage happened to be occupied by a good company . . . It starved good companies, owing to lack of accommodation for a paying house, and it filled people for hours at a stretch with vitiated air'. [58]

Having bought the Empire Palace Chapman formed a limited liability company, the Grand Theatre and Opera House, with a capital of £10,000. His fellow directors were Joseph Grimes of Chorlton-cum-Hardy, James Milnsthorpe (malster, Doncaster) Richard H Hodgson (merchant, Doncaster), Richard F Hepworth (merchant, Doncaster) and Mrs Martha Chapman of Scarborough. The Circus was demolished at the beginning of July 1898 and work began on the erection of the new theatre in early August. [59]

The old theatre closed on 25 March 1899 after its final touring production, J H Morton's company in *Behind a Mask*. Two nights later, on 27 March 1899 Chapman's Grand Theatre and Opera House opened. Chapman had secured one of the most popular musicals of the day, *La Poupee*, presented by E Lockwood's no. 1 touring company, for the first week and the opening night was under the patronage of the Mayor, Councillor Burkinshaw, and the Corporation. The evening was rounded off with a dance, held on the stage.

The new theatre was wholly up-to-date. Chapman himself sketched the plans before commissioning John P Briggs as the consultant architect. The local firm of Harold Arnold and Sons was the building contractor. The auditorium had a ground floor consisting of five rows of orchestra stalls in front of the pit. The first tier above this held the dress and first circles. Above this was an upper tier divided into balcony and gallery. The stage, which was on a level with the street, was 70' wide and 32' deep with a proscenium opening of 26' width. There was a basement, 8'6" high, for storage of scenery and properties and there were nine dressing rooms. The theatre was lit by electricity and had hot water central heating. It was fitted with fire sprinklers.

The Grand Theatre and Opera House was, as its predecessors had been in its last decades, a receiving theatre, built simply to host touring productions. The fare was, like that in other provincial towns of the period, remarkably varied, largely depending on what companies happened to be available. Chapman secured contemporary dramas such as *The Sign of the Cross*, musicals such as *The Lady Slavey* and *The Belle of New York*, Edmund Terle's company with a week of plays by Shakespeare, F S Gilbert's Opera Company and, for occasional weeks between Christmas and Easter, touring pantomimes. Whilst providing primarily 'legitimate' drama, the Grand also sometimes offered variety entertainment and, reflecting this, in some advertise-

Figure 3. Demolition work had already begun when this photograph was taken in March 1900. *Brian Elliott*

ments during Chapman's sway was styled the Grand Theatre and Empire.

The old theatre was demolished in March 1900 (Figure 3) to make way for a cold meat store and a urinal.

The Grand (Figure 4) remained Doncaster's sole theatre until 1911 when the New Palace Variety Theatre in Silver Street opened on 28 August, providing twice-nightly shows, under the management of John William North (1878–1930). Built by the Palace Theatre (Doncaster) Ltd, a company associated with successful music halls in Grimsby.[60], the Palace was designed, in the English Renaissance style, by the Birmingham practice of Ward and Ball and the principal contractor was the Doncaster firm of Arnold and Son.[61] Its stage was unusually wide at 62' and was 30' deep. The auditorium, which seated 2,300, was divided into orchestra stalls, pit stalls and pit with a grand circle and a balcony in two tiers above. Adjoining the circle were a

Figure 4. The Grand Theatre whose future now hangs in the balance. *Brian Elliott*

lounge and cafe. The company rebuilt the *Young Union Inn* next to the theatre to provide bar facilities. Entertainment was chiefly of variety shows with a 'slot' for moving pictures during the evening's programme.

Chapman's tenure of the Grand lasted less than a year after the opening of the Palace and, having been taken over by its rival company, after a week's closure, it opened on 29 April 1912 as the Grand Picture Theatre under the management of J W North, then also manager at the Palace.[62] Conversion to a cinema did not last long, however, and the Grand reverted to live shows embracing straight plays, musical comedies and the increasingly popular revues amongst its fare (Figure 5).

The Palace offered live entertainment for only nine years. It closed on 11 September 1920 after a week of Ernest Dottridge's revue *My Son Sammy* and re-opened on 18 October as the Palace Cinema with *J'Accuse* as its first feature film. J W North remained as the manager and the former stage-manager, W H Borrill, became the chief electrician and operator. The theatre's fourteen piece orchestra was retained. The building had been provided with a new operating box, the old one becoming the re-wind room, and two kalee Indomitable projectors.[63] In 1947, after a buy-out, its name

Figure 5. Poster for a popular revue of the 1930s, from Kate Taylor's collection.

was changed to the Essoldo and, after its closure on 24 November 1962, at a time when numbers of cinemas were closing throughout the country, it was demolished.[64]

The Grand, then under the management of A E Dobney, remained alone in providing live entertainment in Doncaster for less than two years. On Whit Monday, 5 June 1922, the Arcadia in Waterdale opened as a single-storey concert pavilion under the management of Fred G Ingleby whose career in entertainment had begun in 1897 and who had experience in music hall, revue and repertory. The first show was *Rolling Stones*, billed as a musical comedy fantasy. The managing director of Arcadia (Doncaster) Ltd was Henry Russell. Seating 600, on tip-up chairs, and with a 30' wide proscenium opening, the building was designed in such a way that the lower sections of the walls could be removed to provide an open-air feeling whilst the upper portions were painted with woodland scenes.[65] Soon the Arcadia was presenting touring dramas and other productions similar to those at the Grand albeit often of a more upmarket character.

In 1931 the Grand underwent alterations. The cinematograph box was removed, gangways were re-arranged, new exits were made from the circle connecting with the main staircase to enable swifter evacuation and 'unnecessary' cornices and proscenium decoration were removed. A new booking hall was created from the old engine room in Factory Lane making a separate entrance for the pit. Patrons for the stalls and circle were still admitted from Station Road and a new passage from the foyer provided access to the stalls without traversing the pit. It re-opened on 31 August 1931 with an Archie Pitt revue, *London Revels*. Shows were booked at this time by Fred Walford of the Palace Theatre, Grimsby.[66]

The Grand remained under the control of the Palace Theatre Company until 1947 when both it and the Palace Cinema were acquired by the Tyneside company, Essoldo.[67] The weekly diet at the Grand at this time was largely confined to touring pantomimes, revue and variety (Harry Secombe played there as an embryonic star in October 1947).

The immediate post-war period saw the emergence of a Civic Theatre movement nationally. Early in 1947 the Council was 'negotiating for the use of a building' for this purpose[68] and in June 1948 Doncaster Education Committee expressed a wish to buy Arcadia, which had gone over to films in the 1930s (fitted with Western Electric sound-system, it had opened on 12 September 1931 with Maurice Chevalier in *Playboy of Paris*) and was valued at £8,500.[69] It was opened as an Arts Centre, seating 622 in March 1949 and in its first year saw eighteen amateur productions, performances by professional companies, including the Young Vic, films and a Youth Drama Festival.[70] The Arcadia remains in use as a Civic Theatre.

In 1958 the Grand closed as a live theatre and was opened by Essoldo as a cinema on 28 July with *Satchmo the Great*. There was, however, very substantial competition from the other long-established Doncaster picture houses. The Grand took on a brief new and distinctive life when, in March 1959, it became a news theatre, providing a ninety minute programme of news and cartoons, under the management of Kenneth Scourfield who was also manager of the Essoldo. This was no more successful and in October the Grand reverted to live performances with a six-week repertory season by George Hewitson's Famous Players under the direction of Peter Adamson. An attempt to foster support came in the formation of Doncaster Repertory Theatre Club, under the chairmanship of Myers Thomas, manager of a Doncaster dress shop and a shareholder in Birmingham Repertory Theatre. The Grand closed again, however, on 21 November 1959 except for performances of *Showboat* by Doncaster Operatic Society in March 1960 which was urging the Corporation to buy the theatre for the benefit of the town.[71]

On 3 September 1961 the Grand Theatre opened, as so many cinemas and theatres were doing at the time, as a bingo hall, operated by Ladbroke's. In May 1978 the stage was refurbished to allow for live shows in combination with the bingo activity.

It looked as though the end for the Grand, now owned by the Rank Organisation, was imminent when bingo ceased in 1994 and the Prudential Assurance Company, owners of the adjacent Frenchgate Centre, applied for planning permission to demolish it. However, local people have fought a rearguard action. The theatre was spot-listed by the Department of the Environment in January 1995 and, under the leadership of violin-maker Brian Laurence, the Grand Theatre Restoration Group, formed at a protest meeting on 22 February 1995, has since campaigned vigorously for the retention and reinstatement of the building. Support has come from the national organisation, the Theatres' Trust. A Theatre Strategy Group was formed in April 1995, bringing together representatives of the Restoration Group, Doncaster College, the Civic Theatre and amateur dramatic and operatic groups as well as council officers. A feasibility study was commissioned from the Uccello Partnership and, whilst this claimed that the Grand was unsuitable as a Civic Theatre, it suggested a variety of other possibilities including a venue for old time music hall or cabaret, a nightclub or theatre museum.[72]

As this account is completed (May 1997) the fate of the Grand Theatre still hangs in the balance.

Notes and References

1. Phyllis Hartnoll (ed.), *The Oxford Companion to the Theatre*, 2nd edit., 1957, p 639.
2. Charles William Hatfield, *Historical Notices of Doncaster*, 3rd Series, 1870, pp 154–57.
3. Derek Linstrum, *West Yorkshire Architects and Architecture*, 1978, p. 380.
4. Tate Wilkinson, *The Wandering Patentee*, 1795, Vol. 1, pp 210–11.
5. Doncaster Archives, lease of 12 October 1776.
6. *Kelly's Post Office Directory*, 1861.
7. York Minster Library, Hailstone Collection of Playbills.
8. Wilkinson, *op cit*. Vol. 2, p 65.
9. C M P Taylor, *Right Royal: Wakefield Theatre 1776–1994*, 1995, pp 291–92.
10. George Hauger, Theatre General and Particular, p 169 (checked against Hailstone).
11. Wilkinson, op cit, Vol. 2, p 75.
12. Hailstone Playbills.
13. Doncaster Library, collection of playbills.
14. Hailstone Playbills.
15. Doncaster Archives, Doncaster Courtiers Vol IV, pp 326–27.
16. *Ibid* (p 404).
17. *Doncaster Gazette*, 16.9.1833.
18. *Ibid* (23.9.1831).
19. Sheffield Archives MS account book of Sheffield Theatre.
20. *Doncaster Gazette*, 20.9.1833.
21. *Ibid* (25.9.1835).
22. *The Times*, 26.4.1836.
23. *Liverpool Mercury*, 19.9.1848.
24. *Doncaster Gazette*, 15.10.1833.
25. Harold Oswald, *The Theatres Royal in Newcastle-upon-Tyne*, 1936, pp 97–102.
26. Lou Warwick, *Theatre Un-Royal*, 1974, pp 167–78.
27. J E Cunningham, *Theatre Royal, Birmingham*, 1950, pp 33–35.
28. Doncaster Library, collection of playbills.
29. *Ibid*.
30. *Ibid*.
31. *Doncaster Gazette*, 4.9.1846.
32. *Ibid* (7.3.1851).
33. *Kelly's Post Office Directory*, 1861.
34. *Doncaster Gazette*, 6.9.1867.
35. Hatfield, *op cit.*, p 165.
36. Doncaster Archives, lease of 11 Aug 1848, AB 7/4/1008.
37. Doncaster Archives, Estates Committee minutes, 7.5.1855.
38. Doncaster Archives, lease of 1860, AB/7/4/1011.
39. Obituary, *Era*, 23 Apr 1904; J Copley, 'The Theatre in Hunslet Lane II', *Publications of the Thoresby Society*, Vol. LIV, part 3, 1976, pp 196–208.
40. Specification, Doncaster Archives, AB7/4/1012a and report. *Doncaster Gazette*, 6.9.1867.
41. *Doncaster Gazette*, 27.9.1867.
42. *Ibid* (10.6.1870 and 1.7.1870).
43. Doncaster Archives, AB/7/8/4/2.
44. Doncaster Archives, Letters, AB7/4/1014.
45. *Liverpool Daily Courier*.
46. *Era*, 1.3.1874.
47. *Ibid* (11.4.1885).
48. *Doncaster Gazette*, 6.2.1885.
49. *Ibid* (23.4.1886).
50. *Ibid* (21.5.1886).
51. *Ibid* (18.2.1887) and for an account of Mrs Booth's visit, 25.7.1887, see also *Doncaster Star*, 8.8.1995.
52. *Kelly's Post Office Directory*, 1888.

53. Doncaster Archives, Doncaster Corporation Estates Committee Minutes, 17.10.1892.
54. *Ibid* (10.8.1894).
55. *Doncaster Gazette*, 11.3.1887 and 29.7.1887.
56. *Ibid* (11.1.1895).
57. *Ibid* (31.3.1899).
58. *Ibid* (11.3.1900).
59. *Ibid* (8.7.1898).
60. *Ibid* (10.8.1961).
61. *Ibid* (13.1.1911 and 11.8.1911).
62. *Ibid* (26.4.1912).
63. *Ibid* (10.9.1920 and 15.10.1920).
64. Ron Curry, *Lets Go to the Pictures*.
65. *Doncaster Gazette*, 26.5.1922 and 2.6.1922.
66. *Ibid* (28.8.1931).
67. *Ibid* (20.2.1947).
68. *Ibid* (27.2.1947).
69. Doncaster Library, Doncaster Council Minutes, 1947–9, p 572.
70. W H Petty, 'A Unique Educational Experiment', *Education*, 24.2.1950, p 306–7.
71. *Doncaster Gazette*, 28.4.1960.
72. Doncaster Library, Local History Section, files on the Grand Theatre.

11. THE ENCLOSURE OF MEXBOROUGH

by John Goodchild, M Univ

DURING THE EIGHTEENTH AND NINETEENTH centuries, the physical appearance of many West Riding villages changed radically. The construction of a new canal, a new turnpike road, of a railway; the effects of industrialisation and hence of increased housing; all markedly changed how our villages – and indeed smaller towns too – appeared. But there was another major cause of change, which was the division of what had once been large, fence-less commons, strip fields and water meadows, into fenced fields – a real taming of the landscape in visual terms (Figure 1). In fact, the whole of these factors were to affect the village of Mexborough during the

Figure 1. Plan of a 'typical' open field village.

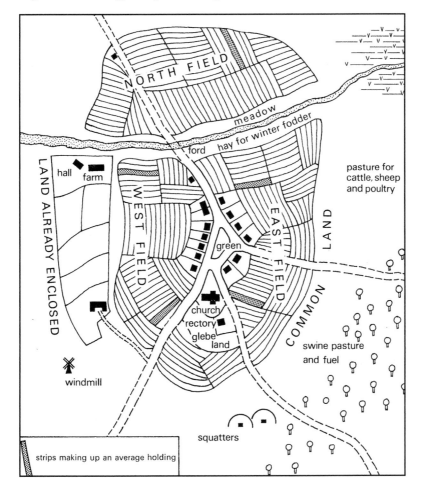

nineteenth century: a tiny village (population in 1801 417, and 1901 10,430)[1], huddling round its parish church on the banks of the Don, was to change as a direct result of the building of a new Don Navigation cut, the construction of a new road which also bridged that same river, the opening of new railways, and the development of new potteries, glassworks and other industrial undertakings, and the development of housing on a large scale, with the necessary pubs, schools, chapels and other facilities. A largely nucleated agricultural village became a small but busy industrial town. To provide, in part, sites for the new developments, the enclosure of hitherto open areas of land was essential: industrial and housing growth was only able to occur alongside enclosure.

But the story is not quite as simple as might be anticipated. Any idea of a simple nineteenth century enclosure providing room for growth is incorrect: research shows that a Parliamentary-powered enclosure did indeed occur in Mexborough in the mid-nineteenth century, but the overall story of enclosure in that township is also far more complicated and also more unusual, more interesting – indeed, more

Figure 2. Dolcliffe Common, Mexborough, prior to enclosure. *John Goodchild Collection*

significant – than might be initially expected. For what emerges is a situation where ancient landholding practices survived far into Victorian times, even beyond the time of 'official' enclosure: enclosure in Mexborough was essentially a long-term process of nibbling at common rights. Some unenclosed lands were taken in 1834 for the building of the new line of canal;[2] some for the new turnpike road, opened in 1840,[3] and more for the railway when it came later in the 1840s; but open fields, commons and water meadows survived the Parliamentary enclosure of Dolcliffe Common (Figure 2) in the 1860s, leaving in the 1870s over 396 acres of common, some one third of the total area of the township, and part of that area survived as common land into the 1880s.[4]

There were, of course, other areas where Parliamentary enclosure was of little overall significance, and indeed where it never had any effect: from Denaby and Mexborough northwards through Bolton and Clayton and Hooton Pagnell to Upton and Ryhill and on to West Hardwick and Sharlston and Warmfield cum Heath, near Wakefield, and including a number of adjacent townships, the process of Parliamentary enclosure did not occur, and there are still commons, and lands owned (if not cultivated) in strips, in those areas. A number of factors occasioned this situation – and agricultural and tenurial conservatism was not one of these. In the outcome, it became possible to consolidate holdings via purchase and exchange in relation to strip lands and common meadows; but the open commons of some of these townships remain visually significant into our own day, even if the rights of depasturing cattle and so forth on them are perhaps not exercised so much as hitherto.

Returning to Mexborough: the purpose is to discuss the situation in that township before Parliamentary and 'informal' enclosure, and then to look at how those same processes were implemented in Mexborough, and what the effects were. From study of published lists of enclosures, one would gather that here enclosure took place in the 1850s, but we will find that here – as indeed elsewhere – enclosure was not only a much longer process, with its marked beginnings long before that decade, but that the enclosure of the 1850s did not by any means end the older system, and that subsequently there still existed Mexborough Pastures or Spittlefield Leys and the Great Leech and Little Leach by the river Don, near Strafford Sands, water meadows described on the mid-nineteenth century Ordnance Survey map as 'Liable to Floods',[6] with the right to turn out cattle there still belonging to owners of individual old houses in Mexborough, while the open fields, still divided by their metes and bounds, still became

common for pasturing cattle after scythe and sickle times, and Bull
Green Common still existed too; the pinfold was still necessary for
impounding straying cattle in 1877. Then there occurred a radical
change, when common rights were bought out extensively, especially
by Mr Mortague of nearby High Melton Hall.[6]

The earliest detailed survey of Mexborough which the writer has in
his Local History Study Centre at Wakefield, is one of 1697,[7] prepared
incidentally by one Robert Willson (sic), who describes himself as
'Philomath'. His survey was of the estate of Thomas Silvester, of an
Ecclesfield family in which several brothers made fortunes in one
generation as Government armaments dealers. Each of the brothers
invested his profits in land, and Thomas Silvester had bought the
Manor of Mexborough estate – some 374 acres plus the commons, in
all some half of the 1300 acres of the township's area. There were
other, smaller, landowners, of whom one was the vicar of
Mexborough, whom we shall meet again, and the Savile family of
Methley Hall, near Leeds, who were to take their title of Earl of
Mexborough from this place upon ennoblement in 1766. Among
smaller areas was the Bell String Flat, some six acres, the rent of which
provided pasture for a bull which would be baited for the amusement
of the inhabitants, as a document says, but which animal possibly
doubled up (as was not uncommon) to serve the cows of the inhabitants. Thomas Silvester owned long, narrow strips in the (apparently)
four open fields of Mexborough, called the Wood Field, the Middle
Field, the Swinton Field and the Wheat Croft: of these strips (individually called doles) Silvester owned 147, each about one-eighth of
an acre in area and marked out by boundary marks (probably stones)
at the head and tail. Where they lay next to each other, some of these
strips had already been consolidated by 1697 into larger holdings, the
largest being of seven and a half strips. They were, of course, let to
tenant farmers, and the largest Silvester tenant was Charles Laughton,
of the Manor House Farm, who was also to be appointed in 1736 to
keep the pheasants and game of the Manor. Silvester also owned areas
in the water meadows by the Don, in the Low Ing and the North Ing,
in areas called butts, each with its own name: rich meadow land, used
for grazing. Each owner of a house in Mexborough had rights to allow
his or her own (or tenant's) cattle – and only cattle – to enter these
water meadows from early July until the beginning of April in the year
following, when they were completely closed until May Day to allow
the grass to grow, and then their owners had rights to graze then until
the common right was exercised from July – Old Midsummer Day.
They were to survive into the 1870s, when they covered some 82 acres

and accommodated the grazing of 51 owners' cattle.

In the strip fields, which in the 1870s still covered 227 acres, almost one fifth of the township area (Figure 3), the farmers had a right to turn in their livestock – cattle, sheep, geese, hens are specified – after the corn had been cut, and then again at the end of September – after 'scythe and sickle', as the periods were called (Figure 4). If a farmer had not cut in time, the livestock were still entitled to enter, and no doubt fattened well on the grain and grass rather than as otherwise they did, on the stubble and the fog or late grass.[9]

The 1697 survey refers to field-names which were to survive a couple of hundred years later – Short Clay, Long Clay, Grimes Croft, Old Moor, and many others; it identifies too the North, Middle, Low and Wood Fields, and the North Ing, and it refers to both the Manor House and the Court House. In 1697 the Silvester estate was in seven tenancies of between 15 and 133 acres; in 1810, the same estate was in six tenancies of between 38 and 88 acres, roughly then half ploughed and half grazed.[10]

When a detailed list of the properties of the Vicar of Mexborough (ex officio) was made in 1764 – a terrier of church property – it was recorded some 38 acres of the vicar's glebe or supporting farm, the parsonage with its coachhouse and stabling for two horses, its cattle

Figure 3. The old strip fields and several ancient field names are still evident on this post-enclosure map.

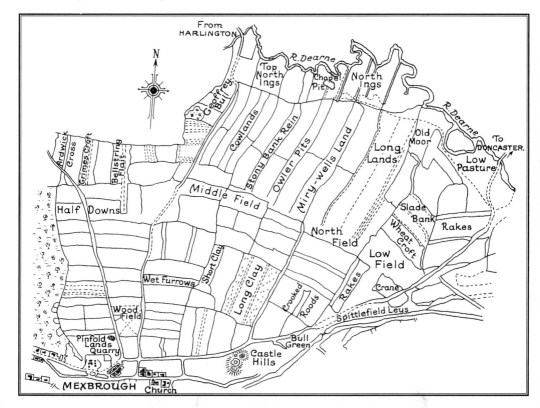

house, its two large barns, its orchard and fishpond, a newly-built farmhouse (for a tenant farmer), a house in the churchyard formerly used as a school, and the timber on the parson's estate – 49 ash, 12 walnut, 2 elm and 2 pear trees.[11]

The records of the manor court at Mexborough give useful detail of the situation from time to time.[12] A pinder was appointed to control straying livestock – a nuisance to the community – and two bylaw men looked after the other agricultural and local government concerns of the village. In 1738 at the court Joseph Newton was charged with taking his cattle into the ings or common pastures when he possessed no right to do so. In 1735 the (then new) Don Navigation was presented for allowing water for their cut to flood the ings, so that in part it could not be used for grazing cattle. Another man was presented for using the land when he had no right, and John Clark, Joseph Newton (again) and Matthew Lister were in trouble for putting in more cattle than they had cattle gates, or rights. A horse could be pastured there, but it had to be tethered, and in 1783 the court found that there were 41 such rights, the owners of which had to pay for the maintenance of the fences round the commons and water meadows. The court was held as late as 1848, when William Booth, local government functionary as assistant overseer of the poor and surveyor of highways, was appointed by the court as pinder; there were still two bylaw men.

In the strip fields, strips belonged as freeholds to the individual owners, but in the ings or pastures, although the rights could be sold or let, the land belonged to the lord of the manor. In Mexborough the estate and manorial rights passed from Thomas Silvester by will, then by sale, and again by will, to the Reeve family (in successive genera-

Figure 4. Strip farmers harvesting crops.

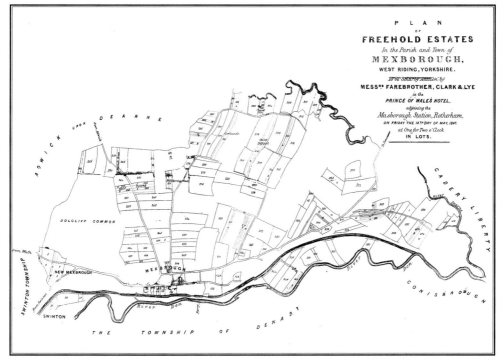

Figure 5. Sale plan of 1847, showing Mexborough fields and strips. *John Goodchild Collection*

tions a doctor and a barrister in London), coming to a Mrs Frances Reeve whose papers the writer possesses.[13] She was to die in 1830, and her daughter was to marry Henry Kater, an army captain, of Wycombe in Buckinghamshire and later of York Gate in London. In 1834 he sold some 4 acres by compulsory purchase to the Don Navigation for £708 for their new Mexborough Cut, and in 1835 his son Edward Kater inherited the 620 acres of the Mexborough estate[14] – and in 1847 put the whole up for sale by auction. But Mexborough was still largely agricultural, and not many lots found a purchaser; the sale plan (Figure 5) shows the strip fields being offered for sale, along with several Mexborough farmhouses and cottages, the *Red Lion Inn*, stone quarries, extensive coal rights, and 58 cattle gates.[15]

Dolcliffe Common in Mexborough was included in the proposed sales of 1847, but it too found no purchaser. With Banks Common it extended over 118 acres, and there had already been shallow coal mining on it.[16] In the 1820s Beevers & Hague had leased coal from Mrs Reeve under the Clay Field in Mexborough, working their mine until about 1830 and working coal under adjacent owners' strips too.[17] Dolcliffe Common was by the 1850s regarded as suitable for formal enclosure: not only was its surface scarred with mine workings and hence largely useless for grazing, but slowly increasing industrialisation was bringing new demands for both industrial sites and workers' housing. In April 1858, application was made, with the lord of the manor's approval – if not on his actual behalf – to the newly established body of Government Enclosure Commissioners in London, who had come into existence in 1845. A minimum of two-thirds of those interested in the common among those who possessed such rights, and working quickly, an Assistant Commissioner held an inquiry in May 1858, and the enclosure was authorised to go ahead by a Provisional Order of October 1858 – itself, along with twenty-three others of a similar nature, confirmed subsequently by an Act of Parliament. The usual proportion of one-sixteenth of the total surface was to be awarded to the lord of the manor, in recognition of his ownership of the freehold hitherto; four acres were to be laid out as recreational ground, and three acres as garden allotments for the working poor. George Dyson Simpson, a professional land surveyor from Loversall, was appointed to value the Common with a view to its enclosure into private plots, and supervise the allotment.

The procedure which Simpson followed at Mexborough was a standard one: he asked for and then received claims from those who believed they had rights of commoning on Dolcliffe Common, and he then heard objections to those claims, holding any meetings in the process. Ultimately, he submitted a report, approved by all the claimants, to the Enclosure Commissioners in London, in August 1861, and only three weeks later, they approved it as the Mexborough Inclosure Award. It provided first for the closure of old roads across the Common, and the opening of new ones, both public and private, and of public footpaths. Four acres were allotted for the recreation of the inhabitants of Mexborough and its neighbourhood (vested in the churchwardens and overseerers of the poor): this land was in fact rough and stony, and it lay useless until in 1887 at the time of Queen Victoria's Jubilee it was let to the Mexborough Local Board, the local authority, for a token one shilling a year rent, and was developed as a public park. Another three acres were allotted for use by the labouring poor of the parish (which included Denaby); later, a public meeting decided to use the ground as garden allotments and 47 such were laid out, let at three shillings a year a-piece. But as three of the largest claimants and allottees objected to this part of the scheme at enclosure, there was an annual £3 to be paid out of this allotment land to them. The allotment garden scheme was highly successful, even though by the 1890s three of the gardens were tenanted by gentlemen who had houses opposite to them, and two were used by well-to-do tradesmen as clothes drying grounds. Also at this enclosure – which included Banks Common – an area was awarded as a site for a West Riding Police Station and Lockup, that necessity of any growing Victorian town.

The costs of the enclosure were recovered by the sale of some of the allotments of land, and the occupations of some of the purchasers of these new enclosures show how Mexborough was changing: there were still tradesmen such as a joiner and a builder and a butcher, but also two pottery manufacturers, a brickworks owner, a master brewer, as well.[18]

Soon after enclosure of Dolcliffe and Banks Commons, Edward Kater sold the manor and estate of Mexborough in 1863 to Andrew Montagu of High Melton Hall, for £20,000, exclusive of the coal mining rights; these were sold in 1871 to J P Makin, auctioneer, estate agent and farmer, of Mexborough, for £10,000, and sold by him in 1872 for £18,250: the property included all the coal below the common lands enclosed or unenclosed. But a report of 1891 by John Warburton, M.E., of Denaby Main Colliery, claimed that the coal in Mexborough was too split up in ownership to warrant the Development of a colliery there: he suggested further, and apparently seriously, that as so much coal was being worked by neighbouring collieries illegally and by stealth, a colliery company might be formed, not to work the coal but to buy up the manorial coal rights and derive its income from suing such other collieries for theft of its coal![20]

Some 400 acres of land remained over which common rights existed, and long before they disappeared, Mexborough had got its large-scale potteries and glassworks, its School Board, its Local Board, its water supply and gas companies, its own newspaper, its chapels and pubs and houses and shops. What happened now?

When the manor and estate of Mexborough came by sale to Andrew Montagu in 1863, they came into possession of a well-to-do owner who could afford to develop his property carefully, slowly and to his own financial advantage, over a period: indeed, such a situation was necessary, as demand for so many development plots was necessarily slow. Montagu was a fairly young man, born in 1815 and so still below fifty when he made his £20,000 purchase in 1863, having succeeded his father when he was in his early thirties.[20] He was well able to acquire land – the New Domesday survey of 1873 shows him with nearly £30,000 a year gross coming from his West Riding estates.[21] He never married, and was to be succeeded on his death in 1895 by his brother's son: the nephew was still letting, leasing and selling land in Mexborough into the twentieth century. In 1907, for example, he entered into an agreement to sell (for £108) land with a forty-eight foot frontage to Park Road, formerly part of Dolcliffe Common, on which the purchaser was to build two houses, at a cost of (at the least) £500.[22]

There were, of course, other developers in Mexborough: Samuel Barker, a local earthenware manufacturer and ironfounder, who died in 1856 leaving nine children, owned the Mexborough House estate and other land, and a family Chancery suit led to an auction of his estate in 1877. The Mexborough Freehold Land Society bought and laid out Victoria and Albert Streets in sixty-seven lots, sold at four shillings [20p] a square yard, to be paid over ten years. William Cresswell's trustees owned seventy-one houses and some shops in Mexborough, and George Smith's trustees twenty-six cottages, which in 1895 brought in a nett profit of just under £4 a house.[23]

In 1880, a deed still was able to convey fifteen and a half strips in the open field, and to refer to Bull Green Common,[24] and other common rights remained. In course of time, these rights were to (entirely?) disappear, but they proved to be resilient reminders of a system which had only slowly collapsed, and which had survived in considerable part while the new Victorian town of Mexborough grew alongside it.

Notes and References

1. WRCC, *Report of County Medical Officer on Sanitary Condition of Doncaster Union*, 1925.
2. The John Goodchild Collection, Wakefield (hereafter JG Colln), M141
3. JG Colln, William Aldham MSS
4. JG Colln, M141
5. Ordnance Survey six inch to one mile, first edition (sheets in JG Colln).
6. JG Colln, M141
7. JG Colln, Newland MSS
8. *Ibid*
9. JG Colln, M141
10. JG Colln, Reeve MSS
11. Borthwick Institute of Historical Research, York: Archbishop Drummonds Visitation Returns, 1764
12. JG Colln, M141
13. JG Colln, Reeve MSS
14. JG Colln, M141
15. JG Colln, William Ald (Figuresam MSS)
16. JG Colln, Wharncliffe Mineral Estates MSS
17. JG Colln, M141
18. JG Colln, M141 West Riding Charities, vol 1, 1897, sub Mexborough
19. JG Colln, M141
20. Burkes Landed Gentry 1906 (and later) edition.
21. Owners of Land Return, vol 2, 1875.
22. JG Colln, M141
23. *Ibid*
24. *Ibid*

12. By the Instigation of the Devil: The Doncaster Borough Coroner's Records

by Jenny Moran

ALTHOUGH THE EXISTENCE OF THE OFFICE OF CORONER has been traced back to 1194, the earliest information relating to the Doncaster Borough coroners is contained in the charter of Edward IV granted in 1467 (Figure 1). This charter authorised the mayor to act as coroner for the borough and soke and this power was not abolished until the *Municipal Corporations Act* of 1835. This makes tracing the coroners easier as far more records relating to the mayor and his office are likely to survive through the ages than to the relatively obscure post of coroner. The last mayor who also acted as coroner under the terms of the 1467 charter was William Sheardown who was mayor between 1834 and 1836 (Figure 2).

Coroners were not paid a salary until the *County Coroners Act* of

Figure 1. The initial letter of the 1467 charter which authorised the mayor to act as coroner for the borough and soke of Doncaster. *Doncaster Archives AB/4 Photograph by B Elliott*

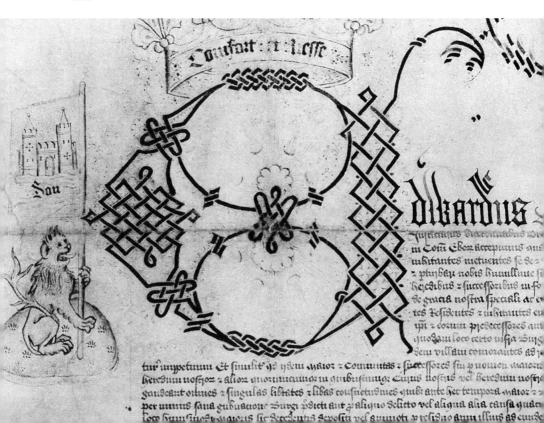

1860, they were, however, able to levy some fees for the service they provided. A statute of 1487 allowed the coroner to take a fee of thirteen shillings and four pence for conducting an inquest into homicide, although he could not impose a fee for any other kind of death. This fee was paid either out of the goods and chattels of the felon responsible or, if he had none, imposed on the township to which he belonged. It was also possible for the coroner to make money from forfeitures and amercements.[1]

In theory inquests were originally held with the coroner and jurors gathered around the body and it was a stipulation that all participants view the body. The condition that the coroner must physically view the body in order to gain jurisdiction is theoretically, at least, still a requirement. In the past, it appears that inquests were held in the nearest convenient building to the place where the body had been found. Often this was a public house. In Doncaster borough, for the period of the later surviving inquest papers (1890–1930) inquests were held at the Guild Hall.

A borough oath book dating from the early sixteenth century gives details of the particular responsibilities of the coroner saying that he 'shall go to suche bodies as be slayne or sudenlye dede drowned or mischeved and also to suche places where it is said tresor[2] shuld be foudon'.[3] It also stipulates that in a case of suspicious or unexpected death a jury of twelve men living in the borough must be summoned and 'enquere theirof by all means and weys to knowe the certeyntie and cause of his dethe'.[4] These directions are surprisingly sophisticated as the coroner is instructed to look for a less obvious cause of death in drowning cases:

> *Also if he* [the coroner] *sitt uppon a bodie drowned he shall enquere and serche if he wore sleyn afore by thrtlyng with corde or other thyng or wounded and then equire in the maner aforesaid arestying the first fynders and other persons suspecte* [5]

As well as investigating suspicious deaths and having a judicial function, the coroner was also involved in collecting revenue arising from the verdicts returned by juries. For example, a deodand was the object which caused the death of a person, for example, in cases of homicide it could be a knife or sword, or in cases of fatal accidents a cart or horse. In theory the deodand was given to the

Figure 2. William Sheardown, Mayor of Doncaster 1834 and 1836. The last mayor who also acted as coroner under the terms of the 1467 charter.
Doncaster Archives AB Photograph by B Elliott

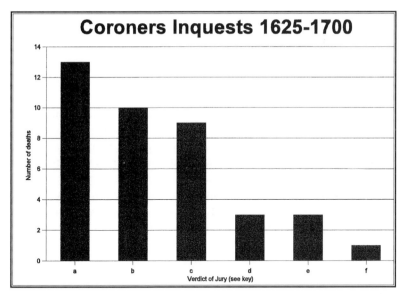

Key:
a	Accidental drowning		d	Sudden death	
b	Other accidents		e	manslaughter/homicide	
c	Suicide (Felo de se)		f	not specified	

Figure 3. Coroners' Inquests 1625–1700.

crown to be used for some pious purpose or it could be sold and the proceeds given to the dependents of the dead person by way of compensation. In some cases, the lord of the manor or person of similar standing had acquired the right to keep deodands, either by official grant or according to custom. On 22 March 1621/2 the Doncaster borough courtier[6] records:

> *... that the maior that now is such other persons as heantofore hath beene or hereafter shalbe maiors of this Corporation shall accordying to Anciente right usage & prestription retayne & keepe all such Deodands as have or shall respectyvely fall in their severall tymes to their severall uses, And if any suit or controversye aryse thereabout the Corporation is resolved to defend the same.*[7]

Unfortunately, inquest papers survive for only thirty nine cases during the entire period in which the mayor acted as coroner for the borough and these cover the dates 1625–1700. As Figure 3 shows, most of the deaths investigated were accidental, with accidental drowning accounting for a third of the cases. Any items found to be deodand are noted with their approximate value, for example, the case of Robert Alvy in September 1700:

The said Jury finde that the decd. in rideinge over the River at Wheatley ford fell from the mare hee ridd on into the River & was drowned by misfortune and that the said mare was a moveinge cause to carry him into the water by meanes whereof hee was drowned, and the said Jury finde the said mare to bee an old mare, blinde of an Ey & that shee is of the value of six shillings & eight pence.[8]

Apart from deciding which articles were deodand and valuing them, the coroner also appraised the goods and chattels of felons as these were also forfeit to the crown. This included the goods of people who had committed suicide and were therefore judged to be guilty of the crime of felo de se – a felon with respect to oneself. This meant that the person would be buried without any religious rites. Such a verdict was returned against William Vickars in 1632 and it is interesting to note that, in contrast to more modern coroners' inquests there is no mention of any attempt to find out the reason for his suicide (Figure 4):

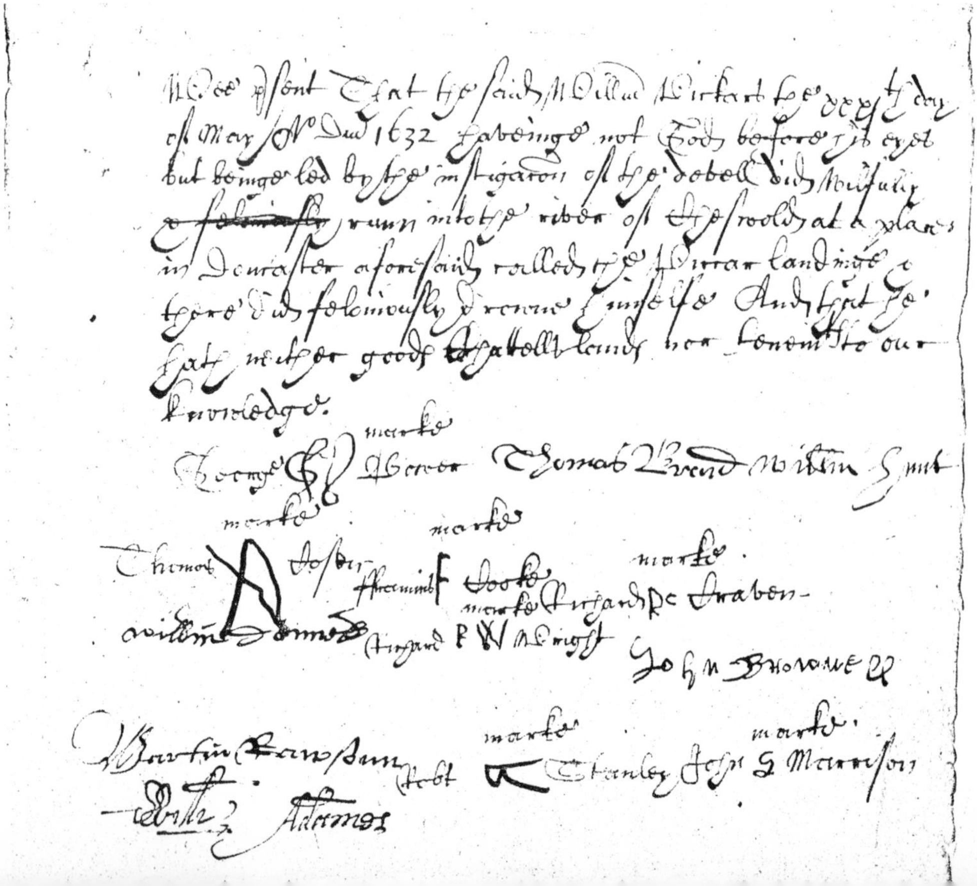

Wee present That the said Willm. Vickars the xxxth day of May Ao dm 1632 haveing not God before his eyes but beinge led by the instigacion

Figure 4. Inquest into the death of William Vickars. The jury concluded that he had committed suicide having been 'led by the instigation of the devell' in 1632. *Doncaster Archives AB/4/1 No 34*

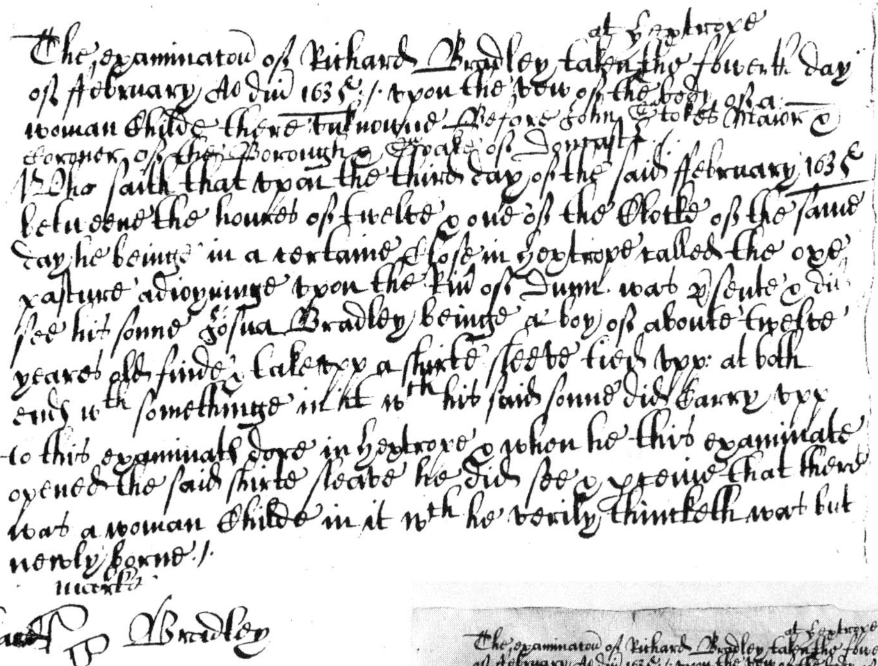

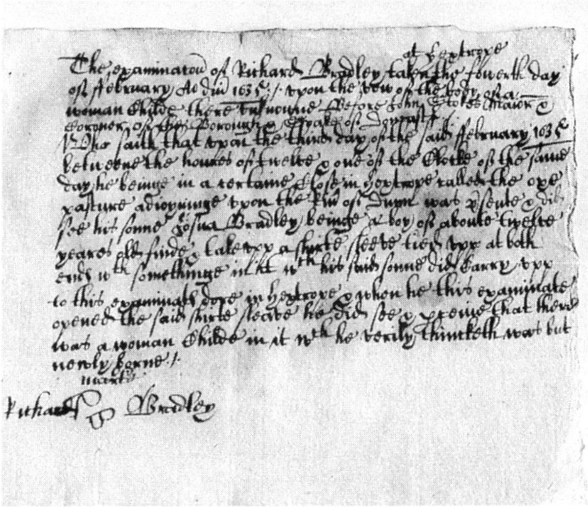

Figure 5. Witness statement of Richard Bradley during an inquest into the death of an unknown female infant found in the River Don in 1636.
Doncaster Archives AB/4/1 No 3

*of the devell did wilfully runn
into the river of Cheswold at a
place in doncaster aforesaid
called the Viccar landinge there
did feloniously drowne himselfe.
And that he hath neither goodes
Chattells landes nor tenements
to our knowledge* [9]

Of the three deaths classified as homicide or manslaughter two were deaths during fights: Abraham Ponton was killed by Robert Wilson of Doncaster and Margaret Carr died as the result of an affray between her husband Thomas and a number of other people. It is likely that the victims in these two cases were not deliberately murdered by their assailants and can be regarded as victims of manslaughter. The third case concerns the discovery of the body of a newly born female infant in the River Don in 1636.[10] The child was found by Joshua Bradley, the son of Richard Bradley of Hexthorpe. The examination of Richard Bradley describes the discovery of the body (Figure 5):

*. . . upon the third day of the said February 1635 betweene the houres
of twelve & one of the Clocke of the same day he beinge in a certaine*

Close in hextrope called the oxe pasture adioyning upon the River of Dunn was presente & did see his sonne Joshua Bradley beinge a boy of aboute twelve yeares old finde & take upp a shirte sleeve tied upp at both endes wth somethinge in it wch his said sonne did Carry upp to this examinates dore in hextrope & when he this examinate opened the said shirte sleave he did see & perceive that there was a woman Childe in it wch he verily thincketh was but newly borne.[11]

The child may have died naturally or been stillborn, but the implication from the attempt to conceal the body is that the child had been murdered and was probably illegitimate. The coroner and his jury could not rely upon the medical evidence that would be available today to find out how the child had died so were unable to say for certain that it had been murdered and recorded only that it had been thrown in the river shortly after it was born 'by some wicked person unknowne'.[12]

Although these documents are useful for showing the procedure followed by the coroner during this period, because there is such a small number surviving it would be meaningless to draw statistical conclusions from them. In the seventy five years between 1625 and 1700 details of inquests survive for only fifteen years with the dates of three of the inquests not given. Of these, it is impossible to say if the surviving papers form a complete record for the year in question: for example, there are records of four inquests for 1625 but we do not know if more were actually held in that year.

As the mayor acted as coroner, the Doncaster Borough courtiers sometimes contain information about inquests he held, but this, again, is far from being a complete record. There is a very detailed account of the accidental shooting of Jane Sausby which took place in Doncaster on 25 December 1685 but few other inquests are noted.

Parish burial registers are another source of information regarding the number of deaths in a particular place, although they frequently do not record the cause of death. Even where the incumbent has made a note of suspicious or unusual deaths, the information cannot be regarded as complete or comprehensive. Some of the people who were the subjects of these surviving coroner's inquest papers were buried in the parish of Doncaster, St George but the burial register does not record that the deaths were suspicious in any way.

There are no surviving coroners records before 1900 relating to places now within Doncaster Metropolitan Borough but outside the ancient boundaries of the borough and soke. This means that the main source of information about causes of death in these places comes from civil registration records after 1837 and parish registers before

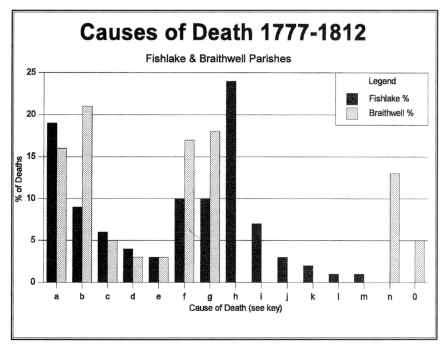

Key:

a	Fever	**h**	Infant (not specified)
b	Consumption (Tuberculosis)	**i**	Wearing (A wasting disease)
c	Smallpox	**j**	Not given
d	Dropsy	**k**	Accidental including drowning
e	Fits	**l**	Childbirth
f	Other (fewer than 10 deaths from any one cause)	**m**	Apoplexy
		n	Convulsions (usually infants)
g	Old age	**o**	Paralysis

Figure 6. Causes of Death, 1777–1812.

this date. Not surprisingly, some parishes noted unusual deaths whereas others either had none or did not record them. It is uncommon for burial registers to note the cause of death in each case, although there are a few examples in the Doncaster Archdeaconry covering the period 1777–1812. The recorded causes of the 363 deaths in Braithwell and the 877 in Fishlake are shown as percentages in Figure 6.

As well as highlighting deaths that may have been the subject of a coroner's inquest such as accidents, drownings and sudden deaths, they also put these into context alongside deaths resulting from disease or childbirth. It is also useful to see the total number of burials in the parish. However, there are a number of problems for the researcher using these records, for example: we do not know how accurate they are as we do not know where the incumbent obtained the information as to the cause of death in each case. Additionally, some of the causes given do not make medical sense today: such as death from a 'sore throat' recorded in Braithwell parish in 1788.[13] In Fishlake for the period 1777–1812 causes of death recorded include: 'cholic', 'a burning', 'gripes', 'grief' and 'a broken heart'. There was also a tendency to record the main symptom of the illness as the cause of death which makes the identification of the illness difficult. In both Braithwell and Fishlake there are a number of deaths from 'fever' by which we can assume that the main symptom was a raised temperature. This means that we do not actually know if any of the deaths recorded were suspicious.

Fishlake records a high number of infant[14] deaths: 209 out of 877 but does not give specific causes. Presumably infant deaths were so common that the incumbent felt it unnecessary to state a particular cause for each death, so it is possible that some of these deaths may not have been from natural causes. The coroner would only investigate if the death was considered to be violent, unnatural or unexpected.

A further series of Doncaster borough coroner's papers survive and cover the dates 1890 to 1930. The records begin without explanation in August 1890 and the surviving statistical return to the Home Office for that year covers the period 28 August to 31 December 1890. The minutes of the council show that at a meeting on 28 August, a new Town Clerk who would also hold the office of Borough Coroner was appointed: Thomas Babington Sugden, solicitor.

The previous town clerk and coroner was Thomas Atkinson who died in August 1890, but it is not known what happened to the records of inquests held by him or previous borough coroners. The absence of records may be partially explained by the ancient custom of inquest papers being regarded as the personal property of the coroner in question and required mainly in order to claim fees and expenses. Once payment had been approved, therefore, the inquest papers were no longer required, so inevitably some coroners retained their records while others did not. The minutes of Doncaster town council record a number of instances where the coroners fees were considered and either approved or rejected, including one instance in 1843 when payment was refused because the coroner had not complied with the correct procedure even though an inquest had been held:

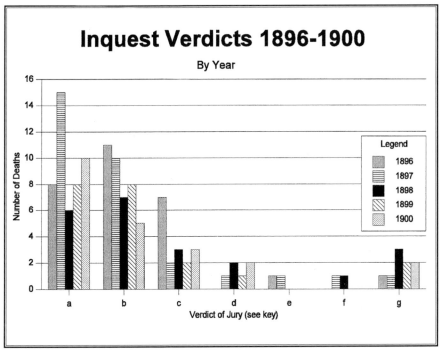

Key: **a**   Accidental drowning   **d**   Sudden death
          b   Natural causes   **f**   Manslaughter
          c   Suicide   **g**   Other
          d   Found drowned

Figure 7. Inquest Verdicts, 1896–1900 (By year).

> *It was ordered that the Coroner's charge of £2.6.8 on the Inquest held on the body of Mrs Sarah Hall be not allowed the Coroner not having taken a view of the body as by law required.*[15]

The later inquest papers are far more detailed and often include witness statements and a list of the jurors summoned at each inquest. The copies of the annual statistical returns to the Home Office make it easier to determine if the surviving inquest papers for each year constitute a complete record.

Verdicts of the juries fall into certain categories with natural causes and accidental death or death by misadventure being the most common followed by suicide. These verdicts are shown by year for the period 1896–1900 inclusive in Figure 7 and consolidated in Figure 8. The inquests indicate the level of medical expertise as they record deaths from causes which would be unlikely to be fatal today such as

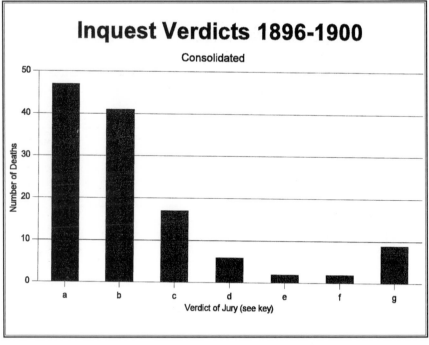

Key:
a	Accidental drowning	**d**	Sudden death	
b	Natural causes	**f**	Manslaughter	
c	Suicide	**g**	Other	
d	Found drowned			

Figure 8. Inquest Verdicts, 1896–1900 (Consolidated).

injuries sustained after a fall downstairs. Less surprising in the Doncaster area are the number of deaths connected with the railway: mostly as a result of accidents, although suicides and people simply being found dead at Doncaster station are also recorded.

Records of the accidental deaths of people working on the railway or in mines are important as they often reveal information about working conditions and safety procedures and sometimes apportion a degree of culpability to the employer and indicate where improvements could be made. In some cases a plan showing how the accident occurred is included with the inquest papers. The inquest papers also show the age of the deceased and the kind of jobs given to young men after they had left school at the age of fourteen. Two fifteen year old apprentices died in separate accidents while working on railway waggons in 1905 although their employers were not considered to have been negligent by the jury.[16]

An accident took place on 14 January 1892 in which an uncontrolled Great Northern Railway engine threw trucks through the wall of a workshop killing Richard Kelly a labourer aged thirty two.[17] The jury concluded that while the death had been caused by accident 'the trucks were upon an unprotected siding' and 'the company should provide a proper stop on catch points to the siding'.

On 30 June 1917 Marlborough Lunn aged thirty five died of loss of blood and shock as a result of being knocked down by a derailed empty coal tub in Askern Main Colliery.[18] The detailed inquest gives a great deal of information about the signalling equipment used and type of signals given to the engine drivers. From the statements of the witnesses it appears that the accident was caused by a signal being given too late and the deceased failing to move to a safe distance at the appropriate time.

Another inquest into a death which occurred on 2 July 1896 held the Doncaster Agricultural Society responsible and referred to more general national concern about public safety at firework displays.[19] Alfred Morris aged twenty two died after he 'was struck by a missile attached to a firework' while attending the Agricultural Society's Doncaster Show on the racecourse. The coroner's jury issued the statement that although the death was accidental:

> *The jury consider that great blame attaches to the committee of the Doncaster Agricultural Society . . . for the inadequate measures employed for the protection of the public from accident in carrying out the display of fireworks.20*

After a similar incident at Brighton the previous year there had been an investigation and a government report had been issued to firework manufacturers recommending certain safety precautions. A copy of the report is included among the inquest papers as well as posters advertising the show and a plan of the racecourse indicating where the accident occurred and marking the public areas.

In cases where a number of people were killed in the same accident one inquest could be held. This happened in mining accidents such as the explosion at Cadeby Colliery which occurred on 9 July 1912 resulting in eighty eight fatalities. Another disaster at Bentley Colliery on 20 November 1931 claimed the lives of forty five men and boys. Although one inquest was held in these cases, the instructions to the coroner when compiling the annual statistical return to the Home Office stipulated that the deaths should be specified individually as if an inquest had been held on each body.

Similarly, reflecting the importance of Doncaster as a railway town, a number of accidents resulting in multiple fatalities occurred. A train collision in St Leger week 1887 at Hexthorpe junction claimed twenty five lives and injured ninety four people. The inquest laid most of the blame for the accident on the lack of care shown by a train driver and his fireman who were both committed for trial for manslaughter. They were acquitted after other factors were taken into consideration such as the excess rail traffic because of the races and an inherent design fault in the train's braking system. This indicates the power of the coroner's jury to decide if a crime had actually been committed. Another serious accident which took place on 16 March 1950 at Balby Bridge killed fourteen people and seriously injured twelve. A contributory factor to this was the poorly maintained track, although this was attributed to shortages after the war.

An inquest in 1899 details what was almost certainly the first fatal motor car accident in the borough.[21] John Edmond Wilson aged eleven was knocked down by a car travelling at about eight miles per hour in St Sepulchre Gate, Doncaster on 18 October 1899. After recording a verdict of accidental death, the jury also stated that in their opinion 'greater care should be exercised in the speed of the vehicles and thoroughly competent men should be engaged in the driving of the car'.[22]

The inquest into the death of Emmeline Hirst in July 1917 is an example of the coroner's papers themselves failing to fully explain the circumstances surrounding the case and the reasons for the verdict of the jury.[23] Fortunately, *The Doncaster Gazette* reported the case in detail so it was possible with this supplementary information to understand the conclusion reached.

Emmeline Hirst was aged nineteen years old and employed as a schoolteacher. At the time of her death she was living with her parents in South Kirkby and was last seen alive on Friday 6 July 1917. She had told her mother that after school she was meeting a soldier called George Tee. Later that afternoon she was seen with a young man and they hired a boat from Hexthorpe Flatts and went up the river towards Sprotborough. The empty and upturned boat was found at about eight o'clock in the evening by the occupants of another boat. An investigation was made by the owner of the boat house who having examined the river banks came to the conclusion they had got out safely.

Her body was found on Sunday morning in the river. The police investigated and a statement was taken from Doris Davies, one of her friends who claimed that Emmeline Hirst had fabricated the story about meeting George Tee in order that her mother would agree to let her go. In actual fact she was meeting another soldier of whom her mother disapproved called Frank Chalmers. The statement from the police says that Frank Chalmers 'is now supposed to be at Lady Sheffield's Hospital, near Doncaster'. The verdict of the jury was that: 'Emmeline Hirst was drowned in the River by falling from a Boat in which she was being rowed at the time'.[24]

This does not suggest that the circumstances under which she died were suspicious, which is surprising as from these records it appears no attempt was made to trace Frank Chalmers and take a statement from him. Given the fact that according to witness statements Emmeline Hirst had deceived her mother to meet this man obtaining his version of events would appear to be crucial for the jury to reach a verdict. From the information given in the inquest papers, therefore, it would seem that an open verdict rather than one of accidental death would have been more appropriate.

The *Doncaster Gazette* featured the story on 13 July 1917 and recorded the fact that the soldier's body had been found on Monday 9 July but the lock keeper Herbert Earnshaw had acted in an unorthodox manner after finding it. The *Gazette* reported that in order to claim fees for two bodies, Mr Earnshaw notified the Doncaster Borough Coroner when he found the body of Emmeline Hirst, but the County Coroner of the death of the soldier. The Borough Coroner Mr R Tovey was disgusted by this action as it meant that two inquests were held instead of one and he refused to allow expenses to be paid to Mr Earnshaw. The newspaper reported some of his remarks:

> . . . *the lock-keeper for reasons of his own, had complicated the matter and caused the holding of two inquests, caused the friends of the deceased two lots of trouble and the County and Borough of Doncaster two lots of expense simply that he could make more profit out of two bodies than one. This man should be taught that he was not to be allowed to traffic in the death and misfortune of other people.*[25]

Verdicts of 'Accidental Death' were returned in both cases although without surviving inquest papers into the death of Frank Chalmers and the local newspaper report the verdict in the case of Emmeline Hirst seems extraordinary given the evident suspicious circumstances of her death.

In many cases, the cause of death turned out to be natural and often as a result of a pre-existing condition such as heart disease. A number of the deaths from natural causes are those of infants who sometimes died of convulsions or were suffocated whilst in bed with their parents. The latter cause was reasonably common and was of national concern indicated by the fact that it was given a separate heading in the annual statistical returns to the Home Office.

Where the verdict reached was natural death the most common causes given were heart disease or 'syncope'. The term 'syncope' in a modern medical dictionary means a fainting or brief period of unconsciousness. In the context of these coroners records it appeared to mean a sudden collapse leading to death probably from a heart problem or internal bleeding which would not be immediately apparent to an observer.

Suicide was the third most common verdict reached and the jury was required to decide if the person had unlawfully taken their own life or whether they had done so as a result of being of unsound mind. It is unclear from many of the inquest papers as to exactly how the distinction was made, but in most cases a verdict of unsound mind was reached. In most of these cases it appears that witnesses who knew the deceased were asked if that person was generally regarded as being unstable or anxious or if they had any particular problem which might have unbalanced them. It appears that juries were, not surprisingly, reluctant to bring in a verdict of felo de se and were keen to accept any evidence of unsound mind. The relatives of the deceased would also want to avoid the stigma of felo de se so would perhaps have exaggerated or fabricated evidence to show the person had been at least temporarily unbalanced.

In May 1898, inquests were held into the deaths of two girls who had committed joint suicide by drowning themselves in the River Cheswold. Amy Gabbitas aged eighteen and her friend Agnes Weston aged fifteen were seen together on 10 May and found dead in the river the following day. Two suicide notes, one of which was identified as in the older girl's handwriting were found on the river bank. Despite questioning family and friends of the two girls the inquest could find no evidence to show that they had been of unsound mind and no clear reason for the suicide was uncovered as all the witnesses called stated that both girls appeared to be in their usual good health and spirits on the day of the tragedy. According to a newspaper report in *The Doncaster Gazette* on 13 May, the coroner had ruled that a medical examination of the bodies was unnecessary, although it seems curious that a more obvious hypothesis such as the possibility that one of them could have been pregnant and hence taken her own life was not investigated. A verdict of felo de se was returned, although several letters published in *The Doncaster Gazette* on 20 May expressed the opinion that it was barbarous judgement and that the act of suicide in itself ought to be taken as sufficient evidence of unsound mind. The crime of felo de se was not abolished until the 1961 *Suicide Act* although the

Borough of Doncaster,
IN THE
County of York.
TO WIT.

An Inquisition, taken for our Sovereign Lady the Queen, at the Guild Hall, in the Borough of Doncaster aforesaid, on the *twelfth* day of *December* One Thousand ~~Eight Hundred~~ and *nine hundred*

before *Thomas Babington Sugden*

Gentleman, the Coroner of our Lady the Queen, for the said Borough, upon the oath of the several Jurors whose names are hereunder subscribed and seals affixed, being good and lawful men of the said Borough, who being duly sworn to inquire for our Lady the Queen, on view of the body of *Daniel Jackson Wilson*

as to h *is* death, upon their oaths do say :—

THAT on the *Eleventh* day of *December* One Thousand ~~Eight Hundred~~ and *nine hundred* in the Borough and County aforesaid, the said *Daniel Jackson Wilson was found dead in a Great Central Railway Carriage at Doncaster and that such death was caused by a wound from a revolver self-inflicted and that deceased committed suicide whilst in a state of unsound mind*

Figures 9 and 10. Different verdicts of the juries into the deaths of William Frederick Simonette and Daniel Jackson Wilson, both found shot dead in railway carriages in December 1900 in apparently unrelated incidents. *Doncaster Archives CR1/8/23 & 24*

Borough of Doncaster,
IN THE
County of York.
TO WIT.

An Inquisition, taken for our Sovereign Lady the Queen, at the Guild Hall, in the Borough of Doncaster aforesaid, on the *seventh* day of *December* One Thousand ~~Eight Hundred~~ and *nine hundred*

before *Thomas Babington Sugden*

Gentleman, the Coroner of our Lady the Queen, for the said Borough, upon the oath of the several Jurors whose names are hereunder subscribed and seals affixed, being good and lawful men of the said Borough, who being duly sworn to inquire for our Lady the Queen, on view of the body of *William Frederick Simonette*

as to h *is* death, upon their oaths do say :—

THAT on the *fifth* day of *December* One Thousand ~~Eight Hundred~~ and *nine hundred* in the Borough and County aforesaid, the said *William Frederick Simonette was found dead at Doncaster Railway Station in a Lancashire & Yorkshire Railway Carriage and that such death was caused by a wound from a pistol but there was evidence to shew by whom such wound was inflicted* verdict became increasingly less common during the twentieth century.

There are two intriguing inquests held in December 1900 where the deceased in each case had been found in a railway carriage at Doncaster station and had died of a gunshot wound. William Frederick Simonette aged thirty two of Huddersfield died on 5 December 1900 and the verdict of the inquest was that he had died of a gunshot wound but there was 'no evidence to show by whom such wound was inflicted.' (Figure 9)[26] A few days later on 11 December Daniel Jackson Wilson aged thirty three was found dead of a gunshot wound in a railway carriage and the inquest concluded that he had committed suicide whilst in a state of unsound mind. (Figure 10)[27]

In both cases the gun was found in the carriage and the coroner's inquest papers do not give a clear reason why the juries reached such different conclusions in two such apparently similar cases. Even the witness statements provide few clues: the father of Mr Simonette stating that his son had recently sent him a letter saying that he 'was doing very badly indeed' and that his son 'has been eccentric from a child'.[28] In the second case, however, further information is recorded in the local newspaper *The Doncaster Gazette*, which makes it clear that Daniel Wilson had left a suicide note. Interestingly, the inquest papers mention the presence of a note addressed to the wife of the deceased, but do not categorically state that it expressed his intention to take his own life. The newspaper report is extremely detailed and even includes the text of the note which refers to his financial problems. In fact, without the additional information contained in the newspaper report the different verdicts seem completely inexplicable.

The records of the inquest into the death of Daniel Wilson do not refer to the case of William Frederick Simonette or look for any possible link between the two deaths. This seems a little odd by modern standards of detective work, especially as the jury had recorded an open verdict in the former case. Although Daniel Wilson could have read about the first death in the newspapers and decided to copy the method, it appears that the similarities between the two cases were entirely coincidental.

Predictably, there are very few cases of manslaughter or murder among the inquest papers. Where an open verdict was reached, for example in cases where people were found drowned or there was not enough evidence to show how they died it is possible that murder or manslaughter had been committed. In 1894, Luke Leaf aged twenty nine was found unconscious and badly injured on the railway line near Moss station and later died at Doncaster Infirmary although there was no evidence to show how he had come to be there.[29] A case in 1898 recorded that Albert Edward Chamberlain had died of an opium overdose although there was no evidence to show under what circumstances it had been taken.[30] There are also several instances of people, some of them unidentified, being found drowned in the River.

The inquest in 1890 into the death of Annie Edwards (alias Crabtree) aged twenty nine was one in which the jury were asked to decide if she had been the victim of murder or manslaughter.[31] Included with the other inquest papers are notes defining the terms murder and manslaughter presumably made by the coroner to assist the jury in reaching a conclusion. These notes also state that the jury must be satisfied that the death was caused by the blow or kick to the head that she had received and that the prisoner John Harrison had been responsible for delivering it. Once they were convinced of this, they must then decide if she had been murdered 'with malice aforethought either express or implied' or if the fatal blow had been struck without malice possibly 'from sudden transport of passion'.[32]

Before she died, Annie had been able to give a detailed statement about what had occurred and this was read out at the inquest and reported fully in the *Doncaster Gazette* although a copy does not survive among the coroner's papers. She stated that she had married John Crabtree, a professional singer and dancer, but that he had deserted her and her child two years previously. She had been living with John Harrison and, according to the inquest papers, working as a prostitute. She then alleged: 'he had assaulted me many a time before' saying that he was of a jealous nature and had heard that she proposed to return to her husband. She reported that he had threatened her saying 'you shall not go away from here alive with your husband'.[33]

In the early hours of 11 September 1890, Annie Edwards received the blow which led to her death. She alleged that John Harrison kicked her in the head while she was asleep. He claimed that she had received the wound accidentally during an altercation between himself and another man who was present known as 'Belfast Ned'. From the newspaper report it appears that Annie and Belfast Ned had been found together by John Harrison who had then attacked them both. She had not died immediately of the wound, but became gradually weaker and died on Saturday 4 October at Doncaster Royal Infirmary. The jury were in no doubt that the injury had been inflicted by John Harrison but believed that he had not intended to kill her and returned a verdict of manslaughter.

A tragic case which occurred in 1924 the parish of Adwick le Street, and therefore outside the jurisdiction of the Doncaster Borough coroner was extensively reported in the local newspapers. George Brecknock aged thirty one killed himself after cutting the throats of his wife Sabina, aged twenty six, and his son Royce, aged four. According to the *Gazette* the note left by George Brecknock read: 'I have taken my wife's life because I believe I have ruined her, and I do not want to leave the lad without a mother'.

Sabina Brecknock did not die immediately and was taken to Doncaster Royal Infirmary so her death was recorded in the Area Health Authority registers. The *Doncaster Gazette* recorded on 15 August 1924 that although the death of Mrs Brecknock at the Infirmary brought her into the jurisdiction of the Borough coroner he had arranged to have the body transported to Adwick so one inquest could be held on all three bodies by Mr Frank Allen the District Coroner. This is valuable information about the degree of autonomy the coroners had in deciding the most sensible or expedient circumstances of an inquest. In several previous cases, people had died at the Infirmary or had somehow been brought within the domain of the Borough Coroner although the events leading up to the death occurred elsewhere.

In a few instances information survives about deaths reported to the coroner where no investigation was held. These can also be interesting as they show how the coroner reached his decision and in some cases explain why the coroner was asked to inquire into the death. Occasionally these records express the suspicions of close friends or family that the death was not from natural causes.

In 1897 the coroner decided that an inquest into the death of Anne Johnson was unnecessary having received a report from the doctor who conducted the post mortem examination stating that her death was as a result of 'chronic inflammation of the liver brought on by most excessive drinking' and that he had 'no reason whatever to suspect any foul play'.[34] A statement to the coroner from Mrs Golding the dead woman's cousin indicates a darker side to the case and suggests that she may have been the victim of incest if not manslaughter and states that 'her father had been caught in bed with her'. The statement asserts that Anne Johnson appeared to be pregnant and that her cousin suspected that 'something had been administered to her' possibly to induce a miscarriage and that the girl's father refused to allow a doctor to be called for a few days after she fell ill. Presumably the post mortem established that she had not, in fact, been pregnant and therefore further investigation was deemed unnecessary.

Coroner's records are public records and are therefore subject to rules made by the Lord Chancellor. Under these rules access to records under seventy five years old is not permitted without permission from the relevant coroner. The proceedings of the coroners inquest are, however, open to the public and this is the reason for the detailed newspaper reports which sometimes contain more information than the inquest papers. In the past, the records were treated as the personal property of each coroner although the current legislation stipulates that they must be kept for a minimum of fifteen years. From 1 April 1974 Doncaster County Borough and Doncaster District both came under the jurisdiction of the coroner for the newly created South Yorkshire (East District).

Notes and References

1. An amercement was a financial penalty. Townships could be amerced for failing to report the discovery of a body or for allowing a suspected homicide to escape.
2. The coroner was also responsible for holding inquests into treasure trove, a function which that office still retains.
3. Doncaster Archives AB4/4 (oath book: early sixteenth century)
4. *Ibid.*
5. *Ibid.*
6. The Doncaster borough courtiers are five volumes containing the principal record of the corporation from 1559–1822.
7. Doncaster Archives AB2/1/1 fol 259 (borough courtier volume I)
8. Doncaster Archives AB5/4/1 no 39 (coroner's inquest 1700)
9. Doncaster Archives AB5/4/1 no 34 (coroner's inquest 1632)
10. In England, until 1752, the new year began on 25 March (Lady Day) so the 3rd February 1635 was 1636 by the modern calendar.
11. Doncaster Archives AB5/4/1 no 3 (coroner's inquest 1636)
12. *Ibid.*
13. This may have been diphtheria which was sometimes described as a 'putrid sore throat'.
14. Children under one year of age.
15. Doncaster Archives AB2/2/3 p 646 (council minute book)
16. Doncaster Archives CR1/11/4 & 5 (coroner's inquests 1905)
17. Doncaster Archives CR1/2/1 (coroner's inquest 1892)
18. Doncaster Archives CR1/19/27 (coroner's inquest 1917)
19. Doncaster Archives CR1/4/20 (coroner's inquest 1896)
20. *Ibid.*
21. Doncaster Archives CR1/7/25 (coroner's inquest 1899)
22. *Ibid.*
23. Doncaster Archives CR1/19/28 (coroner's inquest 1917)
24. *Ibid.*
25. *Doncaster Gazette* 13 July 1917
26. Doncaster Archives CR1/8/23 (coroner's inquest 1900)
27. Doncaster Archives CR1/8/24 (coroner's inquest 1900)
28. Doncaster Archives CR1/8/23 (coroner's inquest 1900)
29. Doncaster Archives CR1/3/14 (coroner's inquest 1894)
30. Doncaster Archives CR1/6/3 (coroner's inquest 1898)
31. Doncaster Archives CR1/1/3 (coroner's inquest 1890)
32. *Ibid.*
33. *Ibid.*
34. Doncaster Archives CR1/5/35 (coroner's papers 1897)

Acknowledgements

The writer would like to acknowledge the assistance of the following individuals: Andy Moran for patience, advice and graphics; Mary Pearce; Mrs G Jennings and Mrs W Bulmer and members of the New Beginnings Group; Brian Barber, Becky Andrews and Marie Kirk of Doncaster Archives; Carol Hill and Helen Wallder of Doncaster Local Studies Library; Martin Taylor of Hereford and Worcester Record Office; Paul Shaw and Julian Pooley of Surrey Record Office; Andrew George of Southampton City Archives and Christopher Hayes. This account is dedicated to my grandparents Hilda and Jack Mawson and their daughter Mary, my mother.

13. Corn Windmills of the Doncaster Area

By Alan Whitworth

IT IS SAID THAT WINDMILLS were first introduced into Britain by returning crusaders. Possibly this is true, as the earliest written reference to a windmill in England, dated 1185, relates to a windmill at Weedley, in Yorkshire, let at a rental of 8s.0d. a year.[1] At that time the mill and manor of Weedley, a small sheep farming community located towards the eastern end of the parish of South Cave in the East Riding, was owned by the Knights Templars, a militant religious order founded at the beginning of the tenth century in Outremer, an arid sandy region on the border of Iran and Afghanistan, which was noted for windmills as early as the ninth century – a coincidence which lends credibility to this supposition. Interestingly, in the same year, 1185, Robert le Waleys was the tenant, under the Templars, of a mill at Burghwallis. However, it is not known whether this was a wind or water-powered mill.[2]

Figure 1. Drawing of an early post mill from a medieval manuscript.

Notwithstanding the dating of Weedley windmill, there are a substantial number of early references to windmills in Yorkshire in general, and from the thirteenth century they are mentioned frequently in documents (Figure 1), and indeed, by the end of the century they are being recorded in the Doncaster area. In 1277, an inquisition mentions a Margaret de Stainton who held 'one windmill worth yearly 20s' at Tickhill.[3] In 1320, this windmill still existed, but its location within the manor is unknown. A view of Tickhill Castle drawn in 1562, shows a four-sail post mill on a mound to the east of the castle, near Tornewood. This was the site of a brick windmill in the eighteenth century, but was not the site mentioned in the fourteenth century. A windmill at Tickhill was mentioned in the seventeenth century, owned by the king, and was one of three corn mills in existence at that period, two of which were water-powered. The three mills together were let at a rental of £12.10s per year.[4] In

1962, the tower of a derelict windmill stood on rising ground near The Spital, east of Tickhill. This was shown on Greenwood's map of 1817. It has been suggested that it was working during the early years of this century and later was dismantled to avoid being rated and chargeable to the owner of the land when redundant.[5]

At Hooton Pagnell, a windmill was first referred to as early as 1297, which stood at least until 1762, when, according to a deed concerning the sale of certain lands at Hooton, Patience Warde purchased from Michael Anne of Frickley, 'two pieces of land near the windmill'. For a time there were two mills at Hooton, a windmill and a horse mill, both of these being rented from the Lord of the Manor in 1704, for a total of £6 per annum, which the miller would, of course, recover from the lord's tenants in a toll or mulcture which he took by permission from each sack of grain brought to the mills for grinding. The windmill, a wooden structure, stood at the junction of the Bilham road and Watchley Lane; the site of the horse mill is unknown. In 1595, Wind Mill Field was the name of a parcel of arable land to the south-west of the manorial hall, later known as Wind Mill Close.[6]

Both the horse mill and the windmill passed through an unhappy period at the beginning of the eighteenth century, and both had extensive repairs carried out on them. The accounts for the repair of both mills in 1710 are extant, and those for the windmill are herewith given:

REPAIRS TO WINDMILL AT HOOTON PAGNELL, FEBRUARY 1710

	£	s	d
Allowed Th. Marriott p. work done at ye Mill	0	7	2
" Robt. Pearl " " " " " "	1	0	0
" Ben Winfield for a pr. of Millstones from Thos. Holmes	11	10	0
P'd Richd. Bannister for his charges & pains in buying the millstones	0	10	0
Allowed Tho. Hall for setting up the stones & other work done at ye Windmill	11	0	0
To Tho. Moor for loading wood & p. Nails & Expences at the Boon for leading it	0	16	3
Tho. Marriott p. nails & iron work at ye Mill	0	2	2
To Wm Day for a cable weighing 4 stones & 13lb. at 6d. p. lb to be lined with sacking into the bargain, besides Wood p. cross trees with	1	14	6
	£27	0	1

The work on the windmill unfortunately did not survive long, for less than five years later it was blown down in a violent gale of wind. A second Patience Warde made the following memo in an old Rent Roll:

My windmill was blown down Feb. 1st 1714/5 there being the strongest
S. W. wind that I have ever heard which began to rise about 12 at noon
and continu'd violent till between 3 & 4 a clock. Elmshall Windmill
was also blown down ye same day with many others.

In rebuilding the windmill at Hooton Pagnell a bill of £25 16s 4d was
incurred, the principal item therein being one of £19 for work undertaken by Woodall & Lister, for which we have no details; deal, nails
and iron work, together amounted to £5 2s 10d whilst amongst the
remaining miscellaneous items is a payment of 7s.6d to one George
Atkinson 'for viewing the work'. It is not known when this windmill
was finally demolished.[7]

The erection of a windmill was a privilege granted only to the Lord
of the Manor or the Church, and with its ownership went certain
rights in respect of milling corn, known as 'mill soke'. Under this
feudal custom, as we have previously intimated, tenants of the manor
were required to bring their corn to the manorial mill for grinding.
The miller was allowed for his labour, to retain a predetermined
percentage of the flour he produced with the exception of that
belonging to his lordship, who could have his corn ground free. It was
also the duty of the miller to collect the toll or mulcture, often known
as 'multer' due to the Lord from the tenants using the mill. He was
then bounded to present it at the manorial court either in money or
kind on prescribed dates of accounting.

Failure to abide by and uphold this state of medieval soke law was
a serious matter, and in 1573, William Plewman, a miller of York, was
fined 13s 4d by the manorial court 'for not attending the Court and
for not bringing the Toll Dishe according to custom'.

Through this responsibility, the miller was often the recipient of
much mistrust, and Chaucer drew attention to this aspect, observing:

His was a master hand at stealing grain.
He felt it with his thumb and thus he knew
its quality and took three times his due . . .[8]

Such acts were not without foundation, and in 1725, William Scutard,
the miller of Thornes (Temple Newsam), was accused in his absence
of falsely setting the stones 'in order to steal the flour of the customary
tenants'.[9]

It was of course recognised, that when a miller was grinding the
wheat, there would be some loss in the process. The custom in the
East Riding was to allow wastage at the rate of a pound weight in each
bushel of corn. Some millers, however, did take undue advantage of

the arrangement and the custom was open to abuse, as was explained by a witness called in a court case as late as 1909:

> When the total was weighed up it was weighed back to the farmer a pound bushel less than the grain. If the waste [difference] was more than a pound, the miller made it up. If it were less, he put it aside to make up for future shortage over the pound.[10]

There was another early windmill mentioned at Hatfield, which in the eighteenth year of the reign of King Edward II (1320–21), was let at an annual rent of 8s.0d.[11] This was a manorial mill and in the same manorial accounts is an item of 13s.0d paid out each year 'For ye Wind Milne'.[12] Two windmills were mentioned in 1606, one sited at West Hatfield; there was a further mention of a windmill at Hatfield in 1608 which was recorded in a grant dated 24 May 1626–27 from King Charles I to Cornelius Vermuyden, worth 13s 4d per year in rent, and which was previously in the ownership of Edward Ferrers and Francis Philipps, esquire.[13]

In 1337, John, son of Peter de Stainford, rented thirty-one and a half acres of corn land in Thorne and Hatfield, from John de Warenne, Earl of Surrey, for an annual rent of 10s 6d, and he was allowed to make 'a way for his carriage to the mill of the said Count', but it is not clear whether this reference is to a windmill at Hatfield or to one at Thorne.

Mill-ways, mentioned above, were an important consideration in the siting of the mills. They would have had to have had free access along their entire length, with no obstacles such as stiles, particularly where the route formed the only means of approach to an isolated

windmill. This was necessary to enable the manorial tenant to transport his grain to the mill and flour back again. Medieval documentary evidence shows that the principal form of transport was the horse, consequently, a mill-way would have had to at least have had the width and substance of say today's bridleway.[14]

In later centuries, other windmills were built at Hatfield. In 1771, stood Ling's Mill (Figure 2), a four-storey brick mill which was rebuilt in the nineteenth century, and which in 1977, still showed signs of rendering. Today, a windmill still exists on Moss Croft Lane (Figure 3 & 4),

Figure 2. Ling's Mill, Hatfield, photographed in August 1934. This windmill dates back to the seventeenth century. *David Muggeridge Collection*

shown in 1771, which forms part of the property now known as *Tower House*. This has a ground floor of rough coursed limestone rubble, with four storeys of brick above. The windmill stands in its entirety, and has a brick dentil course around the top, to which the crenellations have been undoubtedly added at a later date. By 1932 the windmills at Hatfield were no longer in operation.[15] The windmill at *Tower House* is used as a store, and is a Grade II listed monument.

Mention of Thorne brings to mind that here stood six windmills at one time, all shown as still standing on the 1853 Ordnance Survey map. The earliest documentary reference to a windmill is that given in a royal grant of King Charles I to Cornelius Vermuyden dated 1626/27, which mentions a windmill worth 15s 0d a year in rent, once owned by Edward Ferrers and Francis Philips, esquire.[16] In 1771, only four windmills are shown at Thorne on Thomas Jeffreys' map.

The town of Thorne developed along a low ridge of sand lying roughly north and south. The ridge, known as High Trod, is only about two miles in length and nowhere is more than thirty feet above mean sea level, yet its height in an otherwise flat expanse of landscape, was sufficient to encourage the

Figure 3. Hatfield Woodhouse, more correctly Moss Croft Lane, Hatfield, photographed 22 August 1934. Today, this windmill still survives in much the same condition as it did in 1934. *David Muggeridge Collection*

Figure 4. The superb surviving windmill at Hatfield, in the garden of Tower House, Moss Croft Lane. It is shown on Jeffreys' 1771 map, and is only one of six remaining windmills in the Doncaster MBC area. *The Author, 1997*

building of windmills. In 1629 a mill was erected at the top of Brooke Street, or Crust's Mill Road as it was called in the nineteenth century, and was known as Bellwood's Mill. It was a wooden post mill, the stones turned by four cloth sails. At a later date, the open space beneath the mill between the cross-trees which held it up, was enclosed to provide storage space. Unfortunately the sails of this windmill blew down at an unknown date last century and it fell into disuse causing it to be pulled down in 1913, just before the First World War.

Only one windmill remains standing, a brick tower mill on North Eastern Road (Figure 5). It is remembered today as Oate's Mill, after the last family to work it. It stands five stories in height, and had an ogee Dutch cap surmounted by a tall ball finial. The exterior was tar rendered, giving it a distinctive black appearance. The sails broke off about 1880, after which time, the windmill was powered by a steam engine.

Past Oate's Mill and just before the crossroads, stood Casson's Mill; then over the crossroads to the right stood Hemmingway's Mill. The fifth mill recorded was Oldfield's Mill which stood in Southfield Road, not far from the top of Oldfield Road. The final mill was called Far Post Mill and stood just to the south of Thorne North Railway station. By 1907, however, only two windmills are shown surviving.

The windmills, as most mills, often take their names from the miller families working them, and in common practice, often changed their names as the family died out or left the mill and it changed ownership. In 1822 William Baines's *Directory* lists the following corn millers and flour dealers in Thorne: Abraham Bradbury; Curtis Casson; Timothy Harrison; James Moore; John Oldfield; Samuel Sails. Rather aptly, one of the few named inns in Baines's *Directory* for Thorne, was the *Wind Mill*, run by George Hoyland, victualler.

During the sixteenth century the number of windmills increased considerably, and there are frequent references to them in a number of places and in numerous documents, particularly the Fleets of Fines, which provide a wealth of data on property transactions. At Adwick-le-Street in 1564/65, the 'third part of a messuage and a windmill with lands' was owned by William Wilson and Anne, his wife.[17] This may have been the successor to one recorded earlier, but without date, when a document mentions 'Ralph Haket gave two oxgangs of land . . . and

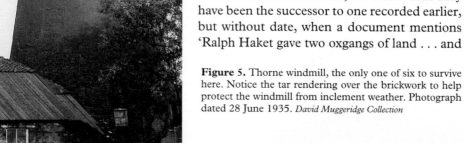

Figure 5. Thorne windmill, the only one of six to survive here. Notice the tar rendering over the brickwork to help protect the windmill from inclement weather. Photograph dated 28 June 1935. *David Muggeridge Collection*

the moiety [share] of the mill, together with Ralph, the miller . . . and all their families and cattle to the said priory' [Monk Bretton].[18] On the six inch to one mile Ordnance Survey map, Windmill Balk is given as a place-name at Adwick-le-Street, and in 1907, Windmill Balk Lane was still in existence.

In Stainforth in 1579 there were two windmills with lands in the joint ownership of Henry Darcy, knight, and several members of the Darcy family.[19] A windmill with appurtenances, at Stainforth was granted by letters patent by King James I on 29 April 1611/12, to Felix Wilson and Robert Morgan, of London, gentlemen, 'there heirs and assigns for ever, under the annual rent of 13s 4d.'[20] This windmill was mentioned again in a document of property grant from King Charles I to Cornelius Vermuyden, dated 24 May 1626/27.[21] In 1771, a single windmill was shown on Jeffreys' Yorkshire map, just south of the village. No doubt this was the windmill which survived into this century standing beside the Doncaster Road. This was a wooden post mill with four sweeps, as sails were often called. These were not cloth sails, but consisted of wooden louvres or shutters, a method of sail construction patented in the late eighteenth century. This windmill at Stainforth stood on a particularly high post supported by four open cross-trees. On Greenwood's map of 1817, a single windmill is shown south of Stainforth and marked Sandhole.

The moity of a windmill for grain at Armthorpe was owned by Jervas Wyrrall, gentleman, and Francis Holme, gentleman, in 1586.[22] In 1591, a windmill with lands in Stainton, was in the possession of Ralph Bowes, esquire, and Johanna, his wife.[23] At Askern, a windmill stood in 1580, owned by Cottonius Gargrave, esquire.[24] It was last mentioned as 'ruinous' in 1958.[25]

During the seventeenth century several windmills were recorded in the Doncaster area. In 1604 there was a windmill with lands at Brodsworth, in the ownership of George Holgate, gentleman, and Mary, his wife,[26] and a year later one is recorded at Barnby Dun.[27] At Bessacarr, William Chauntrell, esquire, and Dorothy, his wife owned a windmill in 1608,[28] and in the same year, Hugh Wirrall, knight, and his wife Elizabeth, owned a windmill at Loversall.[29] In 1610 a windmill at Campsall was owned by George St Poll, knight, and Frances, his wife.[30] This was no doubt the same one recorded in the year 1621.[31]

In the following century, a number of windmills were shown on Jefferys' map of Yorkshire, published on 25 March 1771 (Figure 6). Among the examples featured in this area was one at Fishlake, shown west of the village. Interestingly, by 1932, two windmills existed here

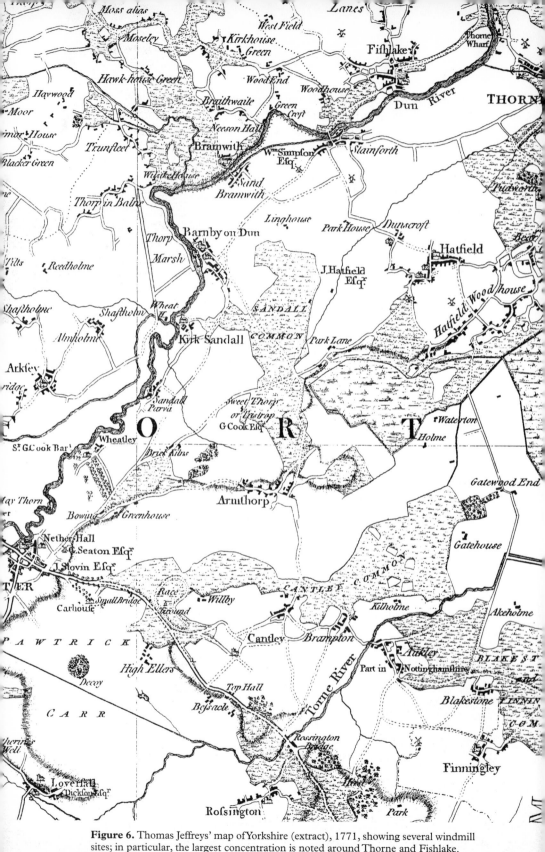

Figure 6. Thomas Jeffreys' map of Yorkshire (extract), 1771, showing several windmill sites; in particular, the largest concentration is noted around Thorne and Fishlake.

(Figures 7, 8 & 9), both painted by Karl Wood, who captured in paintings over several hundred windmills throughout England. The windmills at Fishlake were shown derelict and named Nabb's Mill and North Mill.[32] A windmill was shown at Frickley, sited toward Hooton Pagnell, and there was a windmill shown at Branton, south south-west of the village, while a windmill was shown west of Finningley. On Greenwood's map of Yorkshire, published 4 June 1817, a windmill is marked at Trumfleet, north north-west of the village on the road to Askern, and a windmill is shown north north-west of Fishlake toward Sykehouse.

Figure 7. Fishlake windmill, photographed 22 August 1934. *David Muggeridge Collection*

The achievements of Karl Wood, who was born in Nottingham in 1888, and who later moved to Gainsborough, where he became an art master at the Grammar School there, provide us with details of several windmills in the twentieth century. He painted in total 1,394 windmill pictures, and no less than 139 in Yorkshire.[33] The majority of these were produced during the 1930s, and among those he recorded was one at Conisbrough, which was a tower mill, stood derelict in 1932, another at Sykehouse, which at that date was a full working tower mill, and he painted a windmill at Norton (Figure 10), ruinous in 1932. Today, a mill still survives at Norton (Figure 11),

Figure 8. A second windmill at Fishlake, also photographed 22 August 1934. *David Muggeridge Collection*

Figure 9. Fishlake windmill today. *Brian Elliott*

Figure 10. This photograph of the remains of the windmill at Norton was taken on 2 August 1934 *David Muggeridge Collection*

restored outwardly to a semblance of its original glory. Standing six storeys in height, it is built of brick and rendered, and has an ogee-shaped cap. The rendering of a windmill with either tar or cement was necessary to provide a weather-proof exterior as a majority of windmills were, of course, erected in open elevated and thus exposed positions, and took the full brunt of inclement weather, as a consequence, both stone, and especially brick needed to be further protected.

Other windmills which survive to this day are examples at Branton; one at Fishlake, two at Hatfield; Moss; and one at Thorne, all shown on the current Ordnance Survey Landranger map. Many of these, however, have been converted to residential or other uses.

Finally, concerning the windmills of Doncaster. Here, water-powered mills were more prevalent in the medieval period, and the Corporation records provide a great many details as to their whereabouts and history. Owned by the Burgesses of Doncaster, only one windmill is mentioned at an early date, and this, in a dispute between the town and Wheatley, dated c1322, where it was given as forming the bounds between the two, stated, 'the manor of Wheatley . . . by the Oak Bush, and so by Fulsham Hill, and to the Windmill, and so over the Heades to Hobcross Hill'.[34] In 1546, 'three roods of land near the wynd mylnes' were recorded in their sale to William Faram, and two years later, in 1548, a windmill with lands in Doncaster was owned by Wilfred Pygborne and Isabel, his wife.[35]

All these references may relate to the windmill mentioned in the writings of William Sheardown, when he records the testimony of John White, of Cantley husbandman, of three score years, or thereabouts, called to give evidence in a land dispute. White recalls:

> . . . *From a footsty or path leading a little from the windmill in Wheatley, at the Bull Dole Ends, and which footway goes at the west end of Long Newton, and so by the close end sometime John Pigburn's, and then William West's, Esq., and from*

Figure 11. Today the Norton windmill, a listed building, is outwardly restored to its former glory. *The Author*

thence to Hobcross-hil[36], and so down the Hades between Carhouse Fields and the Brecks, within the lordship of Wheatley, which he knew to be true because all his land for which he did service to Wheatley did lie in the Brecks . . .[37]

Sheardown suggests that Bull Dole Ends was probably a piece of land originally set apart for the maintenance of a bull. In 1637, 'three roods lying in a close called the Bull Butts, alias Shorthreade, near the windmill' were conveyed by Rd. Carlill to Margery Pigott and Edward Sheppard, son of Margery, and Edward Shepherd, son of the said Edward. Mentioned again in the same year, as Bull Butts, alias Short Heades, near the Sandpit Windmill, in the territories of Doncaster or Wheatley. In 1640, Edward Sheppard, the elder, gave, by deed, to his son Edward an inn, called *The Bull*, in French Gate, wherein Margery Pigott and said Edward Sheppard did dwell.[38] It is probable that the 'three roods near the windmills' in 1546 are the same mentioned in 1637, and relate to the windmill recorded around 1322, and that John Pigburn was possibly a relation of Wilfred Pyborne.

In 1617, a windmill was mentioned at Doncaster in the ownership of John Robinson and Anne, his wife.[39] In the following century, the Corporation Rolls of 1712, record Joseph Hall of Fishlake, paying rent of £110 'for a farm rent for the water corn mills, wind Mill, Chapell and Chapel Gate and Salmon Hecks'.[40] These were owned by the Burgesses of Doncaster. In 1771, Jeffreys' map (Figure 4) shows a windmill east of Nether Hall.

A Windmill Close was mentioned in Doncaster in 1717, in relation to almshouses which were erected upon what was then waste ground, but which later formed part of a sale dated 4 September 1717, between George Gibson, of Doncaster, gentleman, and Dorothy Errat, of York, spinster, 'All that, &c. two closes, known as Hall Cross Close and Windmill Close',[41] again mentioned in 1718 and last recorded in 1720.

The almshouses consisted of three cottages, and stood in Hall Cross Close, on the Thorne road, nearly opposite to what was called the sand-pits (at the west of Christchurch church yard). Today, some of the lands of Hall Cross Close lie under part of Regent's Square.

The parcel of land comprising of Windmill Close and Hall Cross Close adjoined Doncaster Town Field on which one of two nineteenth century windmills stood. James Bennett had the Town Field windmill in 1822.[42] The other windmill at that date stood on Balby Road, and was in the operation of Ann Hopkinson.[43]

Lastly, there was a windmill at Cantley, the stump of which adjacent to a tall chimney, can be seen as you drive over the M18 into

Figure 12. Cantley windmill with its familiar chimney adjoining, dated 1849. Photographed 2 July 1961. *David Muggeridge Collection*

Figure 13. The Cantley windmill today remains an impressive landscape feature. *Brian Elliott*

Branton from Cantley (Figures 12 & 13). This windmill is associated with Mill Farm. The age of the windmill is not known precisely, but it appears on Greenwood's map of 1817 and carries a datestone inscribed 'WC 1820', however, this has been inserted into an existing opening, so may commemorate some refurbishment or change of ownership. The millers at this time were James Brock in 1813 and Thomas Hill a year later, still listed in William White's *Directory* of 1837 as a corn miller at Cantley.

The tower windmill, like the one surviving at Hatfield on Moss Croft Lane, is built of brick on a Magnesian Limestone base. The stump stands five storeys, and measures forty-six and a half feet high, approximately twenty-three feet across at the base internally, tapering to eleven feet across at the top. The brickwork is fourteen inches throughout. Several of the window openings have sandstone dressings and cills. At first-floor level there is a fireplace with a flue running up the inside wall. On top of the mill is a cast-iron curb of eight joined segments, each with nineteen integral teeth forming the gear circle for the cap to move on.

It was necessary for the cap to turn, in order to position the sails, which were fitted to the cap, into the wind. With tower windmills being static, this was the only means of doing so, and on the rear was often a fantail sail, which automatically carried out this manoeuvre as the wind changed direction. In post mills, the whole body of the windmill was turned physically by hand into the wind by the miller.

Inside Cantley windmill, remains of the milling gear (in 1993) consisted of some bearings and supports, one pair of French burr mill-stones with stone spindle and iron bridging and the sack hoist drum. In about 1845, the mill appeared to have been converted to steam, and the engine drive entered the windmill on the east side through a wall box, which still survives, and which carried the shaft bearing. While the windmill was powered by steam from the mid-nineteenth century, it is said the sails were not actually removed until they were blown off in a gale of wind about 1908.[44]

It is thought that the windmill was originally worked with three pairs of stones on the second floor, and that the surviving pair of stones on the first floor, were probably steam-driven.[45] The chimney, bearing a datestone 'WC 1845', is all that remains of the steam engine and boiler house which stood between the windmill and the chimney to the east of the mill house.

It is supposed that the initials 'WC', which can also be found on a barn in Chapel Lane, Branton, inscribed 'WC 1814', refer to William Carr, esquire, who owned the mill and barn in 1849,[46] and was recorded as having ownership on Land Tax returns of 1808 and 1834 of three parcels of land, one being occupied by Thomas Hill.[47] Later millers of Cantley have been Aaron Shaw, c1850; Francis Lynas c1861–71 and John Holmes, from about 1878 until 1923. The wind-mill finally ceased around 1927, when most of the machinery was removed.

The location of windmills referred to in the text are marked on the map, shown as Figure 14.

Notes and References

1. Yorkshire Archaeological Society, *Records of the Knights Templars*, p. 131.
2. *Monasticon Anglium*, vi, 831,*b*.
3. Brown W (ed) Yorkshire Archaeological Society Record Series (YASRS), *Yorkshire Inquisitions*, 1892.
4. Hunter J *South Yorkshire*, Vol I, 1828.
5. *The Dalesman*, Vol 22, 1962, p. 305.
6. Ruston A G & Witney D *Hooton Pagnell: The Agricultural Evolution of a Yorkshire Village*, 1934.
7. *Ibid.*
8. Chaucer G *Canterbury Tales* (The Miller's Tale), c1378.
9. Baildon W P (ed), YASRS, vol 29, 1901, *Court Rolls of the Manor of Wakefield*, Vol 1, p. 129.
10. *Hull News*, 26 June 1909.
11. Hunter, *op cit*, gives the figure £8 but I feel that this must be an error on his part, as in my research I have found no windmill rent at that period ever totalling more than one or two pounds.
12. *Ibid.*

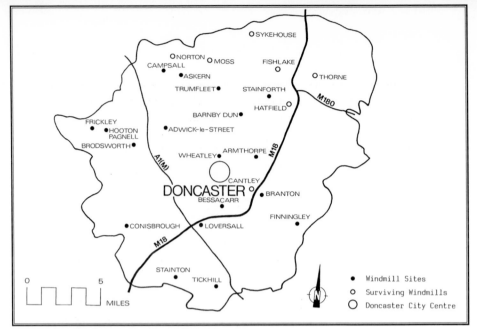

Corn Windmills mentioned in the text.

13. Tomlinson J *The Levels of Hatfield Chase*, 1882.
14. West Yorkshire Metropolitan Council, *West Yorkshire: An Archaeological Survey to AD1500*, vol. 3, 1981.
15. Wilson C *A Checklist of Windmill Paintings by Karl Wood*, 1982, Lincolnshire Museums Occasional Papers No. 1.
16. Tomlinson, *op cit.*
17. YASRS, Vol. II, 1887, *Fleet of Fines, Tudor Period*, Pt. 1.
18. Burton J *Monasticon Eboracense* (Ecclesiastical History of Yorkshire), 1758, p.92.
19. YASRS, Vol. V, 1888, *Fleet of Fines, Tudor Period*, Pt. 2.
20. Tomlinson, *op cit.*
21. *Ibid.*
22. YASRS, Vol. VII, 1889, *Fleet of Fines, Tudor Period*, Pt. 2.
23. *Ibid.*
24. YASRS, Vol. V, 1888, *Fleet of Fines, Tudor Period*, Pt. 2.
25. *The Dalesman*, vol. 20, no. 4, July, 1958.
26. YASRS, Vol LIII, 1915, *Yorkshire Fines, Stuart Period*, Pt 1.
27. *Ibid.*
28. *Ibid.*
29. *Ibid.*
30. *Ibid.*
31. YASRS, Vol. LVIII, 1917, *Yorkshire Fines, Stuart Period*, Pt 2.
32. Wilson, *op cit*
33. *Ibid.*
34. Tomlinson J *Doncaster from the Roman Occupation to the Present Time*, 1887.
35. YASRS, Vol II, 1887, *Fleet of Fines, Tudor Period*, Pt 1.
36. Sheardown W 'Collection of Pamphlets', Vol. 3 (Doncaster Local Studies Library).
37. *Ibid.*
38. *Ibid.*
39. YASRS, Vol. LVIII, 1917, *Yorkshire Fines, Stuart Period*, Pt. 1.
40. Tomlinson, *op cit.*
41. Sheardown (Pamphlets).
42. Baines W *History, Directory and Gazeteer of the County of York, West Riding*, Vol 1, 1822.
43. *Ibid.*
44. *Yesterday Today*, 10 April 1993.
45. *Bessacarr and Cantley Times*, 13, September 1991.
46. 'A Childers Family Estate Map', Baxter Papers, Sheffield Archives.
47. *Yesterday Today*, 10 April 1993.

14. A BENTLEY CHILDHOOD REMEMBERED

by Doris Kitching

I WAS BORN IN THE MINING VILLAGE of Bentley, near Doncaster, in 1920. In the evening of my life I find myself remembering with affection my childhood years which were carefree, serene and happy. I was an only child, well-fed and clothed. My father, Thomas Hopkinson, was a miner. He married Lily Robinson at St Peter's Church, Bentley in 1919. When I was about six months old the family moved from a terraced house in New Street to a large and airy council house, 35 Daw Lane, not far from the pit, where I spent my childhood.

My grandfathers and uncles were also miners. Granddad Joe Robinson, for example, started at Bullcroft Colliery at the age of

Figure 1. Mum (Lily), Dad (Thomas) and myself, aged nine, outside our house, 34 Daw Lane, Bentley.

Figure 2. Early days in New Street, Bentley. Grandma is in the centre, standing, Granddad is the second figure to her left (capless). Dad has his arm around Mum.

Figure 3. Four generations are present in this family group, the most senior being the seated lady, mother of Joe Robinson, my grandfather. The standing figure is Joe Robinson junior, and the boy is Dennis, son of the younger Joe.

Figure 4. Granddad Joe, with his daughter, Lily – and 'Pat' the greyhound!

Figure 5. An informal photograph taken after the wedding of my parents in their back yard, New Street. Thomas and Lily who are shown seated, linking arms at the centre of the group. The small figure of Grandma can be seen standing behind the bride and groom, with granddad to her left. The photographer would have required a lot of patience to capture this scene. Notice how the toddlers have been arranged on a rug on the ground.

twelve and worked until he was seventy years old. Work below ground was very hard, picking and hacking at the coal face stripped to the waist and often in water. Family photographs (Figure 1–5) are fond reminders of my childhood and background; and a recent visit to my former Daw Lane home, after a sixty year gap, was a most welcome though emotional experience (Figure 6).

Dad was an excellent pianist and for a while he played in local clubs

Figure 6. Myself outside of 34 Daw Lane, April 1997, over sixty years after I lived there. *Brian Elliott*

Figure 7. Mum, Dad, myself (in front of Mum) and a relative on Cleethorpes beach during a 'club' outing.

on Saturday and Sunday evenings to earn a little extra. He formed a Quartet and every Sunday afternoon they would gather in our large front room to practise. They played for dances and wedding receptions and became very popular.

Holidays in those days were definitely a rarity, and in many families unheard of. The highlight of the year was a day at the seaside, travelling by train (Figure 7). These outings were arranged by the Working Men's Club where my father was a member. As the time approached for the outing my friends and I became very excited, especially the night before when Mum insisted that I went to bed early. Dad would go along to the club to pick up the tickets and draw out the savings which had been building up over several months, and each child received some spending money. I always had new white plimsolls to wear that day. On the journey we would eat some sandwiches, then have a sing-song and keep asking our parents, 'Will we soon be there?'

I loved the long summer evenings when neighbours would gather together in the street to laugh and chat and exchange views with each other, whilst we children played marbles or got out our skipping ropes. We never wanted to go to bed, enjoying the long, light nights and balmy evenings of peace and contentment. I looked forward to school summer holidays in fact I could hardly contain myself. Friends and I would go to the local park to enjoy the swings and see-saw and paddle in the pool. We would watch the tennis players, then attempt a game ourselves, laughing at our feeble efforts.

The beginning of September was the time of the St Leger race meeting, always a memorable week. Many visitors came to town to enjoy the races and all the entertainment. We looked forward to this special time for weeks, Mum always making a batch of fruit cakes in case anyone visiting the town would call in to see us. I found this very exciting and never wanted the week to end. Quite a few of our neighbours prepared for visitors from the North and each year it was lovely to greet them again. On the Sunday afternoon prior to the races starting Mum and Dad used to take me into town and we would walk to the race course, stopping to see the various entertainers on the way: buskers, tipsters, pavement artists, escapologists and the Teale family selling their home-made humbugs. Dad always bought some, then further along a voice would shout 'Parkinson's Butterscotch 5d and 10d a packet'. Visitors to the town usually took some home as a gift for family and friends. On our arrival at Town Moor my excitement grew when I saw the massive fair; there were all sorts of rides, at a penny a go, gaily coloured swing boats, side shows, boxing booths, wrestling, flying chairs and coconut shies – the noise and laughter, music and the happy feeling all added to the magic of the occasion. I remember hot peas cooking in a large cauldron with mint sauce to which you helped yourself. I also vividly remember going home, carried on Dad's shoulders, feeling tired but very happy.

When I was six years old there was the General Strike. Mum talked about the very bleak time everyone had. There were no trains or buses and no pits or factories working. Men hung around street corners feeling desperate. Soup kitchens were set up in schools in villages all around. Dad was one of the helpers, and at lunchtimes people queued with containers to receive a rather small ration of rather watery vegetable soup. Many people resorted to coal-picking from the pit tip. All sorts of improvised containers were used: prams, sacks carried on push-bikes, barrows in fact anything and everything was used to transport the precious commodity home. Dad would mix water with coal debris and make blocks to burn in the grate. It was all worthwhile as it kept us warm. Sometimes, scouring the pit heap, large bright pieces of 'black diamonds' would be found and were a real bonus. Mum told me that they also received a small food voucher for bare essentials. Often two people would unexpectedly turn up on the doorstop and, if they suspected that you were cooking something special, would ask where the money came from. Mum got wise and would cook a late meal when she thought they had finished visiting. Mum and Dad had a few savings which they used for extras. Dad earned a little extra with his piano playing.

When visiting the pantomime I was so excited when I looked onto the stage. How I wished I was there dancing and performing. For weeks afterwards I lived in a fantasy world of make believe. I even stuffed some shoes at the toes thinking I would be able to toe dance, like the girls on the stage. I practised for weeks much to my friends amusement, then gave it up as a bad job.

The excitement of Christmas overwhelmed me. One of my mother's stockings hung by my bed and on Christmas morning it was bulging with goodies. I remember pea and pie suppers in the Co-operative Hall at Bentley organised by the Labour Party Ladies' Committee of which my Mum and Grandma were members. They always worked very hard making pies, along with the other workers and members. After supper Dad's band played for dancing. I was always there with them so was able to learn ballroom dancing at an early age. When I was about thirteen I used to go to the Victoria Rooms in St Sepulchre Gate to learn to perfect the dancing.

On Sunday I had to go to chapel twice. Sometimes I wished that I could be out playing with my friends instead but by 10 a.m. I would be in my best dress and patent leather ankle strap shoes and off to morning service. On arriving home an hour later I had to change my dress and shoes, then I would change back into them again in the afternoon, and, with my collection money in my hand, would return to Sunday School. I loved the Sunday School anniversary time. I always had a new dress and straw hat. The chapel would be packed with parents and grandparents and I always recited a poem, and can remember feeling very nervous as we climbed on to the platform to take our places. I would look into the congregation for my family. Before leaving home Mum would ask at some stage if I knew my poem and when I answered 'Yes' Mum would say don't forget to speak up.

When I got a little older I had to learn how to do housework and do it properly. On Saturday mornings I would have to clean all the downstairs windows and later, if the job was done well, was allowed threepence to go to the matinee at The Coliseum Cinema, twopence to go in and a penny for sweets. It was very noisy and often the film would break down. When this happened we would all shout and then cheer when the film came on again. I looked forward to the matinee, a serial would be on as well and it always finished at an exciting time, to be continued next week. Mum told me each Saturday that if I didn't clean the windows there would be no cinema – it was as simple as that.

Tuesday was washing day. Before I went to school Mum had got the copper filled with plenty of water. The copper was located in the corner of the kitchen when the house was built. Washing was a long and tedious job. Underneath the copper was a small place with a door to close. A fire would be started to heat the water. This would be used to boil white clothes, sheets and towels. Mum was very particular about her washing. When I arrived home from lunchtime I would have a bowl of home-made stew. This was an easy meal for wash day because when Mum had put in the meat and vegetables she could leave it to cook whilst she got on with her work. I know that when I came home about four o'clock my job then would be to clean the kitchen, scrub the floor, empty the copper, scrub the copper lid, sink and draining board before we could sit down for our tea. That was the way of life in those days.

My mother was strict and she loved me very much and my home life was happy and comfortable. My friends thought I was a lucky girl. Some were not so fortunate. I remember one family home where they had no floor covering at all, but their Mum used to scrub the bare boards and then would lay newspapers down to keep the floorboards clean. There were only a small variety of floor coverings, either linoleum or a cheaper kind called oil cloth. A flowered pattern made a room bright and cheery looking; and people made their own pegged rugs, made with odds and ends of cloth of various colours about two inch in length, pushed through hessian with a hook-like tool. They looked quite cheerful when finished, the brighter the colours the better the appearance. Rugs would be laid in front of the hearth, and with the big black shiny range, looked quite majestic.

The range needed cleaning every week to keep it black and shiny. Mum did this task every Saturday morning. A black substance ('Zebra') was mixed with water and put onto the stove with a cloth, then brushed with a soft brush to make it shine. Then she used a silver polish to enrich the metal facings on the oven door. With this job completed, the baking from the previous day stacked away in containers: coconut tarts, apple pies, scones, bakewell tarts, egg custard.

My Dad was a great fellow and I loved him dearly. I was the apple of his eye. He was a St John's Ambulance man and, as can be seen

Figure 8. Dad, Thomas Hopkinson, looking smart in his St John's uniform.

from his photograph (Figure 8) was proud to wear his uniform. If there were any minor accidents in our street Dad was sought after to render first aid and he also gave a talk many times at ambulance classes. He carried a first aid box in the mine when he was on his shift in case of emergency and was affectionately known as Tommy the Ambulance Man.

A skating rink opened in Bentley and Dad and his friends took me along with them to teach me to roller skate. We went in style, by motor bike and side car; I thought this was great as a young child, but the novelty soon wore off, and Dad decided he hadn't really got time for it. He had his band and first aid classes to attend, and was also studying for his Deputy papers, which meant, if he passed his exams, promotion. As he was progressing well in his studies, life continued in a happy and comfortable way.

When I was ten years old my maternal Grandma and Granddad, Martha and Joseph, both of whom I loved dearly, gave up their house and came to live with us. They had their own sitting room and bedroom, but we all ate together. Grandma, like Mum, was an excellent cook and her special dessert was bread and butter pudding. Over the many years I have made it, somehow it never tastes the same, although I follow exactly the same recipe.

I was so happy when they came to live with us. Grandma was a small rounded lady, very old fashioned and she made her own dresses, which were very plain like a shift, nearly always black. The only jewellery was her wedding ring and some black beads. Granddad was good fun; all my school chums loved him and he made us laugh with the stories that he told. We used to go for walks and pick wild flowers which Granddad would make into a posy blending in the different colours. On the way home he would pick watercress from the stream. He worked in the mine from the age of twelve until he was seventy, often in very bad conditions. Grandma would make pads to put on his knees because this is how he sometimes had to spend his whole shift. Sunday morning he would dress in his best pin stripe suit and Homburg hat, flower in the lapel, watch and chain across his waistcoat and walking stick completing his outfit, he looked like the Lord of the Manor (Figure 9).

I remember street vendors shouting their wares. One particular memory is of a man pushing a barrow containing vegetables – lettuce, onions, cress, potatoes and others, which he had grown himself; also the milkman coming to the door with a large container. My mother would hold out a large jug and then the man would ladle the milk into it. I thought how heavy this container looked as he went from door to door. On his dray he had a milk churn from which he refilled this container.

When I was aged eight or nine Dad bought a radio. This was something very new; it was an achievement for us. We were the first in our street to own a wireless and people would gather round our garden gate to listen to the music and hear the news. Dad was so proud he would beam and would open the windows so the neighbours could hear the radio better. On one wall in our big room we had a wind-up gramophone. Dad's earnings from piano playing and also photography helped. He was often asked to take pictures for weddings, of babies and so on. He had a large plate camera on a heavy tripod and used to place a black cloth over his head when he was looking through the viewfinder. His photographs always seemed to turn out well. He did his own processing so was a busy and active person.

I always had a birthday party with a gathering of my friends, the table groaning with goodies. What made one party special was when we had the wireless switched on. Mum had sent a request to the *Children's Hour* to have my name read out. After sitting quietly for what seemed a long time my name was broadcast and everyone cheered, then we enjoyed our tea.

At the age of twelve the popular venue for me was tuning at 5.15 pm everyday to listen to Henry Hall and his band. I even sent for his autograph which duly arrived, written on a sheet of music. Another favourite band leader was Jack Payne. I loved going to the cinema and had many favourites to which I also used to write for their autographs including Warner Baxter, John Wayne, Clark Gable and George Brent.

In the school holidays my parents and I, and two neighbours plus their children would plan a picnic outing to Hexthorpe Flatts (Figure 10). We would be very excited as we watched our parents prepare the sandwiches, off we would go, all happy and excited. We would go by tram from Bentley and then walk beside the River Don towards Hexthorpe singing. When we were almost there the man with a rowing boat would take us across to the other side of the river, filling his boat with as many people as possible and charging a penny each. On alighting, it was just a short

Figure 9. Granddad looking smart on a visit to the seaside.

Figure 10. Rowing boats on the Don at Hexthorpe. *Norman Kitching*

walk and we were at the Flatts ready to enjoy a few hours. We returned home the same way, tired and ready for bed; simple pleasures in those days, giving contentment. On Friday evening, after tea, Mum and Grandma would go to the High Street to do the weekly shop. Sometimes I would go, or perhaps I would decide to stay behind with Dad and Granddad. If Dad was on his afternoon shift (2–10pm) I stayed with Granddad.

On Sunday nights in winter Dad was out playing the piano at the Club. Mum, myself and two or three school friends would sit round our large table and we would play board games; then I would have to prepare for school the next morning. In summer crowds of people would gather around the bandstand in Bentley park to listen to the visiting brass band rendering many favourites old and new, a terrific atmosphere for all ages. Many of the older generation would gossip whilst us children would make a bee line for the swings and slide, not wanting the evening to end. Open air dancing was also featured in Bentley park for a time. It took place on the hard tennis court and coloured fairy lights were placed all the way round the entrance. The entrance fee was sixpence but many people who couldn't dance watched from outside the enclosure. Mum and Dad attended and took me along, often with Eunice, one of my school friends. We would show off rather a lot.

The date 20 November 1931, when I was eleven years old, is a time I will never forget. Dad was at work on his afternoon shift, Granddad and I were playing Ludo, and Mum and Grandma were out shopping. Suddenly Granddad looked up and listened, there was the sound of pit boots on the road, I think it was about 6.30 pm. Granddad thought this was unusual so he went out to investigate and was shocked to learn that there had been an explosion at the pit. He left me with a neighbour and went to the pit yard to see what he could find out. Of course by this time the street was filled with fearful people who were anxious to gain news of loved ones or friends. Mum and Grandma rushed back home after hearing the news whilst shopping. Mum went immediately to the pit head. As the men were brought out injured or dead, Mum scanned each one anxiously, each name chalked up on a board. Dad was the last to be brought out, badly hurt. He had insisted on staying behind to give first aid and assistance to the injured. He was taken to hospital and Mum, Grandma and Mum's brother, Joe, went to be at his side. The sight that met them was horrific; Dad just managed to say a few words, he asked after me and died a few hours later.

The whole village was in mourning, all the coffins were placed side by side in St Philip's Church and most were buried together in Arksey Cemetery where a memorial now stands (Figures 11–15). Forty-five men and boys lost their lives on that dreadful day.

After the disaster the whole village was in mourning. Our household bore such grief and sadness and I was bewildered by it all. In early January 1932 we attended a large gathering of people at Bentley Pavilion for my mother to receive an Order of Industrial Heroism medal and certificate to honour Dad's memory and bravery; along with other presentations. Mum cherished them in her lifetime and they remain as treasured mementoes of my dear father's courage and honour (Figures 16–18).

Looking back, before Dad died, my school friend Evelyn would stand by me besides our piano when he played and we used to sing. One of our favourites was *Wedding of the Painted Doll* and another popular tune was *Carolina Moon*. I used to giggle when Dad said 'When I die I am going to be the man in the moon, so that I can look down on you, so you had better be good'. I cried a lot when he died but when I went to bed I looked through the window at the moon and felt happy because I thought I saw Dad's face and it made me feel safe and happy.

Conditions slowly got back to normality, though many miners who survived the disaster never worked underground again, it shocked them so much. The piano stood still and silent in our front room, there was no band practise, no laughter, no singing. I tried to have piano lessons again but wasn't very successful. We decided to keep the piano because Mum liked to try and play a little and, with her fingers on the keys, she felt close to Dad.

I decided, at the age of twelve, to join the St John's Ambulance Cadets. I felt so proud when I first wore the uniform and imagined Dad was smiling at me. There was a weekly meeting every Thursday evening in a room off French Gate, Doncaster, facing the old Guild Hall. I made some new friends and enjoyed learning First Aid and Home Nursing. I passed exams and at the age of fifteen did voluntary

Figure 11. St Phillip's Church, Bentley where the coffins were placed before burial at Arksey.

Figure 12. Burial of the Victims of the Bentley Colliery Disaster, at Arksey cemetery, 25 November 1931.

Figure 14. The Bentley Colliery Disaster Memorial and graves, after burial.

Figure 13. A mass of floral tributes at Arksey Cemetery.

work at the hospital for a few hours each week. Life took a new pattern and we were happy again.

About the time I started work in a clothing shop in Wood Street the river Don began to rise rapidly and the banks collapsed, water pouring down Hunt Lane like a raging torrent near where the Don Cinema was situated. Householders had been warned and carried their downstairs furniture upstairs and found accommodation elsewhere. The flood water poured into Arksey over the back fields, then to our home in Daw Lane, near Victoria Road church. We were also warned that our homes might be flooded. Thinking to save the piano which was too heavy to carry upstairs, we felt that the only

Figure 15. Myself at the Bentley Colliery Disaster Memorial in April, 1997. The memorial also commemorates a more recent tragedy when seven Bentley miners were killed in 1978. *B Elliott*

solution would be to put it on the table, laid on its back. Many hands volunteered to help with this task. The piano stayed in this position for a month. We returned home after the flood water subsided. The

filth and smell was terrible. The council supplied each home with a strong disinfectant. All the downstairs rooms had to be stripped of wallpaper and left in a bare state till such time as the walls were dry enough to re-paper again.

My mother eventually married Herbert Wright, whom she had known years earlier but had returned to Bentley after living in Australia. They were to be married for forty five years and both lived to the age of eighty six. About the same time Mum bought a small grocery shop for me to run when I left school at fourteen, so we moved from our council house of so many lovely memories and from friendly neighbours to the shop with living quarters behind, about two miles

Figure 16. Order of Industrial Heroism Medal, awarded by the *Daily Herald* 'to the widow of Thomas Hopkinson'. *B Elliott*

ORDER *of* INDUSTRIAL HEROISM

INSTITUTED BY
The Daily Herald
Presented as a mark of
respect and admiration
to T. HOPKINSON.
a brave man who in a
moment of peril thought
more of others than of
himself

date 3ʳᵈ Janʸ 1932.

Figure 17. Certificate to 'a brave man who in a moment of peril thought more of others than of himself. *B. Elliott*

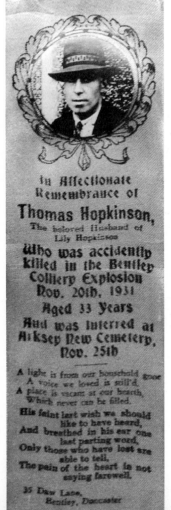

In Affectionate
Remembrance of

Thomas Hopkinson,
The beloved Husband of
Lily Hopkinson

Who was accidently
killed in the Bentley
Colliery Explosion
Nov. 20th, 1931

Aged 33 Years

And was interred at
Arksey New Cemetery,
Nov. 25th

A light is from our household gone
A voice we loved is still'd,
A place is vacant in our hearth,
Which never can be filled.

His faint last wish we should
like to have heard,
And breathed in his ear one
last parting word,
Only those who have lost are
able to tell,
The pain of the heart in not
saying farewell.

35 Daw Lane,
Bentley, Doncaster

away, at 39 Church Street (Figure 19).

I progressed in the St John's Ambulance Brigade and as a nursing sister wore a different uniform (Figure 20). After completing further training I received a medallion, presented at the annual dinner and dance at the *Danum Hotel*.

My best friend was called Dorothy and as teenagers on Sunday evenings during the summer we would go into town and stroll along French Gate, High Street and Hallgate looking in shop windows, meeting friends of both sexes, chatting, exchanging views and then calling at Rossi's Ice Cream Parlour in High Street. Because Dorothy did not like dancing I would go with a group to dance at Bullar's Victoria Rooms on Thursdays and Bentley Pavilion (Figure 21) on Saturdays.

I fondly remember Davys in French Gate, where British Home Stores is now located. It was a popular and tempting shop selling provisions, cooked meats of quality, bread, fresh cream cakes, and scones. On the second floor was a restaurant. Opposite was the Guild Hall and a few yards away was Leesings pork butchers.

Figure 18. *(Right)* Commemorative silk ribbon in remembrance of Thomas Hopkinson. *B Elliott*

Figure 19. Myself outside our old family shop (now Sarah-Louise Boutique) at 39 Church Street, April 1997. *B Elliott*

Moving onward to High Street was the Picture House. People would stand in a long queue on Saturday night to enjoy a film. Facing the cinema was Parkinson's, owned by the factory people who made the famous butterscotch and mouth-watering buttered brazils. Fresh cream cakes of excellent quality were also sold. In Silver Street stood the Palace Cinema which was also very popular. Next was the Ritz in Hallgate, then a very modern building (opened in April 1934) and above it an excellent ballroom. Further along Hallgate was the Majestic Cinema, later rebuilt and renamed the Gaumont (and became the Odeon in 1955). Hodgson and Hepworth's shop, situated in St Sepulchre Gate, was for many years a popular store selling high quality provisions: plump dried fruits, a good variety of wines and spirits and the aroma of fresh ground coffee always present, even when passing the entrance.

I also recall Station Road and Trafford Street, Priestnall's Cafe on the corner,

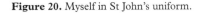

Figure 20. Myself in St John's uniform.

the Co-op buildings selling ladies and gents clothing, children's clothes and shoes; then the Emporium being built; this tall modern store, now the Danum, standing proud, replacing the old Co-op building that was to be demolished, and our lovely Victorian theatre whose future is now in doubt. We used to enjoy the variety shows presented there and the stars who appeared. Having a night out at The Grand was always exciting, especially for the pantomime.

There were many popular shops selling a variety of merchandise. Veritys and Blakes together in Baxter Gate selling clothing, replaced later by Owen & Owen, now Binns and Etam. Woolworths was next door and sold nothing over sixpence (2.5p). To us teenagers it was a very popular store supplying all our needs: stockings, underwear, records, song sheets, make-up, perfume (California Poppy or Evening in Paris), birthday cards; and on the second floor was a restaurant. On a Friday evening, 6 May 1938 a fire, which began in the cellar of Verity & Sons, spread to the Woolworth store causing terrible damage and putting many who worked there out of a job. The glow from the fire could be seen for miles and people flocked to town to view the situa-

Figure 21. Myself outside Bentley Pavilion, April 1997 *B Elliott*

tion. Sills Bazaar was in Baxter Gate, very interesting to walk in to view what was on show on each floor, a walk-in arcade type of shop, selling a variety of goods including sweets, chocolate, haberdashery, cleaning materials and household odds and ends. Bentley also had a Sills Bazaar and every Friday evening when Grandma was doing her weekend shopping she used to call in and buy sticks of licorice for Granddad to chew down the mine.

The grocery shops were also very memorable. The Meadow Dairy was pleasant and popular – as we stood at a long counter we would see a huge dome of butter on a marble slab, pieces cut to customers requirements, two wooden butter pats used to shape the butter. Next to it would be the lard and in front, occupying the whole length of the counter were biscuits of an assorted variety in containers with lift-up lids and we could have them mixed to our own choice. There were also dates, figs, prunes, canded peel, all giving out wonderful aroma and if you asked for a dozen eggs they would give you thirteen, many other shops doing the same. Gallons, Lipton, Melias, Thrift, all tempted us with simple but appetising goodies.

In contrast the corner shop was even more personal and friendly, making deliveries to your door if required, cheerful chatter over the counter gaining local news and exchanging views and ideas made shopping a pleasure not a chore.

When I was about seventeen years old Grandma and Granddad were offered a small new house, 76 The Homestead on Arksey Lane and they decided to take it. I was sad but helped them to pack. It was only a short distance away.

I saw an advertisement for a hairdressers in Hallgate called Segals. They were after models to demonstrate and advertise a new setting lotion the owner had invented called 'Self-Set'. I presented myself at the appointed time and a long queue had formed. The owner interviewed us all and chose three girls, including myself. It was all very exciting, he checked over our hair and with his lady partner arranged the three of us to go to the salon for a perm. The day duly arrived and we all looked smart in our best clothes. Photographers arrived and took pictures for publicity purposes and a few days later we travelled to Sheffield to a demonstration in front of a very large gathering of hairdressers, Mr Segal hoping to sell his product.

Mother decided to sell the now silent piano which hadn't been heard for years. She wrote to a relative at Balby who bought the piano and took it away. We both cried but were happy that it stayed in the family.

My best friend, Dorothy and I quite frequently took advantage of the Sunday afternoon trips to Scarborough or Bridlington by train from Arksey Crossing. The fare was two shillings and six pence (12.5p), leaving about 2.30 and returning around 8 pm. On one outing to Scarborough we went into a Woolworths store there and whilst wandering around noticed the new song sheet was on sale. We used to always buy them from our Doncaster store before it was burnt down by the massive fire. We stood together, turning over the pages, looking at the latest songs and suddenly realised we were singing at the top of our voices *September in the Rain*, getting curious glances from shoppers.

Grandma suffered a stroke in 1937 which took the use out of her left side. Mum spent each day caring for her while I ran the home and shop. Aunt Agnes and her daughter, Beatie, also helped with the nursing and Granddad cared for her during the night. We were saddened that our grandparents couldn't be at Beatie's wedding so after the reception we went to see them, dressed in our wedding clothes (myself as a bridesmaid). Grandma died peacefully, three weeks later.

1938 was a year of unrest and fear, because war seemed imminent. People were panic buying sugar, tea, coffee, tin foods, in fact anything that could be stored and saved. Neville Chamberlain, our prime minister went to Germany and for talks and when he arrived back he alighted from the plane waving a piece of paper: 'Peace in our time' he announced to the waiting media. It was a joyous feeling, making the country feel relieved and happy, wanting to get on with their lives in confidence. A short time after this episode unrest and fear returned when air raid shelters were being erected and the way of life seemed to change. People were asking many questions and not getting answers. There was conscription for young men having to join the forces for training, munition factories working at full speed and tank factories, but even through this apprehension there was an air of excitement and challenge; and a waiting; and more panic buying. Our shelves in the shop were looking bare and the wholesalers, although anxious to supply us, were finding it difficult to oblige. We took every-thing in our stride, thinking that war either wouldn't happen or if it started would soon be over.

Acknowledgements

Many thanks are due to Carol Hill at Doncaster Local Studies Library for encouraging me to write about my memories and for publishing extracts in *Yesterday Today*. Thanks also to Mr Smith for allowing Brian Elliott and myself to visit his home. This edited version is courtesy of Brian Elliott who has also provided modern photographs.

CONTRIBUTORS

1. FROM PACKHORSE TO MOTOR LORRY AND 7. THE EARLY HISTORY OF THE BRASS BAND MOVEMENT IN DONCASTER

Philip Lloyd Scowcroft, born in Sheffield in 1933, was educated at King Edward VII Grammar School, Sheffield and Trinity Hall Cambridge (M.A., LL.M. Cantab.). He was admitted as a solicitor of the Supreme Court in 1959 and from 1956 until his retirement in 1993 worked in local government in Doncaster. Philip was married in 1959 and has two grown-up daughters. He lectures widely on music, transport history, cricket, detective fiction, military history and the law and has written hundreds of articles and reviews on those subjects for fifty-seven different periodicals and for compendia like the *Oxford Companion of Railway History, Crime and Mystery Writing* and the *New Grove*. Philip has been music correspondent for various Doncaster newspapers since 1967. He is a Member of the Council and a director of the Railway & Canal Historical Society and Coordinator of its Rail Transport and Docks & Shipping Groups, Philip has also served as Chair of the Doncaster Arts and Museums Society since 1968, organising local arts festivals and concerts. Independent publications include *The Law and the Teacher* (Sheffield Hallam University), *Sidelights on Sayers* (Dorothy L Sayers Society), *British Light Music* (Thames Publishing) and many items on the local history of the Doncaster area.

2. THE DEMAULEYS: MEDIEVAL LORDS OF DONCASTER

Brian Sprakes was born in Doncaster in 1937. He studied European Architecture and Stained Glass & Heraldry as a mature student in Sheffield and has been a part-time lecturer for the WEA and University of Sheffield since 1973. He is author of several articles for art journals and learned societies. In 1987 he was appointed author for the international *Corpus Vitrearum Medii Aevi*, charged with the task of cataloguing medieval stained glass. South Yorkshire awaits publication, and work is in progress on Nottinghamshire. He is also Stained Glass advisor to the Diocese of Sheffield. An article, 'Medieval and Renaissance Stained Glass in the Vicinity of Barnsley' appeared in *Aspects of Barnsley 4* (1996).

3. AN ABBOT IN RETIREMENT

Tom W Beastall was born in Doncaster and brought up in Tickhill. After attending Maltby Grammar School and Manchester and London Universities he made the study of the Lumley archives a major leisure time interest. He published *A North Country Estate: the Lumleys and Sandersons as Landowners* in 1975 and *The Agricultural Revolution in Lincolnshire* in 1978. He contributed to the *Victorian Countryside*, volume 2 in 1981 and has edited publications on the history of Tickhill for the University of Sheffield. His latest book, *Tickhill: Portrait of an English Country Town* was published in 1995. A churchwarden at St Mary's Parish Church, Tickhill, he was deputy headmaster of Maltby Comprehensive School after teaching history at Chichester High School for Boys, West Sussex. Tom has also contributed articles for *Aspects of Rotherham.*

4. THE LANDED GENTRY OF THE DONCASTER DISTRICT

Brian Barber is the author of a number of articles on local government and archives, including contributions to histories of modern Leeds (1980) and Sheffield (1994), and to the Society of Archivists' *British Archival Practice* (1996). He is, with MW Beresford, the author of the official history of the West Riding County Council (1979) and wrote the guide to the records of the West Riding quarter sessions (1984), which he catalogued whilst employed as an archivist by the West Yorkshire Archive Service. Since 1984, he has worked at Doncaster Archives, where he is now Principal Archivist. In 1994, he persuaded four distinguished historians to write *Doncaster: A Borough and Its Charters* to celebrate the eight hundredth anniversary of the first Doncaster borough charter.

5. CHARLES SABINE AUGUSTUS THELLUSSON AND THE ITALIANATE BUILDINGS ON THE BRODSWORTH ESTATE

Peter Gordon Smith was born in Aberdeen, though he has lived in all quarters of England since. After reading Ancient & Medieval History at the University of Sheffield, and some time spent in working for the British Library in London, he returned to Yorkshire in 1990 when appointed by English Heritage to manage the herculean task of preparing to open Brodsworth Hall to the public. This was achieved in 1995 and now Peter's work involves him in the continuing development of Brodsworth as a visitor attraction.

6. OPEN FIELD FARMING IN FISHLAKE AND HATFIELD: THE EVIDENCE OF THE COURT BOOKS, 1582–1808

Dan Byford was born in Wharfedale and educated at Prince Henry's Grammar School, Otley. He is a graduate of the universities of Oxford and London. He taught in schools for twelve years, starting at Rotherham Grammar before going to Buckinghamshire as Head of History at Aylesbury Grammar School. He lectured in economic and social history at the Harris College, Preston and returned to South Yorkshire thirty years ago to lecture at Doncaster College of Education. Having settled in Hatfield he became interested in the drainage of the area and has worked on its agricultural consequences for many years. He taught, part-time, for the Open University in its early days and after taking early retirement from Doncaster Metropolitan Institute of Higher Education he was a part-time tutor, mainly in local history, for the WEA. He was Conference Secretary of the History of Education Society for four years and on the Executive Committee of the British Agricultural Society for fifteen years. He is married and has three daughters and one grandchild.

8. DONCASTER PEOPLE OF TEN GENERATIONS AGO

David Hey is Professor of Local and Family History at the University of Sheffield, where he teaches in the Division of Adult Continuing Education. Originally from Penistone, he now lives in Dronfield Woodhouse. He was educated at Penistone Grammar School and Keele University and obtained part-time MA and PhD degrees at the Department of English Local History at Leicester University. His books on South Yorkshire include *The Making of South Yorkshire* (1979), *Packmen, Carriers and Packhorse Roads* (1980), *Yorkshire From AD 1000* (1986) and *The Fiery Blades of Hallamshire: Sheffield and its Neighbourhood, 1660–1740* (1991). He has also written *Family History and Local History in England* (1987), *The Oxford Guide to Family History* (1993) and *The Oxford Companion to Local and Family History* (1996). He is, with Martin Olive and Martin Liddament author of *Forging the Valley* (1997), outlining the remarkable story of Sheffield's Lower Don Valley.

9. A FIELD GUIDE TO DOVECOTES OF THE DONCASTER AREA

Brian Elliott was born and educated in the Barnsley area. After an undistinguished spell as an apprentice professional footballer with Doncaster Rovers he obtained a proper job, working for Barnsley Corporation in a Dickensian office next to the Public Cleansing Department. Whilst Head of Geography at Royston Comprehensive School he tutored local history courses for the WEA/Sheffield University and published short histories of Royston parish. Interest in local history continued, researching his own town for an M Phil, awarded by Sheffield University in 1990. His book *The Making of Barnsley* (1988) was the first published history of the town since Victorian times and is now in its third printing. He founded the acclaimed *Aspects* series, edits the Barnsley and Doncaster volumes and is editor of the Aspects Special, *Barnsley's Sporting Heroes* (1997). His other publications include *Barnsley's History From the Air, 1926–1939* (1994). Brian works at Rother Valley College, Dinnington where he is Head of the School of General and Community Education. He lives in Warmsworth, with wife Angela and daughters Natalie and Hannah.

10. DONCASTER THEATRES: AN OUTLINE HISTORY

Coral M P ('Kate') Taylor was born in Wakefield in 1933 and educated at the Girls' High School before going on to St Anne's College, Oxford, where she read English Language and Literature. After teaching in Leeds, at West Park C S School and the City of Leeds and Carnegie College of Education,

she took up a post as Principal Lecturer in English at Wentworth Castle College of Education at Stainborough. Following the closure of the College she became Vice-Principal (Community) at the Barnsley Sixth Form College when it opened in 1979. Since her retirement in 1990 she has spent her time researching local history, in particular in the field of entertainment. Her book *Right Royal: Wakefield Theatre 1776–1994* was published in 1995. She works part-time as a tutor for the Open University and is the Hon Managing Editor of Wakefield Historical Publications, President of Wakefield Historical Society and Chairman of the Mercia Cinema Society. Her article on Barnsley's Wellington Street Theatre appeared in *Aspects of Barnsley 4* (1996).

11. THE ENCLOSURE OF MEXBOROUGH

John Goodchild is a native of Wakefield and was educated at the Grammar School there. He has been active in local historical research since about the age of thirteen, and is the author of over 140 books and published essays on aspects of the history of the West Riding. He was founder-Curator of

Cusworth Hall Museum and subsequently Archivist to Wakefield MDC; in his retirement he runs a Local History Study Centre at Wakefield which houses his immense collection of manuscripts and research materials, and which is open to use, free of charge, by appointment. Mr Goodchild holds an honorary M Univ from the Open University, awarded for academic and scholarly distinction and for public services. He is a regular contributor to the *Aspects* series. Outside historical research, his interests lie in Freemasonry and in Unitarianism – and his dog.

12. BY THE INSTIGATION OF THE DEVIL: THE DONCASTER BOROUGH CORONERS' RECORDS

Jenny Moran (nee Pillay) was born and educated in Hampshire. She obtained her Bachelor of Arts degree in History and Russian Literature from Liverpool University in 1991. She then worked at Southampton City Archives and Surrey Record Office where she discovered her interest in the role and records of the coroner. She gained her Master of Archive Administration in 1994 and has since been working as an archivist at Doncaster Archives. When not working she enjoys drawing and painting, science fiction and travelling the country in order to try different beers.

13. CORN WINDMILLS OF THE DONCASTER AREA

Alan Whitworth trained at Bradford College of Art, from 1977, after a number of years in the world of printing and graphic design and then predominantly turned his attention to promoting the preservation of English parish churches, founding and running a charity to that end, writing and lecturing on the subject, mounting many exhibitions and organising the first national conference dealing with churches and tourism; and yet his interests are wider, and his regard for old buildings and history has led in one area to the founding of the Yorkshire Dovecote Society after a study of dovecotes and pigeon-lofts, about which he has written and lectured often, and in another, to compile a number of visual records about places which he has been associated. He now writes and lectures about local history subjects and his books include *Yorkshire Windmills* (MTD Rigg Publications), published in 1991 and *A History of Bradley* (1997).

14. A BENTLEY CHILDHOOD REMEMBERED

Doris Kitching (nee Hopkinson) was born in Bentley in 1920. Now resident in Barnby Dun, she has had several poems published but has gained a great deal of satisfaction in seeing her account of her early life and times serialised in Doncaster Library's *Yesterday Today* local history magazine. Memories associated with the loss of her father, Thomas, in the Bentley Colliery Disaster, inspired her to record her early life. Doris married Norman, a railway fireman and subsequently furniture salesman, at St Peter's Church, Bentley. She has a daughter, grandson and a great grandson.

INDEX OF PEOPLE

Young,Arthur,106-107,119